AF291169

The Constructed Worlds of
Calum Colvin
Symbol, Allegory, Myth.

The Constructed Worlds of

Calum Colvin

Symbol, Allegory, Myth.

TOM NORMAND

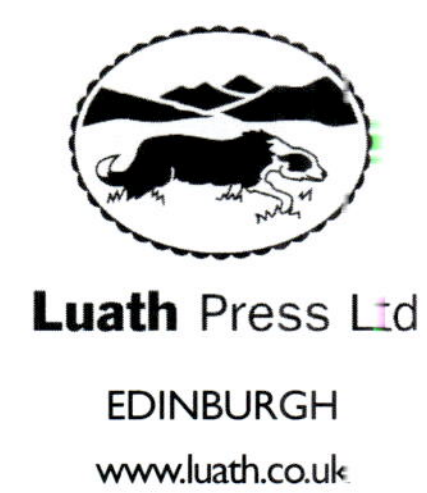

Luath Press Ltd

EDINBURGH

www.luath.co.uk

First published 2019

ISBN: 978-1-912147-89-2

The artist and the publisher thank the Royal Scottish Academy and the Sir William Gillies Bequest Fund for their financial support toward the publication of this book.

The paper used in this book is recyclable. It is made from low chlorine pulps produced in a low energy, low emission manner from renewable forests.

Printed and bound by iPrint Global, Ely.

Typeset in 10.5 point Sabon.

Contents

Calum Colvin, photographer

There is a magical character to the art of Calum Colvin. It might be suggested that there is a magical element to all art, and especially his chosen genre of photography. For photography is that fundamental illusion, promising a truth and presenting a fiction. But Colvin's work has, historically and consistently, conjured a world that is deceptively attractive, subtly alluring, and filled with spectacular enchantments. The multiple manipulations and the artfulness of this photography present a vision that is spellbinding.

Were this quality a mere artifice then it might be questioned, but Colvin's photography has typically explored the most challenging aspects of contemporary life and society. The threads and passageways of his work invoke topics as diverse as the nature of fine art and its alternative in popular culture; the complex attributes of identity in the present day; the historical contests between the arts and the sciences; the pressing discourse on the environment; the hybrid nature of art and culture and politics; and the opaque relationship between history and myth.

This intent, then, is serious, but Colvin's imagery is joyous. Its characteristic quality is comedy and comedy's mischievous twin, irony. His photography deploys metaphor and allegory, combined with a shape-shifting metamorphosis that generates a raw and revelatory laughter. This is the laughter of recognition. The conceit of human action is recognised for its glorious ambition and for its absurd failure. The creative work enthrals its audience by challenging perceptions and petitioning insight, all in a spectacular theatre of illusion, allusion and intimation.

As if to accent these qualities it is illuminating to study the photograph titled *Natural Magick*, from 2009. This is a self-portrait. The image is staged in a three-dimensional set, floored in the optically challenging black-and-white-square-patterned tiling common in the work of Johannes Vermeer's interiors. Already the image is a puzzle. Into this set, the paraphernalia of an artist's studio, a photographer's studio, is distributed

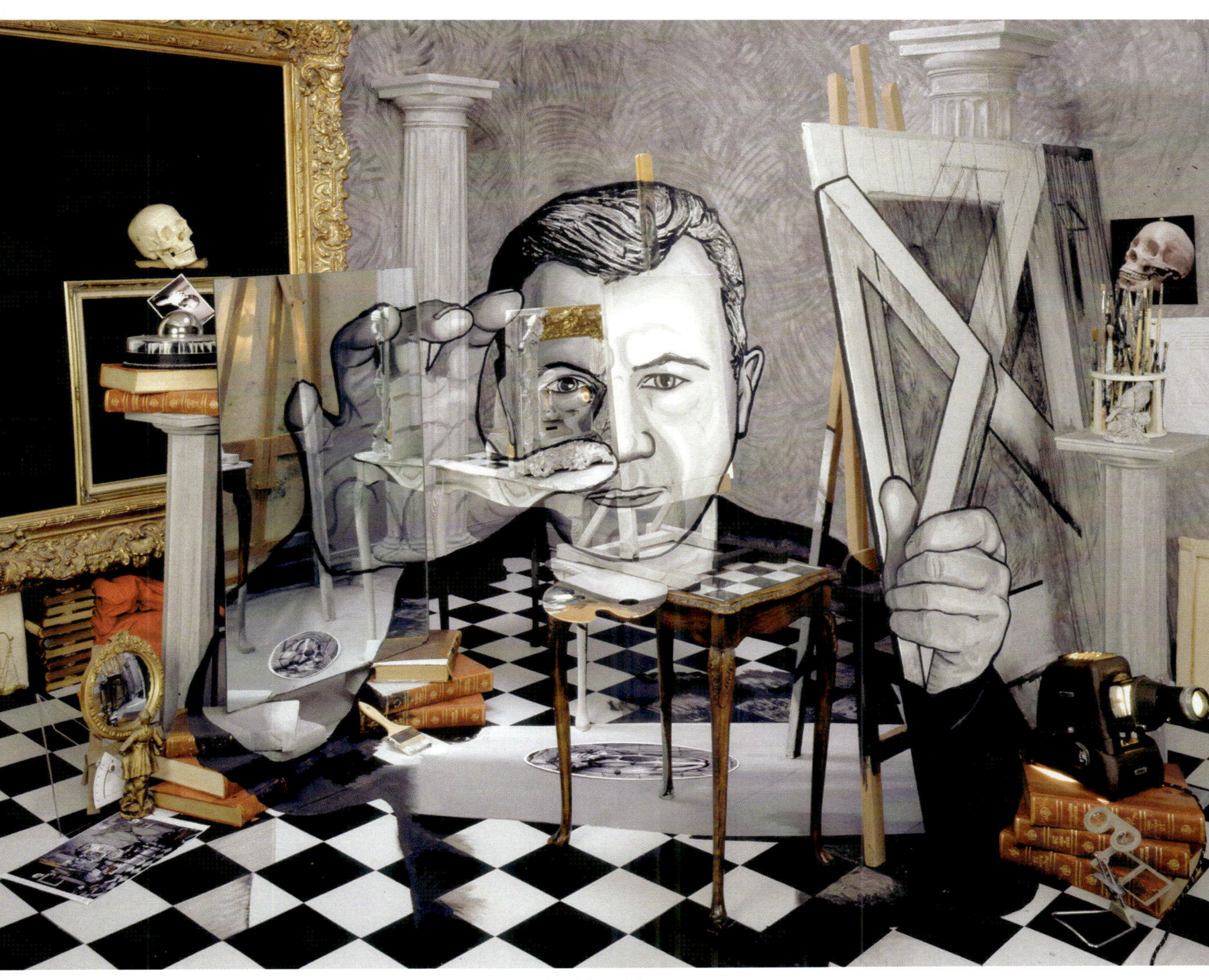

Natural Magick,
2009

in a seemingly random manner. There are pedestals and columns, tables and easels, frames and mirrors. The arrangement appears chaotic and dislocating. The floor-space is strewn with books, a partial edition of the *Encyclopaedia Britannica*, and with mirrored ornaments, stereoscopic viewers, a slide projector, paintbrushes and scales. The arrangement appears random and fluid. On the pedestals these objects are complemented by more brushes, a model bird and a slide carousel. A large mirror, just off-centre, reflects the scene back upon itself but capriciously, as if an unreliable narrator.

Across this mercurial stage Colvin has painted his self-portrait. The outlines and forms of his portrait are written into the objects and backdrop of the setting. The magic here is to promote a coherent image from the inchoate assembly of objects. This is the alchemy of the artist and the wizardry of the camera. Colvin emphasises this artifice in the objects he holds in his outstretched hands: a picture frame that encloses a slide lantern, which in turn is transcribed into his left eye; and a triangular wooden structure that echoes the impossibly complex mathematical models of MC Escher. His self-portrait is that of a conjurer, and so of an artist.

Everywhere, however, the deepest sense of this creativity is acknowledged. The focus on the eye, the very centre of the composition, recognises the unique quality of the visual experience, both its inviolable nature, and its fallibility. The inclusion of the mirror – indeed, multiple mirrors – in the set establishes the complicated web of viewpoints, the substance of competing illusions, and the frailty of recognition in the image. Finally, the repeated motif of the human skull, as object, photograph, and rendered as anamorphic perspective, surely a reference to Hans Holbein's *Ambassadors*, declares that eternal note of self-reflection; the consciousness of mortality.

Evidently *Natural Magick* is a majestic piece of work, and something of a manifesto of Colvin's creative practice. It is replete with signs and symbols, codifications and contests, illusions, allusions and associations. Typical of Colvin's work it is open to innumerable readings. This is its power and intrigue, but, of course, this mature statement has a pre-history.

Colvin came to photography through the unlikely corridor of sculpture. An undergraduate at Duncan of Jordanstone College of Art in Dundee, he was subject to the conventional model of art training in the period. In the early 1980s, students were expected to take a General Course that introduced every kind of creative practice and specialised in an intense engagement with the 'life-class', drawing firstly from the cast, and then from the model. Subsequently, Colvin chose sculpture as his specialism.

In common with most Scottish art schools at this time, photography was not on the curriculum. Dundee, however, was honoured to retain the eminent documentary photographer Joseph McKenzie who was engaged to assist students in the recording of their works. McKenzie's was a subsidiary role within the college, but Colvin came to recognise him as something of a mentor. Certainly, he readily absorbed the profound technical knowledge that McKenzie would offer and increasingly Colvin engaged with the camera, not simply to document his sculptural works, but as a focused element within his creative practice.

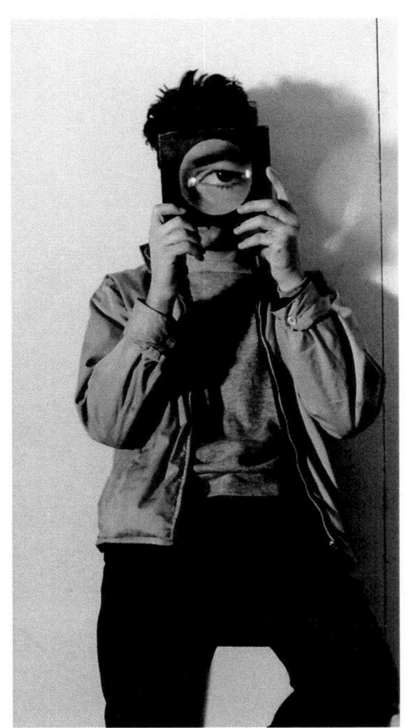

Photograph of Calum Colvin, circa 1982

This fascination with the camera, and the photographic image, led him into a close study of its history and its possibilities. Indeed, his undergraduate thesis explored the work of the great French photographer Henri Cartier-Bresson and, in the manner of Cartier-Bresson, he began to explore the environs of the city of Dundee, searching out subjects and ideas. While his photography, in these student years, did not attempt to mimic Cartier-Bresson's 'decisive moment', it did engage with the French master's humanism and even his muted romanticism. It also introduced some sense of those themes that would become important in his later practice.

These early photographs were black and white images, taken with Tri-X film, renowned for its subtle grain, and tended to reflect areas of the environment that were either ethereal or desolate. All were untitled, but a photograph like *Untitled (Petrol Pumps)*, from 1982, is quintessential. Three abandoned petrol pumps, two standing and one fallen, sit on the horizon. They are framed against the broken clouds of the sky and, in the deep horizon, the distressed tenement architecture of the city. The whin, gorse and shrubbery that grows wild around the central subject is overexposed so that the image has a magical and even a spectral quality. The mood of the piece is melancholic but this is redeemed by the subtle beauty of the image for it is also pensive, and even wistful.

With experiments like these, Colvin was exploring the potential of the camera as a teller of tales, a medium that could evoke ambience and emotion. But these remained a tangential practice within the parameters of his undergraduate study for he remained, in 1982, a student specialising in 'sculpture'. In the event his diploma show of 1983, that moment when each student realises the potential of their learning, combined sculpture, or at least 'installation', with photography.

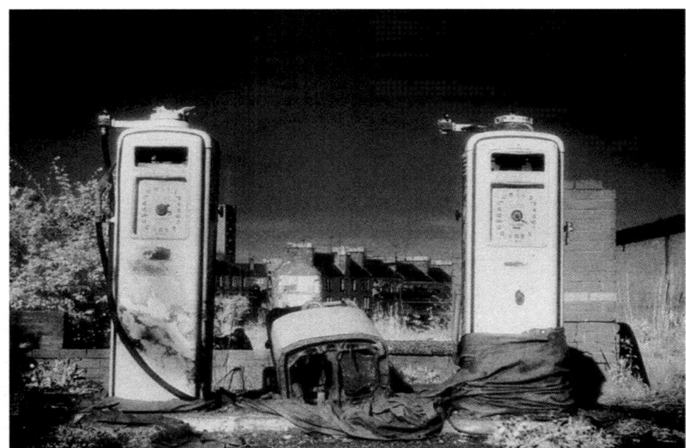

Untitled (Petrol Pumps),
1982

In the early months of 1983, Colvin had been photographing derelict sites within the city of Dundee. He came upon an abandoned school building and rescued some of the desks, chairs, notebooks and related debris from this deserted institution. In his allocated diploma-show space, he assembled these objects as a chaotic schoolroom. He then painted the whole space white. Locking his 'field'-camera on a tripod he set this scene as his subject, but then painted across the three-dimensional installation the outline of a school teacher, his fist raised against the empty classroom. This was *Untitled (Schoolroom)*. The piece then existed as an assemblage, or an installation, but was recorded as a photograph. Moreover this image, in juxtaposition with the discrete symbolism and romanticism of his 'documentary' photographs, explored issues of authoritarianism, institutionalism, social control and anger. In form, style and content, this work would seed those 'constructed narratives' that became Colvin's celebrated photographs of the later 1980s.

The originality of this diploma show, and the obvious creative inspiration of its maker, ensured that Colvin would be accepted into the Royal College of Art in London in the autumn of 1983, and appropriately, it was to

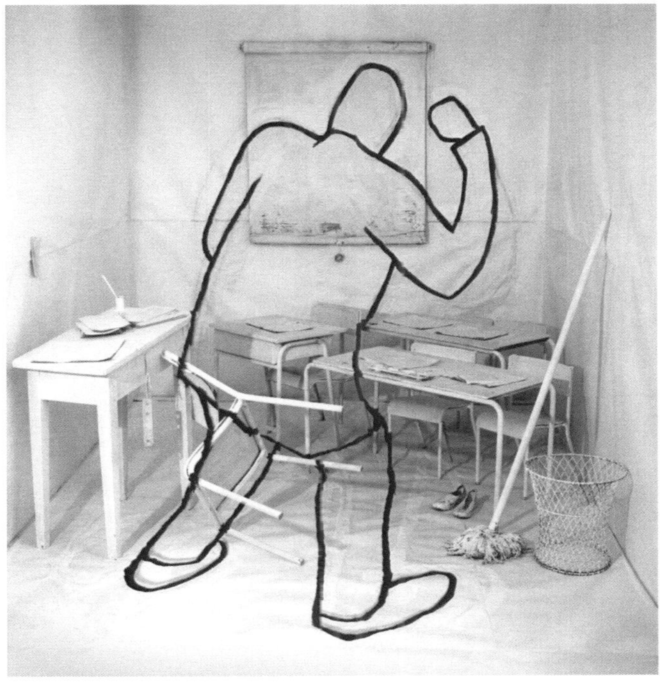

Untitled (Schoolroom),
1983

undertake a Masters diploma in Photography. Here, with guidance from Bill Brandt, and later from John Stezaker, Colvin would mature as a photographer. In part this was shaped by his 'outsider' status within the close-knit London art scene, for this sense of an 'alien' presence within an established order helped generate an impulse towards the 'otherness' of his developing practice.

An early London work, like *Leaf Man* from 1984, connotes those sensations of alienation and isolation that are features of the exile's experience. An interior of a bed-sitting room, a spare single bed, a coat rack with jacket and a floor strewn with autumnal leaves. From this scene the 'leaf-man' emerges; a frail figure, lacking substance, and composed of the very leaves that set the foundations of the image. It remains a black and white photograph, and a 'constructed' assemblage, but it invokes a mood that is dislocated and fragile.

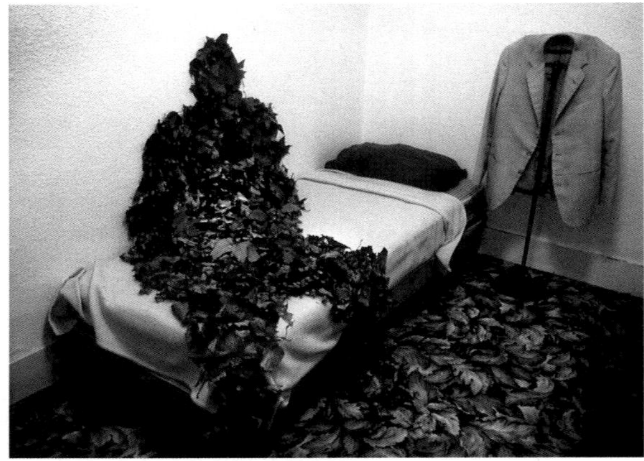
Leaf Man,
1984

It speaks to impermanence and uncertainty. The photograph is also, in an unnerving manner, contingent and inscrutable, and the dark enigma of the work is haunting.

Nevertheless, it was in London that Colvin would come to recognise his signature style and this was a culmination of those forms, themes and approaches that had been maturing from his early student years. In 1985, he would complete a coloured photograph, *Untitled (Head and Room)*, that was both the apotheosis of his earlier experiments and a signpost of future developments.

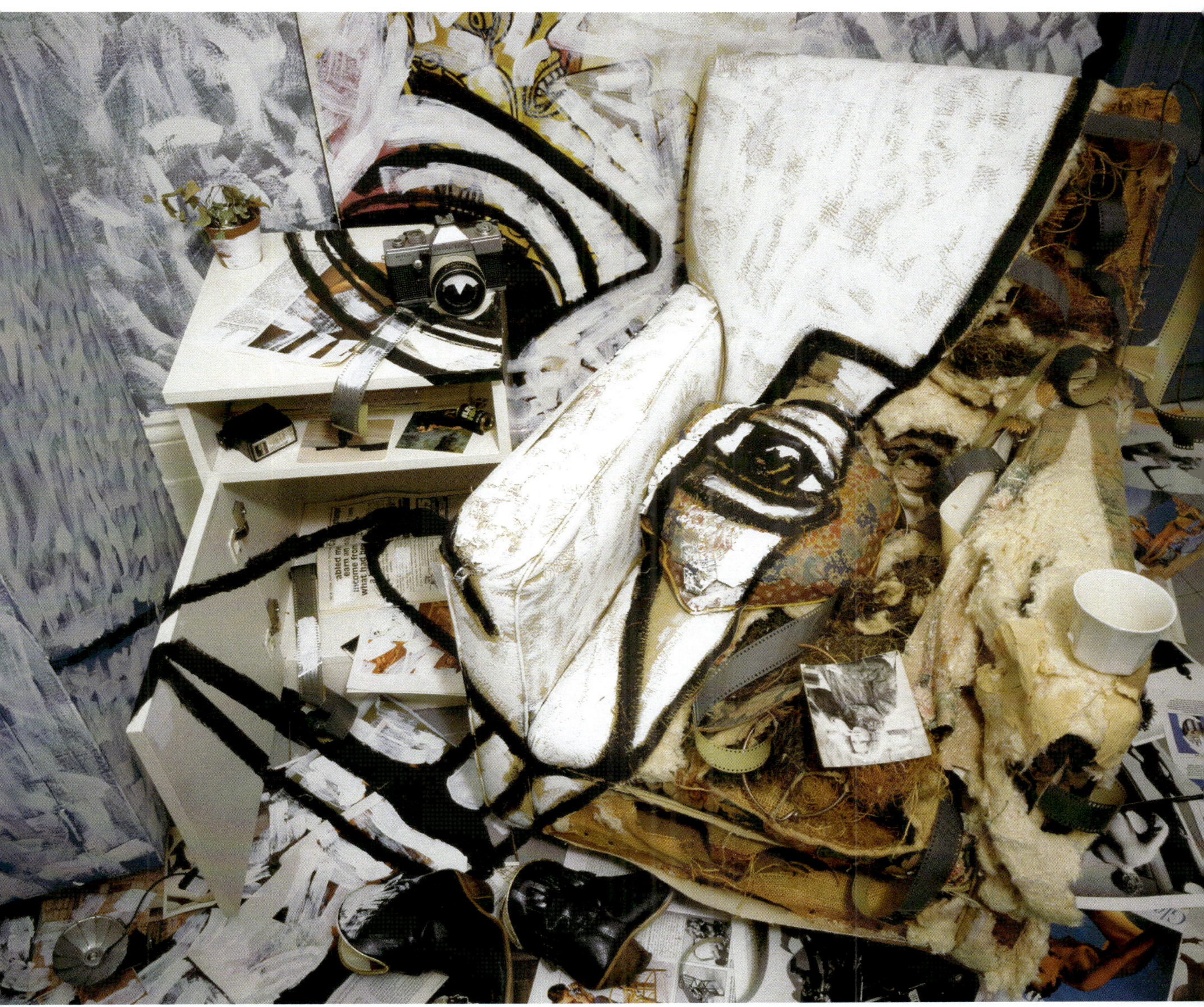

Untitled (Head and Room),
1985

Untitled (Head and Room) is a constructed work. The assemblage consists of a dilapidated easy-chair and a cabinet, with open door, all set against the corner of a room. Across this battered interior, every kind of jumble and litter is strewn. Cups, a dying plant, books and magazines, abandoned photographs, a camera, some exposed film strip and the fragments of a fractured life. Onto this scene a head is drawn in black outline with white highlights and part of the backdrop is scumbled in white paint. The atmosphere of the piece is chaotic, and even fetid. It speaks of turmoil and perhaps despair but the nature of this work, the practical creative engagement, signals a direction that was full of potential and promise. It augured an aesthetic that was ripe with possibilities, and it exploited an energy that had become dynamic and innovative.

This outlines the pre-history of Colvin's mature approach, and his aesthetic. Within this fluid and adventurous style, there is a quicksilver imagination that makes oblique associations and discovers subtle metaphors. Subsequently these things, and more, would become the substance of his magical images and his extraordinary photographs.

Fine Art, Pop Art, Photography

By the mid 1980s, Calum Colvin had established himself as a photographer. But, evidently, he had begun to reframe the very concept of photography as a medium. He could no longer be described as a 'documentary' photographer. He was involved in neither landscape photography nor the celebration of groups, individuals and their actions. Indeed, he positioned himself in opposition to the common tropes of photography while remaining committed to the medium. His was a unique approach that would meld the worlds of photography, fine art practice and the wild paraphernalia of vernacular culture.

An early example of this approach was *The Death of Venus* from 1986. As an image this work is based of Sandro Botticelli's *The Birth of Venus*, created sometime around 1486 and a celebrated denizen of the Uffizi in Florence. This photograph begins to gather the fundamental attributes of Colvin's style. The corner of his studio becomes the platform for a stage set. Into this space a group of disparate objects has been arranged. As a centrepiece, an ornamental podium is positioned. This is composed of a playful dog that leaps upon a human figure who holds a bunch of grapes, presumably this is Bacchus. Atop the figure's head is a podium on which sits a goldfish bowl, complete with goldfish and plant in water. To the left an Action Man toy is positioned; dressed in a kilt, and wielding an axe as if to smash the fish tank. To the right of this episode there stands an incongruous model horse. Finally, a broken rose falls from the podium and some fallen petals drift onto the scenery. Surrounding this tableau there sits a doll, a book that references the source work and idea for the image, a calendar date, and a photograph of the upper torso of a naked woman. Across this three-dimensional construction the head and shoulders of Botticelli's Venus is painted, complete with flowing hair and against the background of a rolling seascape.

Typically, this is an enigmatic and intriguing image. It references the most esteemed work from the fine art tradition, but introduces the confections of popular culture. It pastiches a revered symbol of love and beauty, and

The Death of Venus,
1986

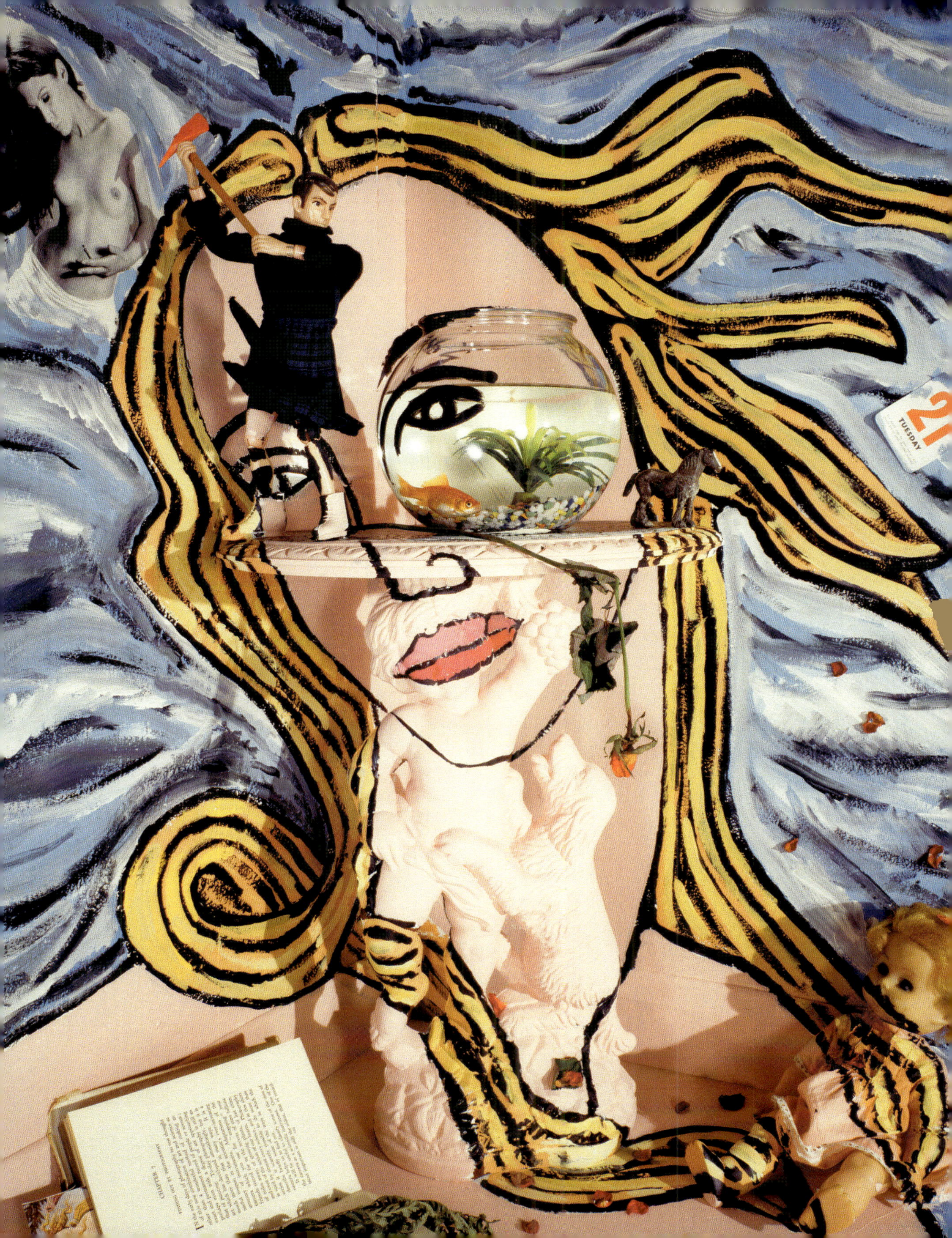

TUESDAY
21
CHAPTER 7

discredits this with actions that intimate violence, loss and tragedy. It usurps the sense of creation and birth by introducing notes of decay and death. At every level, the image questions the elation of Botticelli's vision and reflects a souring of human aspirations.

And, yet, in its 'look', *The Death of Venus* appears comic, even frolicsome. The assemblage looks random and haphazard. The gestures seem to caricature pathos. The painting of the set emulates the bold outlines and intensified colour combinations of Pop Art. Throughout, the artwork establishes a mood that is simultaneously exuberant and plaintive.

This would become characteristic of Colvin's early constructed photographs. His imagination looked for images and symbols, and explored the way these could be manipulated such that they were transformed into competing meanings. In this manner, he was able to produce work that seemed to be in homage to the classical tradition while simultaneously offering a series of contesting thoughts. Often this contest would be determined by the dialogue between high culture and popular tropes. Equally, it might explore the horizon between the esteem given to fine art and the derogation of photography as a 'common' medium. And, finally, his work might highlight a universal, mythic, subject and transform this into a personal narrative.

The leitmotif of this last metamorphosis sits at the very core of *The Death of Venus*. The kilted Action Man doll signifies a kind of doppelgänger and is everywhere in Colvin's work of this period. Of course, it is a narrative character. Taken from a child's toy box it opens up every potential flight of the imagination. But, dressed in a kilt, and journeying through fantastic and uncommon panoramas it subtly invokes the journal of its creator. In this period, Colvin was cast into the maelstrom of the London art scene. An exile and a stranger in this metropolis, he was a traveller in a world that seemed alien. Distinguished by his accent and his history, he came to recognise the 'otherness' of his identity, most specifically, his liminal status as a Scot.

The kilted Action Man becomes the emblem of this status and his journeys within realms of civilisation and culture a perplexing experience. The photographs, then, become both an expression of that condition and its partial resolution.

This crucible of thoughts, ideas and experiences intensified in the middle years of the 1980s. An example of this deepening insight is *Heroes 1* from 1986. In this instance, the image is appropriated from Jean-Auguste-Dominique Ingres' intriguing Neo-classical painting, *Oedipus and the Sphinx*, completed in 1827 and now a memorable component of the vast collection in The Louvre.

Evidently, the array of objects and furnishings in this construction has become more convoluted. The foreground in particular is a mosaic of drinks cans, magazines, comics and toys. References from Coke cans to superheroes to Donald Duck and beyond serve to create a kind of alternative pantheon of heroes. As if to emphasise this, the background is painted with a clouded sky and a Doric column, while, juxtaposed with this classical motif, the right side of the tableau features a curtain decorated with Superman logos. On a sofa sits the large plaster model of a young boy, a 1950s charity advertisement appealing for the Barnardo's Homes, and painted across the scene, the figure of Oedipus staring quizzically at a globe lantern, and his reflection in a mirror. Manifestly, he is asked the fateful riddle by the Sphinx and his own image is the answer.

The layers of meaning in this work became characteristic of Colvin's oeuvre, as did the elements of pastiche, irony and montage. While the style of the imagery paid some homage to Pop Art, there were associated links to Surrealism, most especially in the use of the found object and the disruptive juxtaposition of images. But there remained a fascination with the Classical and the Neo-classical traditions. Indeed, the pendant to *Heroes 1* was *Heroes 11*, an artwork created largely from the same stage set but modelled

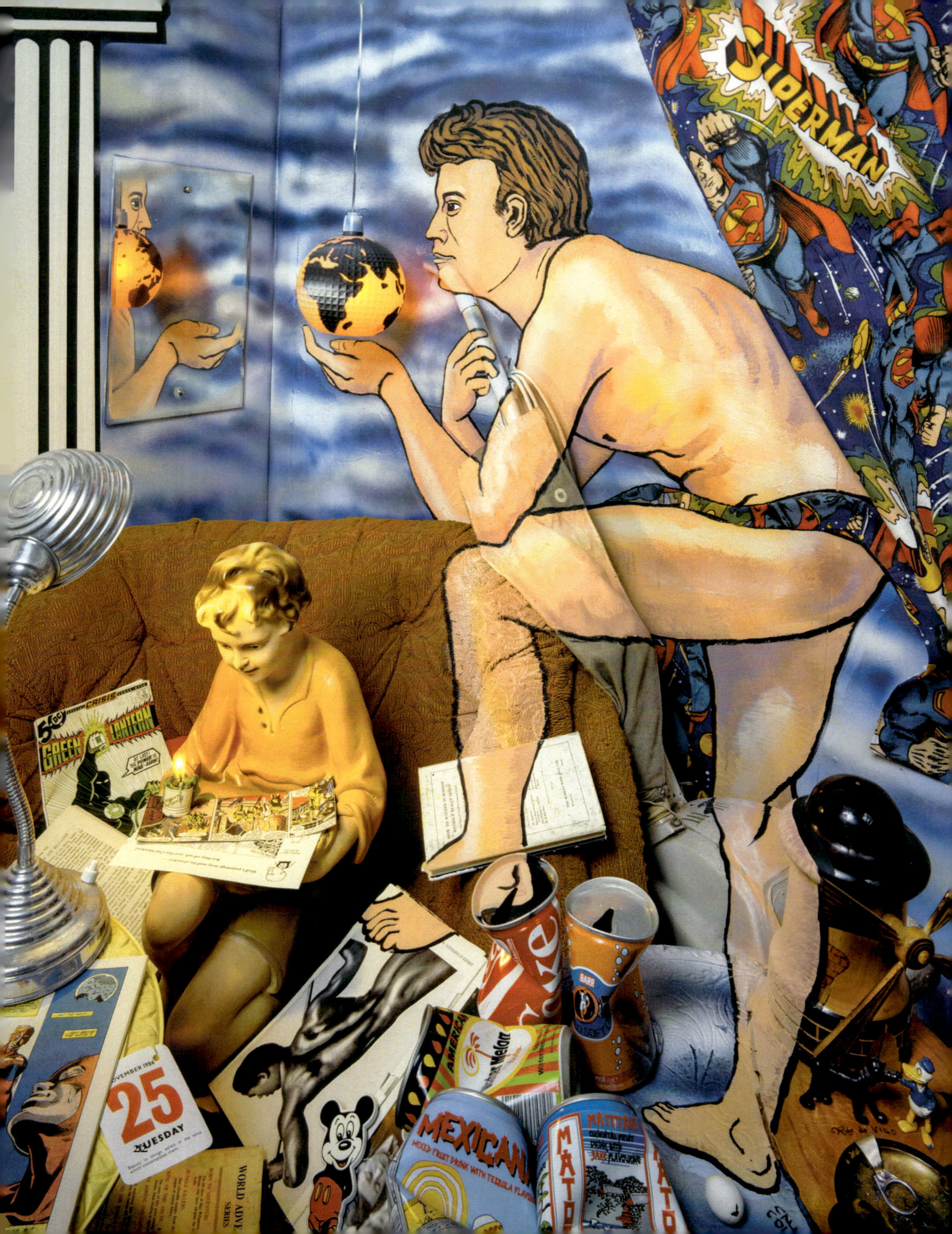

SUPERMAN
CRISIS
50¢
GREEN LANTERN
NOVEMBER 1986
25
TUESDAY
WORLD ADVENTURE SERIES
MEXICANA
MIXED FRUIT DRINK WITH TEQUILA FLAVOUR
BARR
Coke
MATT
MATT
Río de Vito

on Ingres' *Jupiter and Thetis* from 1811. This painting, held in Musée Granet in Aix-en-Provence, features the nymph Thetis in supplication before Jupiter requesting clemency for her son. Her pose is extraordinary, with her right hand on Jupiter's lap and her left hand reaching upward to stroke his ferocious beard. Colvin has excluded the imposing pagan god from his construction and creates only the female figure, her gestures and pose painted across the detritus of magazines, books, discarded cans and cartoon toys.

Both these works, it might be said, are archetypal examples of this collision of styles that became characteristic of Colvin's work but, in some sense, they also recognised the conventions of academicism and the academic tradition. It was an obligation of academic training that the student should display mastery of the painting of the both the male and the female nude, and here Colvin has delivered his catechism.

The vitality and originality of these early photographs was quickly recognised in London and beyond. The Photographers' Gallery in London curated a significant exhibition in 1986 where Colvin was teamed with the Scottish photographer Ron O'Donnell. O'Donnell had, independently, arrived at a narrative style that involved elements of construction and so the title of the exhibition *Constructed Narratives* was uncontested. This exhibition travelled to Stills Gallery in Edinburgh and marked the arrival of Colvin as an important new talent in the world of photography.

The centrepiece of Colvin's contribution to *Constructed Narratives* was *The Death of Venus*, but it was the case that his work was already becoming more intense and complicated. It was also being recognised more widely. In the late summer of 1987, contemporary Scottish art was celebrated in the 'blockbuster' exhibition *The Vigorous Imagination-New Scottish Art* held at the Scottish National Gallery of Modern Art in Edinburgh. Here, a group of 17 selected artists, from the younger generation, were presented as examples of the 'new found Scottish confidence' and the 'enormous international success' of Scottish figurative art.[1]

Heroes I,
1986

Colvin's contributions were key, and among these was the totemic image of *Narcissus* that had been completed in 1986. *Narcissus* depicts a naked male figure viewing his face in a mirror. In this sense, at least, it corresponds to the ancient myth, so evocatively expressed in Ovid's *Metamorphoses*. But, in the spirit of metamorphosis Colvin offers a number of transpositions and alterations in his image. The naked figure is painted across a table-top. On this sit various commonplace objects: a teapot, jugs, tumblers, a clock, a calendar and some playing cards. Behind the figure, a standing lamp connotes the domestic environment. This mood is enhanced by the wallpaper, composed of flower petals, and by a painted patch of sky complete with a fighter-plane carefully montaged into the scene. But the core image is the painted figure who looks towards a circular mirror. Narcissus is transfixed by his own image and is in love.

While the source for this photograph is classical, it is not based on any particular painting. To the lower left of the montage a book can be seen, open on the table-top. This is Magnus Hirschfeld's *Sexual Anomalies and Perversions*, first published in English in 1936. Hirschfeld was a German physician and prominent theorist of gender identities. He was also an early advocate for the rights of homosexuals and transgender persons.

This book was significant for it allowed for 'passages of narrative' that might be introduced to the image. Indeed, increasingly, Colvin would source his imagery in text.

Narcissus, then, is an important example of the ways in which distinctive layers of meaning became written into Colvin's imagery. Moreover, as an artist he was exploring territories that were complex and contemporary. But, the mood of these intriguing and sometimes dark works was consistently leavened by notions of humour, and even the absurd. A key note in *Narcissus* is the placing of the teapot, with its little spout just where the genitalia of the protagonist might be anticipated and so, the tragedy and pathos of the image is undercut by the whimsy and playfulness of the iconography.

Narcissus,
1986

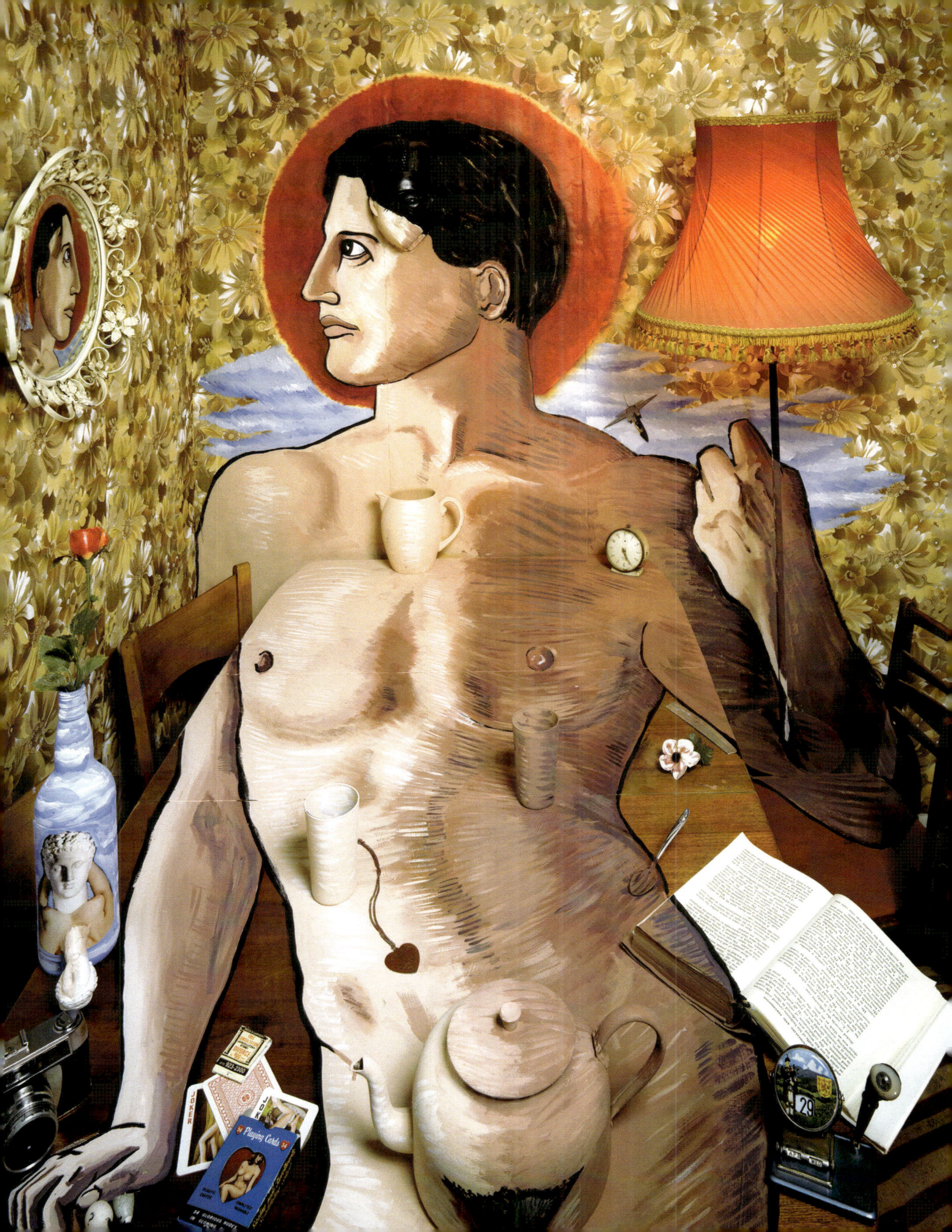

All of this is indicative of the complicated process of making these photographs. From 1986 to 1989, this process became even more convoluted while, as an artist, Colvin became more confident in his method. In this respect, it is important to recognise the role of the studio and the camera in this practice. Colvin's various studios, in London, in Portobello and in Edinburgh, have been furnished with a treasure-house of every conceivable curio, gewgaw and bauble. Odd pieces of furniture, old mirrors, every conceivable kind of ornament, magazines and books, dolls, toys and general knick-knacks. These have been gleaned from waste-skips, refuge throw-outs, second-hand shops and charity bazaars. For this reason, many of the objects have a decayed quality. They are also the common paraphernalia of a domestic home from the 1960s or 1970s. Many of the objects would be described as kitsch, and even more of them would be recognised as bizarre. These things become the decorative materials that festoon the first level of his creative process; the construction of a three-dimensional stage set, or tableau. Central to the studio, however, is the most commonplace of artist's materials: a desk for paints, brushes, pens, palette knifes, solvents and all the equipment that allow for the painted image. Surrounding the set there is, inevitably, a carefully positioned lighting system, throwing the appropriate levels of light and shade into the construction. And finally, at the heart of this kaleidoscopic scene there, is the camera.

Historically, Colvin has used a large field-camera. This accommodates a glass plate on the back of the mechanism and lens. Having established his tableau and reflected upon his subject, Colvin proceeds by drawing the outline of his figures onto the glass surface. This he transposes onto the various surfaces within the set, and so the painted image is stretched across the broken three-dimensional furnishings of the complicated *mise-en-scène*. The transposition involves innumerable movements between the drawing plate and the set, constantly reviewing the coherence and 'sense' of the image in its context. In this way, the singular viewpoint from behind the camera becomes the one point at which the image reads, and may be understood. One step to the left or to the right of this viewpoint and the scene becomes fractured, like a Cubist painting. When all of this is settled, after weeks of construction, the photograph may be taken. Certainly, these were images that were and are 'hard-won'.

By 1989, such was Colvin's confidence in this method that he undertook one of his most complicated photographs to date, the triptych titled *Deaf Man's Villa*. This photograph took some three months to construct and complete. The centre panel depicts a naked figure coloured blue. The basis for this figure is an obscure drawing by the 19th century German painter Julius Schnorr von Carolsfeld, an associate of the Nazarene movement. The drawing was titled *Nude Youth with a Shawm*. The 'shawm' itself was a medieval woodwind instrument that would evolve into the oboe. And, in Colvin's photograph, it transforms into a paintbrush.

This element of complex transformation is replete throughout the work and across the panels of the triptych. The central panel shows the 'blue boy' painted upon and across a record player behind the figure a mannequin, and behind this a panel replete with collaged items. These last include texts, maps, diagrams, cartoon strips and bird illustrations. The bird illustration, a song thrush, is reprised on the open top of the record player, and some onomatopoeic

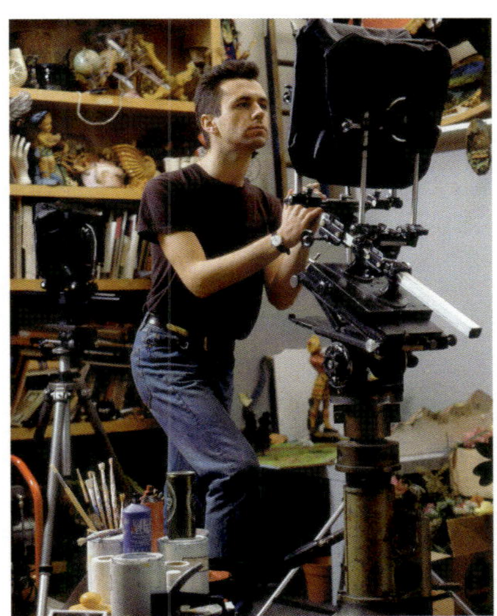

Calum Colvin in his studio, c.1986

words spill from its throat. Surrounding this ensemble, an easel supports a board with a circular mirror; an accordion rests, open, on the floor; a miniature statue of the Venus de Milo echoes the form of the mannequin; an ornamental guitar, a tourist memento made from fretwork, sits to the left and right of the figure; a palette, complete with mixed paint and brush rests at the left foot of the 'blue boy'; and a wild array of masks, ornaments, plastic flowers and unlikely bird models complete the kaleidoscopic scene. Naturally, the kilted Action Man journeys through this wild landscape.

This central image is loaded with symbols, metaphors, puns and associations, and these threads are picked up in the pendant panels. Both of these take the easel, with drawing board, as their central prop. And in both, the board is mounted with a mirror, reflecting diverse scenes and surrounded by collaged images.

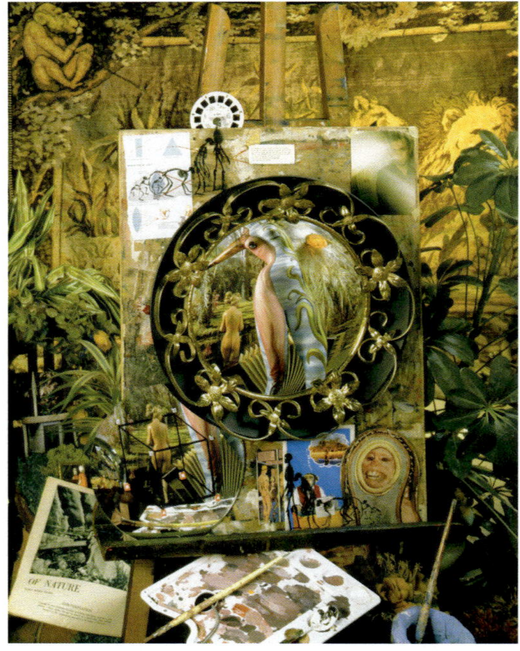

In the left panel, the mirror offers a naked figure that surreally morphs into a parody of a bird form. Just visible in this reflection is the accordion, reprised, and the back of a naked woman, this last caricaturing the Venus motif. The board on which the mirror rests is strewn with diagrammatic papers, postcards, a disc that echoes the imagery in the mirror and an actual photograph depicting the artist. The whole is set in a fecund simulation of nature, an idea repeated in the throwaway magazine that rests on the floor open at a title *Of Nature*. The lower fraction of the panel displays, again, the palette with brush and mixing pot.

In contrast, the right panel offers a darker, perhaps a night-time, scene. In the mirror, the Venus de Milo is re-presented. Situated in a long corridor, she is approached by the kilted Action Man. The sculpture, it is evident, is also accompanied by half-hidden secondary figures. Again, the foundation board that supports the mirror is covered in related collaged elements. A postcard of a song thrush is prominent, a disc that repeats the iconography of the mirrored image, an illustration of a

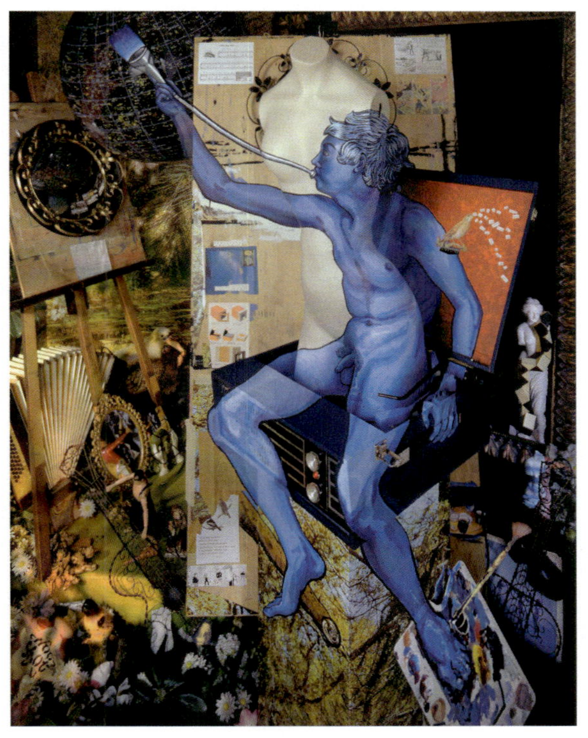

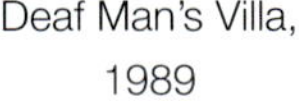

Deaf Man's Villa,
1989

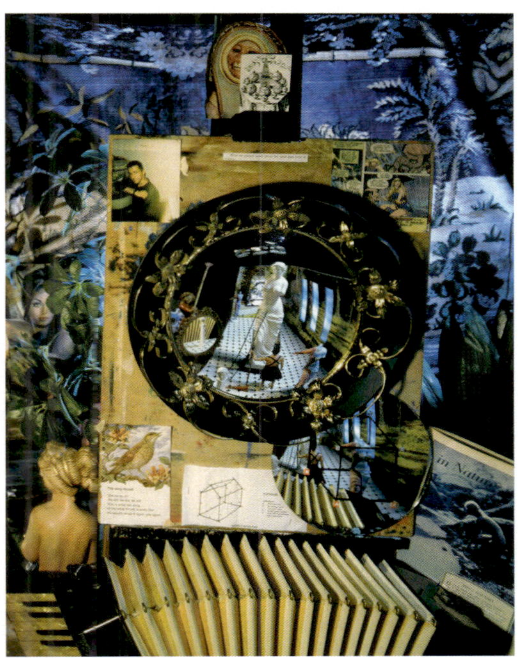

house-frame that references the mechanism of the pin-hole camera, and, a snapshot image of the artist with caged cockatiels. The context of nature is reiterated in the background vegetation and, here, the lower portion of the image presents the open bellows of the accordion.

Unquestionably this work is a *tour-de-force*. Colvin has remarked how

> he wanted to create a painted figure, which would be a central icon, and would have a complex narrative surrounding it. Like a sculpture standing in a town square.[2]

David Alan Mellor has written of

> the impossibility of grasping the narrative of a tableau such as the *Deaf Man's Villa*. Except that you might grasp them (only to lose them again), as the threaded play of returns and permutations of a confused space and its content of dolls, mirrors and reflections.[3]

Yet this triptych contains many of the themes that would become essential to Colvin's developing aesthetic and his thought world.

The title, *Deaf Man's Villa*, is something of a conundrum. It loosely relates to Francisco Goya and the estate near Madrid which he had purchased in 1819, some four years before his death. This is where the Spanish master completed the famous *Black Paintings*, now held in The Prado in Madrid. Goya, of course, had been deaf from 1793 though the villa was actually named Deaf Man's Villa in respect of a previous owner. Colvin has suggested, however, that the title was only elliptically related to the Spanish artist for

> I loved the sound of these words and used them as a title. For me the villa became the earth itself and I wanted to look at ideas concerning human kind and nature, the idea that the one was out of kilter with the other.[4]

This gathering of symbolic meaning in *Deaf Man's Villa* is significant. The triptych, as a whole, considers the condition of nature and the environment in the contemporary world. Its background is set in fertile and abundant spaces. Plants and flowers and vegetation proliferate. The sense of 'mother nature' as a creative energy is channelled through the work and this becomes its context. But everywhere this is threatened. For, here, the natural world is set-upon and destabilised. This is recorded in the conditions of the bird symbols within the photograph. These birds are transformed into surreal concoctions, they are represented as fractured and torn images, they are caged. Most evidently their song, as in the 'voice' of the song thrush in the central panel, is distorted and random. At this level, then, an environmental concern seeps into the work.

But equally the photograph reflects upon creativity. Not simply the creations of nature, but the positive and negative effects of human kind's actions in the world. The journeys of the Action Man are manifestly an intervention in nature and the near chaos of the tableaux may be his doing. Yet, the core sense of the work remains a celebration of the creative act. The 'blue boy' plays his shawm and it transforms into a paintbrush. This paintbrush stretches upwards to an inflatable model of the cosmos. And so humanity embraces this wide creation at the same time as it threatens these resources.

Music sits at the very centre of the image. The record-player, the accordion, the guitar models all allude to a cacophony of expressive sound. This is matched by the repeated palette and paintbrush motif and these tributes to the most abstract of creative practices model the vision of aspirational ingenuity. The mirror glass connotes the sense of the lens, giving photography itself a place in this creative pantheon.

Of course, the layers of meaning in this image can be excavated *ad infinitum*. But there is a sense, here, in which Colvin has found his voice and his subject.

He is reflecting upon the condition of the artist, the photographer, in the contemporary world. He questions both the nature and the purpose of creativity, he challenges the import of human action upon the entire environment and, he recognises his personal situation within a chaotic universe. In *Deaf Man's Villa,* Colvin offers a complex pandemonium that mirrors the world, and he does so with that characteristic wit and irony that shaped his entire practice. Importantly, he configured this vision within the dialectic of fine art and vernacular culture.

Deaf Man's Villa represented a manifesto statement of Colvin's constructed photography and his fascination with the classical tradition in western painting continued. This was an endlessly fruitful resource for his creative imagination. In 1992, he returned to the canonical works from this tradition and created *An Allegory with Venus and Cupid (after Bronzino).*

Bronzino's complex parable, *An Allegory with Venus and Cupid,* had been completed under the patronage of Cosima 1 de Medici in 1545. It was given as a gift, by Cosima, to Francis 1, King of France, and now hangs in the National Gallery in London. This original is an extraordinarily erotic work that reflects upon the pleasure and pain of love. The central figure, a naked Venus, is kissed by Cupid, complete with his arrow of desire. Surrounding this central group are various allegorical figures. To the right, a playful *putto* scatters flowers, while a young girl brings gifts and the symbolic representation of Time drifts above the scene. On the left side, figures possibly representing deception, jealousy and folly are distorted in agony. The whole speaks to the extremes of lustful passion and the despair of failed affection. This allegory is completed as the young *putto,* spreading his joys, steps upon a thorn.

Colvin has freely adapted this scene though his constructed photograph is self-evidently a reprise of the Bronzino. Within Colvin's image, the two central figures, Venus and Cupid, are painted across a leatherette, wingback swivel chair. The *putto* to the right holds a starburst clock, a reference to Bronzino's inclusion of Time and an intimation of love's temporality. Other allegorical figures are omitted but the Action Man figure lies prone at the foot of the *putto* while, juxtaposed to the left side, a forlorn doll-figure seems to paint an illustrative scene. Everywhere comic references are scattered. A miniature 'Jock' ornament is hung above a sign proclaiming that 'Happiness is under my Sporran'. The ubiquitous circular mirror that reflects the scene, like a knowing eye, hangs to the left of the central couple. Beneath this, a series of Donald McGill postcards mock the allusion to sacred love. And, tellingly, the *putto* steps not on a single thorn but upon a carpet composed entirely of upturned nails. In Colvin's work, the discrete content of Bronzino's masterpiece has been opened out, and what is revealed is the hidden torment of love and passion as these intense affections fade. In this sense, he has echoed Bronzino's allegory, and his warning.

For all this tragedy, however, the photograph is a comic-book narrative that deliberately usurps the reverential character of the original. It pulls the divine nature of the original sentiment into an everyday, remarkably kitsch, sitting room and everywhere the furnishings of the ordinary challenge the regalia of the classical.

Recognising the ingenuity of this particular trope, Colvin was invited to work within the National Gallery of Scotland. This project would culminate in an exhibition titled *Sacred and Profane* in 1998. Here, Colvin selected eight compelling works from the esteemed collection held in Scotland's National Gallery and revisioned these pieces in his now inimitable style. He selected, from the array of works available, three paintings by Titian: *Diana and Actaeon*, from circa 1558, *Diana and Callisto*, also circa 1558 and *Venus Anadyomene*, from circa 1520. These were accompanied by *The Feast of Herod*, painted by Peter Paul Rubens in the period circa 1636 and by Antonio Canova's *The Three Graces*, that revered marble sculpture from the early 19th century. Here were venerated examples of Renaissance,

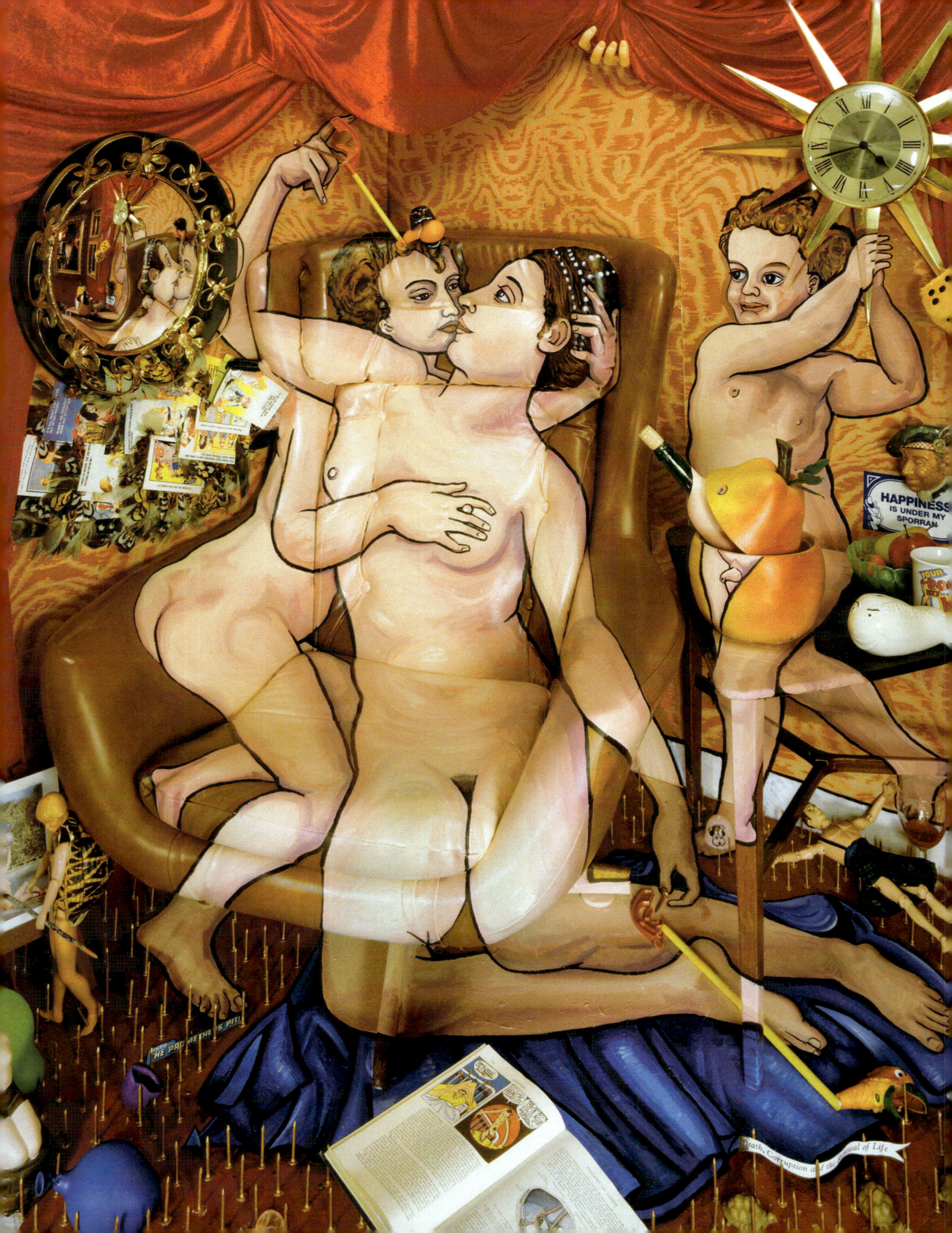

Baroque and Neo-classical art and they would be completed by some more arcane examples from the collection. These last were *The Stoning of St Stephen*, painted by Adam Elsheimer, the German Baroque artist, in 1605, with *The Combat: Women Pleading for the Vanquished*, by the hand of William Etty sometime before 1825, along with David Scott's *Philoctetes Left on the Isle of Lemnos by the Greeks on their Passage Towards Troy*, from 1840.

Intriguingly, the works by Etty and by Scott were less esteemed than the more canonical examples from the historical tradition. But, besides the powerful and symbolic nature of their subject matter, these artists were important figures in the history of the Royal Scottish Academy of Art. The English painter William Etty was a much admired exemplar for Scottish academicians in the nineteenth century. Indeed, the Academy would purchase a number of his major paintings, many of these now destroyed by bitumen abrasion, as ideal prototypes in the art of painting. Equally, the tragic and erratic David Scott became an early member of the Scottish Academy in 1829, where his morose and often theatrical works were exhibited.

Naturally, Colvin was drawn to the melodrama of Scott's painting. This mythic tale, gleaned from Homer's *Illiad*, speaks of Philoctetes' abandonment on the isle of Lemnos. A Greek hero, set to reclaim Helen from Menelaus in the Trojan War, he and his compatriots stopped at the isle of Lemnos where Philoctetes was bitten by a snake. He fell into agony and his groans, not to mention the odious smell from his wound, caused him to be abandoned by his comrades. He lived in agony for ten years, but was rescued when the Greeks were forced to return to Lemnos to gather the weapons of Hercules. David Scott evidently delights in the wild drama of this tale with Philoctetes lying prone on a rock, his foot bathed in the sea water. He is evidently in agony. Beneath a dark and stormy sky the Greek fleet can be viewed sailing off into the distance.

An Allegory with
Venus and Cupid
(after Bronzino),
1992

Colvin positions Philoctetes in a chaotic dressing room. The painted figure of the warrior is drawn straight from Scott's model, but the place of his abandonment is pure fantasy. Philoctetes is stretched across a modern dressing table. The drawers spill open to reveal every kind of gimcrack bauble. In the foreground, a scattering of castoff knick-knacks give the impression of flotsam and wreckage while, on the back wall, a pin-up image of a young woman on a motorcycle speaks, perhaps, to a discount vision of Helen of Troy. On the wall facing the distraught Philoctetes, a heart-shaped logo irradiates a design resembling the pattern of a migraine, an optical anguish. This melodrama of pain and loss is completed with a vinyl record sleeve in the lower left of the photograph, proclaiming the title *Round at Calum's*. And so the epic is allowed to segue into the ordinary, the heroic into the mundane.

This feature remains consistent in Colvin's inventive reimagining of all these canonical works. Titan's masterpiece *Diana and Actaeon* is recreated in a spectacularly distressed parlour complete with ironing board and indoor washing line, hung with laundry and an emblematic 'Madonna' tee-shirt. The hapless Actaeon comes across Diana, with her handmaidens, naked and bathing. His fate for this trespass is intimated in the model stag's head decorously hung on the wall to the right of the scene. Such transformations are reprised in *The Feast of Herod* where the action takes place in a modest, chaotic and crowded dining room and in *The Stoning of St Stephen* where the saint is martyred in front of a *faux* log-burning electric fire and beside a 'Dansette' record player.

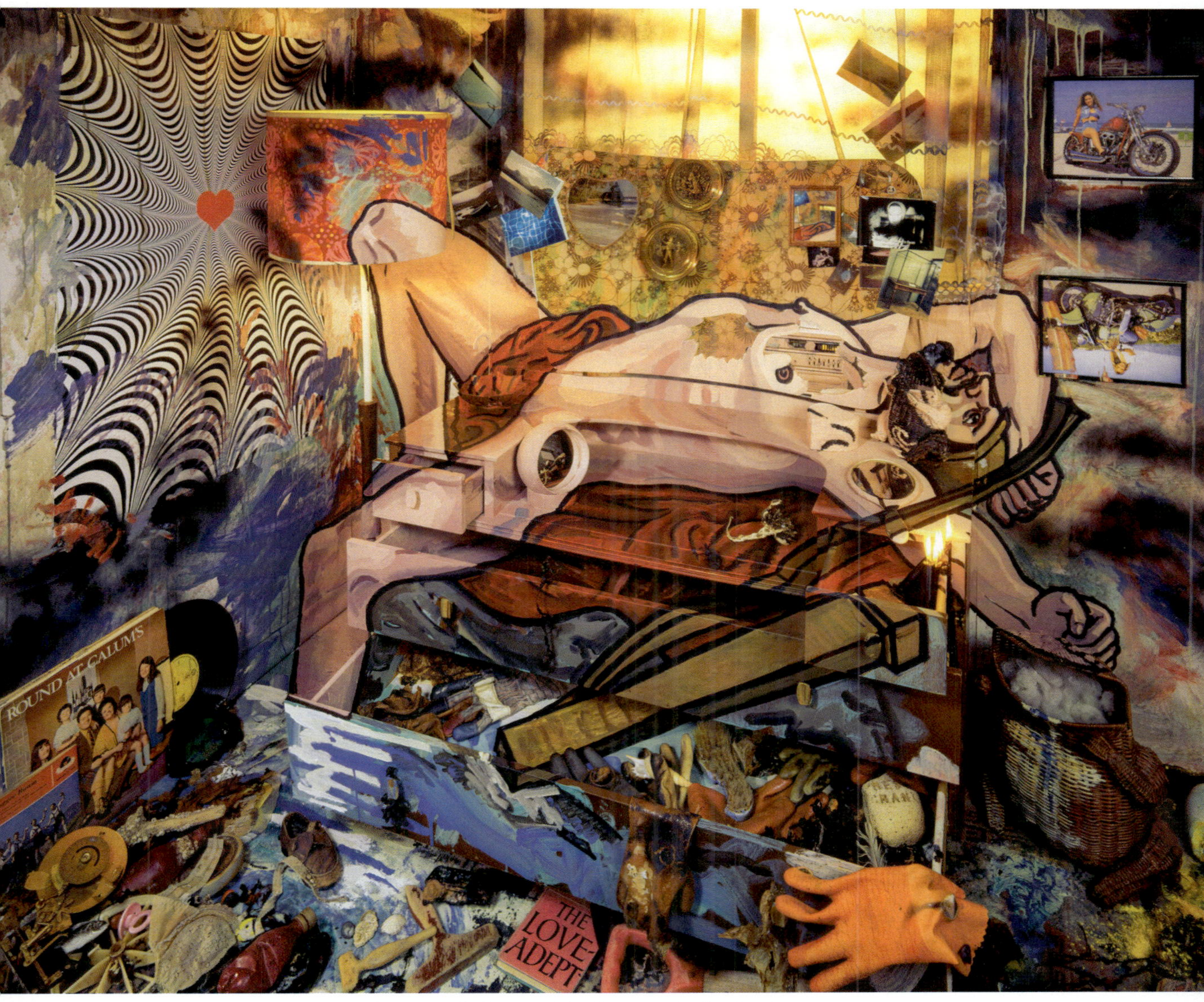

Philoctetes Left on the Isle of Lemnos by the Greeks,
1998

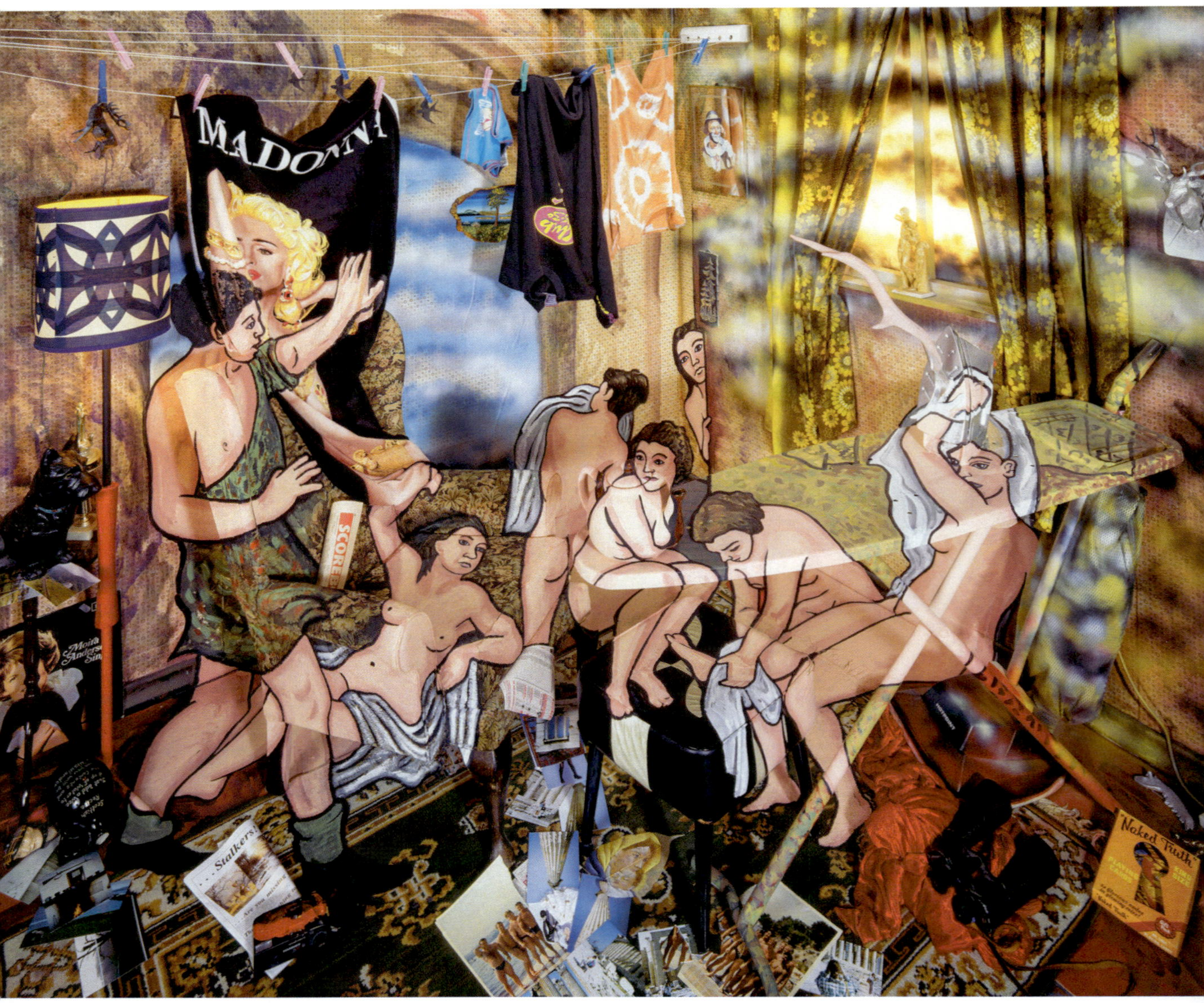

Diana and Actaeon,
1998

In his fine introductory essay to the catalogue for this landmark exhibition, James Lawson has commented that

> Upon the moral or mythic core of the individual works in the National Galleries Colvin lays down veils of narrative, meditation, argument and humorous digression, and … after the manner of the palimpsest, creates a work of resonant thematic colour, always somehow transparent rather than obscuring…[5]

Certainly, this is a powerful assessment of these challenging and provocative photographs, and it remains important to recognise the ways in which the humour of these images cloaks an inherent pathos. In this way, the images do acknowledge the intense emotions and sentiments of their sources. Indeed, where the 'sacred' element of the fine art tradition meets the 'profane' technology of the camera, there is the arena of Colvin's art.

This creative arena has remained a constant in Colvin's oeuvre. Moreover, it is fully acknowledged in two related works completed in the new millennium. Colvin was approached by UNESCO to complete a commission for the organisation's Paris headquarters in 2004. This would be an adjunct to his *Ossian* project of 2002 and would be presented at the opening for this exhibition in Paris in 2005. Colvin's acclaimed reflection on James Macpherson's fabrication of 'the Celtic Homer', the bard Ossian, published in 1765, was an homage to the invention of cultural fictions and the construction of resonant myths. In respect of this commission, Colvin was aware that Napoleon had carried the *Poems of Ossian* in his knapsack while on his many campaigns and so chose to re-imagine Jacques Louis David's epic work of propaganda, *Napoleon Crossing the Alps*. A definitive piece of Neo-classical painting, tinged with flamboyant romanticism, this work was painted in 1805 and is now housed in the Chateau de Malmaison to the west of Paris.

Colvin first projected this idea as *A History Painting* and here he revealed the magic of his art and his ingenious transpositions. In this photograph, the set itself becomes the subject, and the context of studio-space, lighting, paints and materials are all exposed. Moreover, the extraordinary effort in making his photographs is presented and acknowledged. Evidently, he has unmasked his method and declared the nature of his practice.

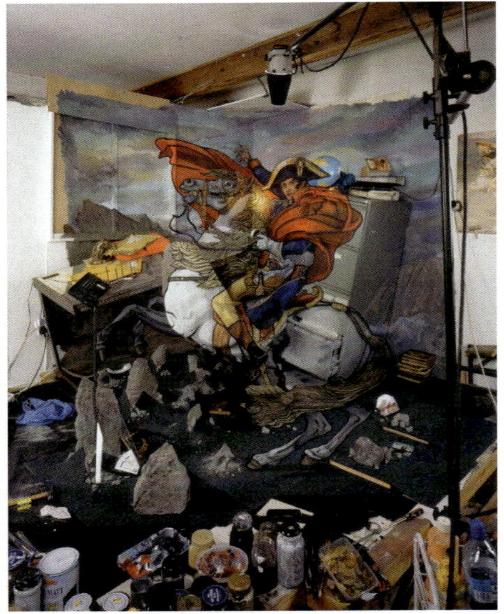
A History Painting,
2005

This creative arena became fully realised in the completed illusion of *Napoleon Crossing the St Bernard Pass (after David)* from 2005. In David's renowned painting, Napoleon sits astride his rearing white charger, in full uniform, and commands his troops forward across the rocky landscape of the Swiss Alps (though it should be acknowledged that Napoleon crossed the Alps several days after his army had advanced, he was taken by a local guide, and he was on a mule). In Colvin's version, the rocky landscape of the St Bernard Pass is suggested by the angular stones that press upward from the carpeted floor in the set, and Napoleon on his charger is placed inside a contemporary, shabby, office space. There is a dull but functional desk, a metal filing cabinet and a cheap office chair.

Subtly, this setting references another propaganda piece by David: his portrait of *The Emperor Napoleon in his Study at the Tuileries* of 1812, a work now held in the National Gallery in Washington DC. In this painting, Napoleon is in a grand study with desk and chair and surrounded by the symbols of his power; a sword thrown across his chair, some maps and documents on his desk and a Neo-classical longcase clock to signify his command

Napoleon Crossing
the St Bernard Pass
(after David),
2005

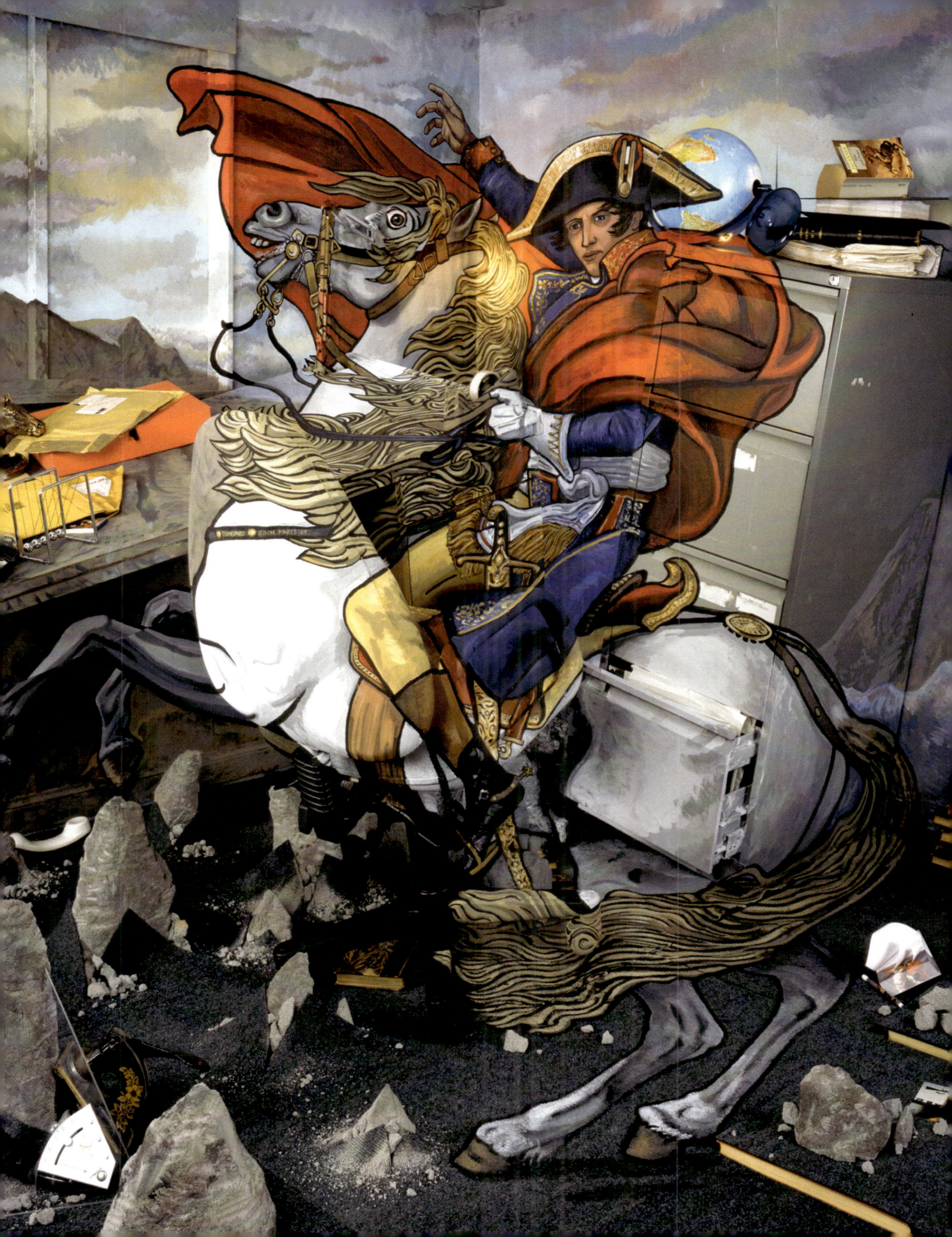

of time and history. This work is the epitome of imperial and masculine power. But in Colvin's work, the trappings of grandeur are reduced and the scene incorporates an old telephone, a fallen globe of the world and a discarded 'executive toy'. Here, the glittering showmanship of David's Napoleon has been transposed into the most mundane of bureaucratic spaces. The solemn and revered has become routine and commonplace.

And so, within Colvin's extraordinary works, the glory of Fine Art crashes into the popular culture. The exclusive aesthetic realm of the connoisseur becomes trapped in the practical world of everyday appliances. The rarefied and exalted becomes prosaic and humdrum. This is the comic irony of these photographs, and this is their insurgent insight. They exist as both culture and as counterculture.

Portraits: some real and some imagined

Given the elements of creative construction and fantasy in Calum Colvin's photography, it might be assumed that his style was unsuitable for the art of portraiture. Portraiture is surely that most representational of the visual arts. It demands a form that is authentic and faithful to its subject. It requires something approaching description; albeit tempered by interpretation, the subtle presentation of an 'interior life', and a sense of the artist's creative insight. But Colvin's mature work had become joyously whimsical. It began to rejoice in symbolism, allegory, metamorphosis and a kind of fantastic shapeshifting. The notion of an image that might speak to the unadulterated 'look' of an individual would seem alien to this aesthetic.

Moreover, the photographic portrait has a history that has prioritised the barely mediated interrogation of the human face. Certainly, in photography, there had existed pictorialist modes of representing people, and even some abstract presentations, but these have been marginal tropes. The earliest photographic portraits, by canonical figures like Hill and Adamson, say, were remarked upon for their indisputable claim to 'likeness'. And, of course, the 'straight' photography of an individual like the great American Paul Strand, in the early 20th century was championed for its unflinching commitment to the authenticity of its representation. The photographic portrait, then, implied the singular virtue of its role as witness.

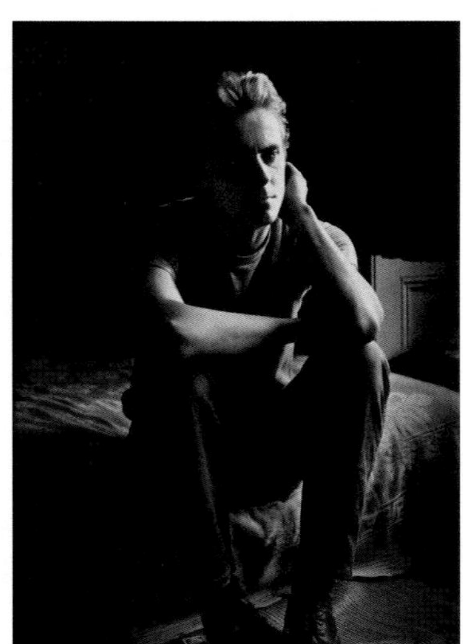

David Kane, film-maker and writer
circa 1981

As a student, Colvin would explore some of these established threads. His earliest formal portrait study, *David Kane, film-maker and writer*, from circa 1981, signals a temper that attempts to capture a likeness while exploring, also, a 'mood'. This image is carefully lit so as to highlight only half of the face and the expressive action of the arms. Much of the background is in darkness.

And so, there is a strong element of chiaroscuro in the setting. These qualities evoke a sense of theatricality in the portrait, one that is significant given the calling of the sitter. They also embody a nuanced romanticism that has been characteristic of portraiture; attempting, as it so often does, to embody the singular creative aspirations of the individual.

But Colvin would orientate his photographic style away from this form of expression, and in the opposite direction. Notwithstanding this development, in the middle of the 1990s, the Scottish National Portrait Gallery proposed an ambitious commission where he would be asked to complete a portrait study of the prominent classical composer James MacMillan. This would become Colvin's *Portrait of James MacMillan*, completed in 1996.

Described as 'the pre-eminent Scottish composer of his generation', MacMillan had, by the mid 1990s, an established reputation and had made significant contributions to the classical repertoire. In 1995, he had newly completed his opera titled *Ines de Castro*, and it was in celebration of this achievement that the Portrait Gallery commissioned his portrayal. Selecting Colvin for this project was something of a risk, but it did allow for the creation of one of the most dynamic and intriguing portraits within the collection.

Colvin undertook some detailed research into MacMillan's working method and was captivated by the fact that he composed at a desk and without the guide of a piano or instrument. He established a set consisting of a desk and chair. The desk was laden with a metronome, some books and some paper. Evidently, MacMillan was researching the history of the 14th century Portuguese noblewoman, and her tragic fate: for she was secretly married to King Peter I of Portugal, murdered on the orders of Peter's father King Alfonso IV and subsequently exhumed from her grave to be crowned as a rightful queen. The subject was, unequivocally, operatic. But, besides the desk, the scene is strewn with sheet-music and a music stand, images of icons and martyrs, candles and bells, a violin, a photograph of MacMillan

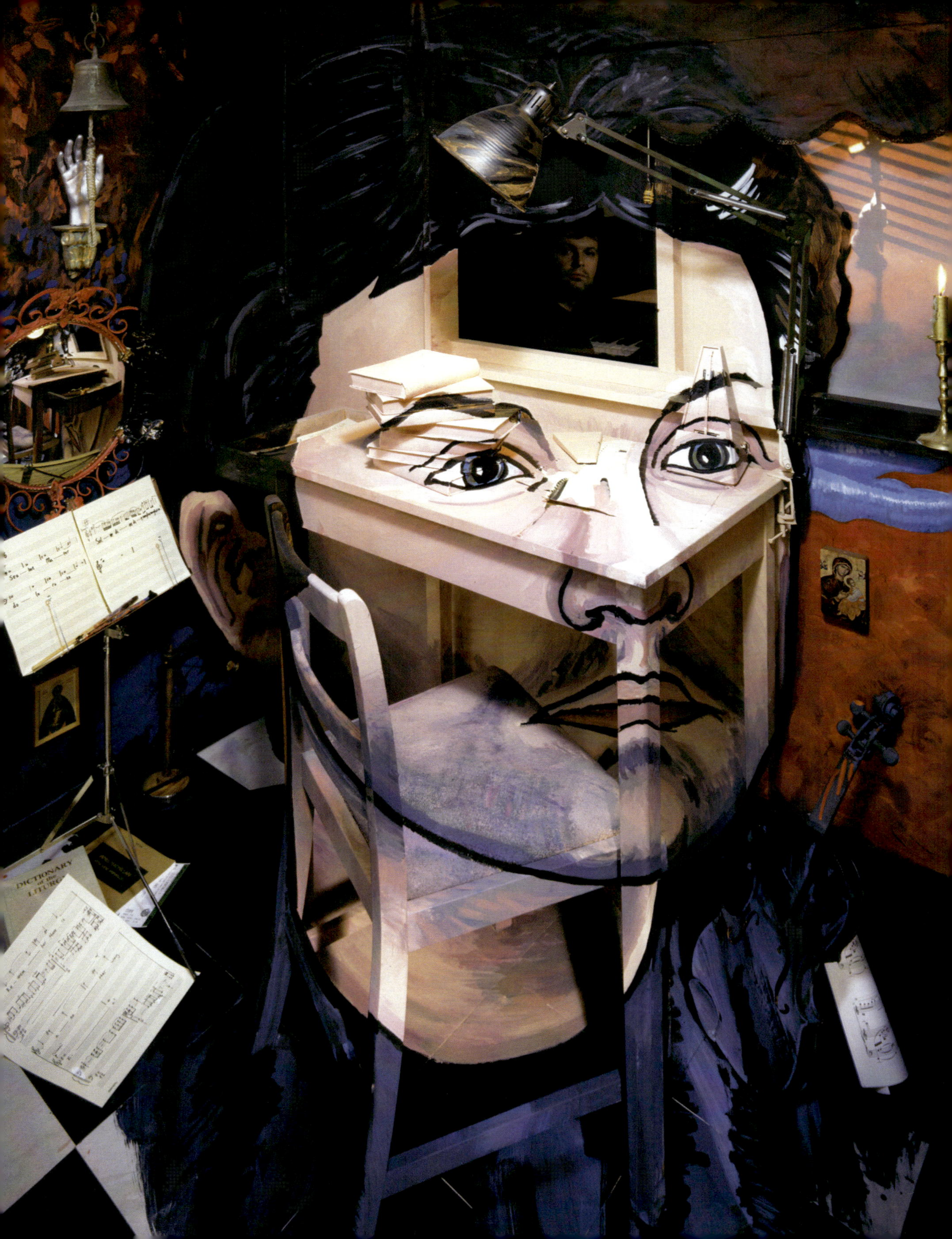

himself, and a round mirror that reflects the scenario. The portrait of the composer is painted across the set on a scale that fills the image. Moreover, as a portrait, it is an uncanny likeness, both in the demeanour of the subject and in the 'presence' of the personality.

In creating this portrait, Colvin has acknowledged the nature of portraiture as an oeuvre, and so has restrained the elements of caprice and humour in his work. But the essential aspects of symbolism and analogy remain. In fact, Colvin has revealed this by locating his image in association with the sitter's 'attributes', in the manner of Medieval and Renaissance icon production. He has selected those emblems that signify the nature and character of the individual, and allowed these to convey the virtue of the subject, in which case appearance and essence are allowed to coalesce in the image, a feature that would remain consistent in his portrait studies.

The initiative of the Scottish National Portrait Gallery in commissioning this portrait demonstrated a commendable ambition, for it displayed a willingness to combine contemporary subjects with contemporary, not to say radical, practitioners. This experiment was surely judged a success for Colvin was again commissioned at the end of the 1990s to complete a portrait study of some of Scotland's most celebrated writers and poets. This became the epic multi-figure photograph titled *The Kelvingrove Eight*, completed in 2000. The subjects were, without question, amongst the most esteemed of Scotland's literary figures, namely, the novelist and poet Janice Galloway; the artist and writer, Alasdair Gray; Tom Leonard, the poet renowned for his exposition of a Glasgow patois; the Glasgow based Northern Irish writer, Bernard MacLaverty; Liz Lochhead, the poet and Scottish Makar; the acclaimed writer and author of *Glasgow Zen*, Alan Spence; the novelist, Jeff Torrington; and Agnes Owens, the august writer whose talent was only recognised late in her life.

Portrait of
James MacMillan,
1996

These figures, in Colvin's complex photograph, stand and sit in a room in what is nominally a west-end flat in Glasgow. From a window, at the rear of the set, the baroque spires of Glasgow's Kelvingrove Art Gallery and Museum can be seen, montaged as a documentary photograph into the scene. The assured figure of Alasdair Gray seems to preside over the event, but it is easy to read this gathering as a literary salon. Each individual reflecting upon potential thoughts and actions. Typically, Colvin has furnished the room with everyday fittings: an easy chair, a small table, some small dining chairs, a standard lamp, a bookcase and a mirror tagged with photographic mementos. Incongruously, he has painted a Doric column to the right of the set, and, mischievously, he has allowed the left of the set to remain open into the studio space.

Each of the authors is presented full-figure and painted across the display. Significantly, each is represented by their 'attributes', those books and publications that give full testament to their combined achievements. And so, a close reading of the image will lead to a kind of résumé of these writers as evidenced in their contributions to the literary canon. Simultaneously, a deep reading of the photograph will reveal those throwaway visual puns and puzzles that reveal Colvin's admiration for his subjects.

This is a remarkable group of portrait studies, both for the likeness afforded to each sitter, and for its ingenious combination of eight figures within a confined space. Importantly, the sense of a relaxed and convivial gathering of these distinguished literati is compelling, and entirely plausible.

In titling this piece *The Kelvingrove Eight,* Colvin was playing with a number of tropes. In the media, this type of phrase would commonly be applied to groups of people wrongly imprisoned. More appropriately, Colvin was surely setting the style and inclination of these authors within a west coast ambit, specifically within a Glasgow culture. But the signal reference within the work is a gentle rejoinder to a painting that already occupied a prominent

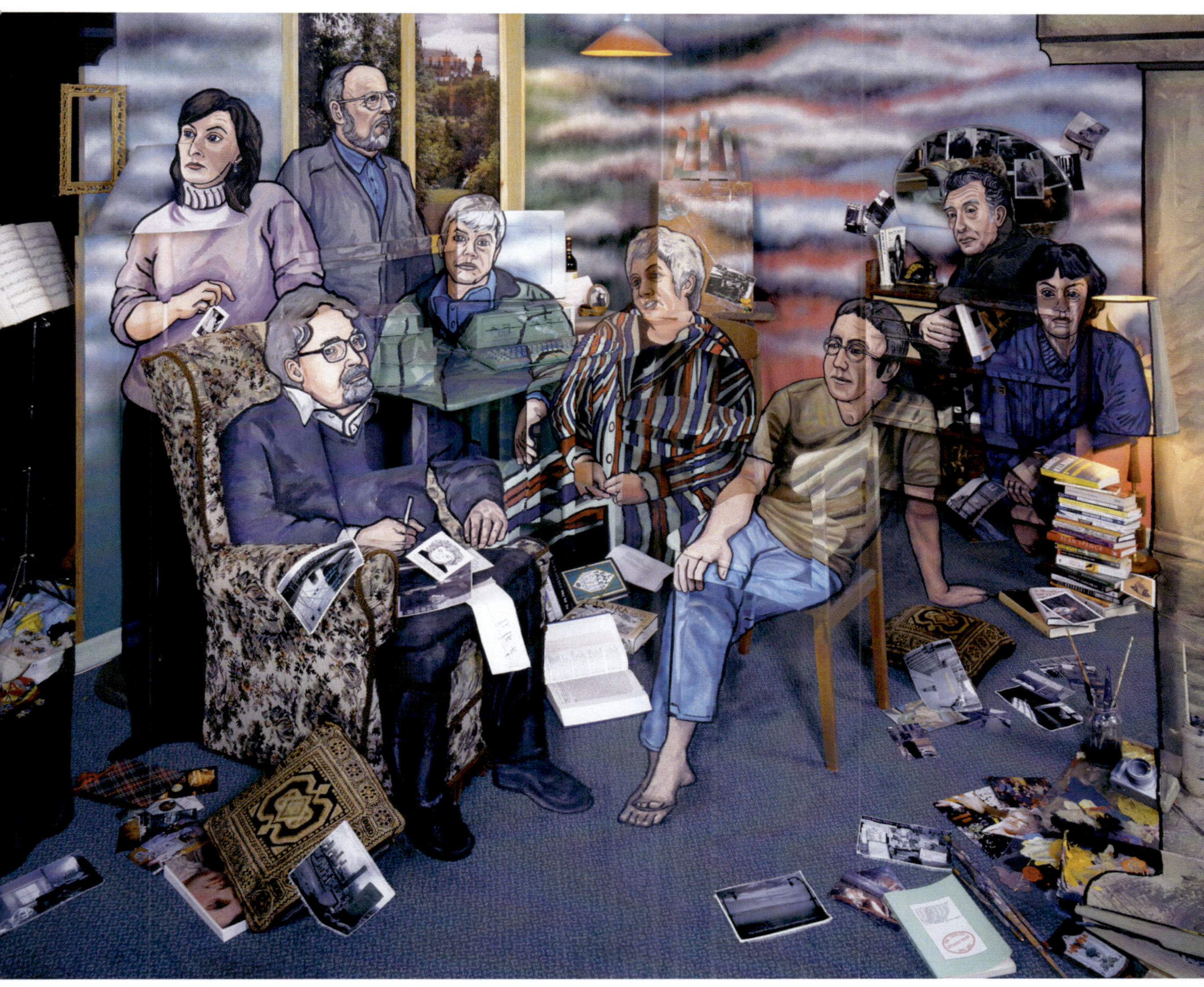

The Kelvingrove Eight,
(Janice Galloway, Alasdair Gray, Tom Leonard, Bernard MacLaverty, Liz Lochhead, Alan Spence, Jeff Torrington, Agnes Owens),
2000

place within the Scottish National Portrait Gallery, Alexander Moffat's *Poets' Pub* from 1980. Moffat is acknowledged as one of Scotland's most acclaimed contemporary portrait painters and his celebrated *Poets' Pub* is surely amongst his finest achievements. A multi-figure composition, it depicts eight poets of the Scottish Literary Renaissance gathered together in Milnes Bar in Edinburgh. These include Sorley Maclean, Norman MacCaig and George MacKay Brown. Notably, they are gathered around the electric figure of Hugh MacDiarmid. Colvin has paid a kind of homage to this work at the same time as he offers an ironic juxtaposition in his 'Glasgow' image, his *Kelvingrove Eight*. Certainly, these two group portrait works stand as amongst the most noteworthy in modern Scottish art.

Beyond these public commissions, Colvin was to perceive a rich vein of creative potential in the genre of portraiture, one that would chime with his visual and intellectual aspirations. It may be suggested that he was mostly drawn to literary figures and, in 2014, he returned to the subject of Janice Galloway. Galloway has been acclaimed for her debut novel, *The Trick is to Keep Breathing*, but she is also recognised as an accomplished poet and a writer of short stories. In 2014, Colvin was curating an exhibition of his work at the Edinburgh Printmakers Workshop. This would be realised as a show titled *The Magic Box*, a tribute to the camera as a creative instrument and its role in his complex fictions.

As part of this exhibition, Colvin chose to undertake the portrait of Galloway in the public space of the printmakers workshop. He established a studio within one of the gallery spaces, dressed his set within this area, and began the construction and painting in the public realm before taking the final photograph. Evidently there was a performative element to this presentation, and again Colvin was content to unmask his techniques as a photographer. Indeed, he engaged with visitors to the exhibition as the project developed and discussed the evolution of the work. The completed image, *Portrait of Janice Galloway*, remains an evocative and telling depiction of the sitter; the eyes visionary, the aspect of the mouth determined. Within Colvin's oeuvre as a whole, it is one of the less ornate stagings. A simple sitting room with table and chairs, a display cabinet with ornaments and, on the adjoining wall, the omnipresent circular mirror, all placed against a geometrically patterned wallpaper. But, it remains a powerful portrait, fully reflecting the strength and character of the sitter.

While this type of portraiture, the depiction of important contemporary artists, would never become a core theme in Colvin's work, he remained committed to the celebration of those individuals he most admired.

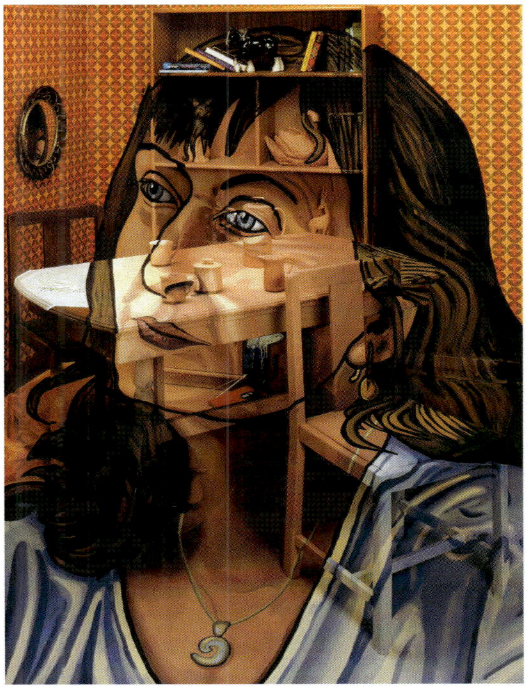

Portrait of Janice Galloway
2014

This would include some interesting commemorative portraits. Both the *Portrait of Michael Marra*, from 2017, and the *Portrait of Colin McLuckie*, completed earlier in 2011, were works that were created following the death of the subjects.

In fact, Colvin had essayed a portrait of Michael Marra in 2011, the year before the singer and songwriter's untimely death. This was undertaken as a project within the McManus Gallery in Dundee, and as part of the Victoria and Albert Museum's 'Masterclass' series; an event designed to promote the establishment of the remarkable V&A gallery within the city.

Created as a public event over a period of three days, Colvin prepared a rudimentary set composed of armchair, small table and lamp. Marra was painted across this stage with blue face and signature black beret; the former being a discrete homage to Vladimir Tretchikoff's ubiquitous image, that kitsch ornament so common in the junk shops that remained Colvin's hunting ground for resources and props.

The more finessed *Portrait of Michael Marra* was completed in 2017. Again, this was undertaken in respect of a project at the McManus Gallery in the city of Dundee. The exhibition titled *Museography* saw Colvin engage in a series of 'interventions' within Dundee's respected art gallery and museum. These intercessions in the museum's collection swept across the range of fine art and material culture. The *Portrait of Michael Marra* was a key work that championed a local figure, one with an international reputation.

Michael Marra,
2011

Significantly, there are important synergies between the artist and his subject. Marra was a highly respected and much admired songwriter and performer, 'The Bard of Dundee'. He was also a fine painter and a gentle cartoonist. His lyrics embodied some extraordinary word play, a feeling for puns and subtle ambiguities. They were at once comic and profound. All this wit cloaked a deep humanism and a discerning radicalism. When Colvin came to reflect upon these qualities in his 2017 portrait, he gathered together the public and the private Marra in a paean to his gifts and his personality.

The *mise-en-scène* is created in a dilapidated interior, part sitting room and part wooden shed. The portrait itself is painted across the floor, a rudimentary chair, a makeshift box-table and the background set. Resting on the chair, and painted as the subject's mouth, is a guitar. On the guitar,

Michael Marra,
2017

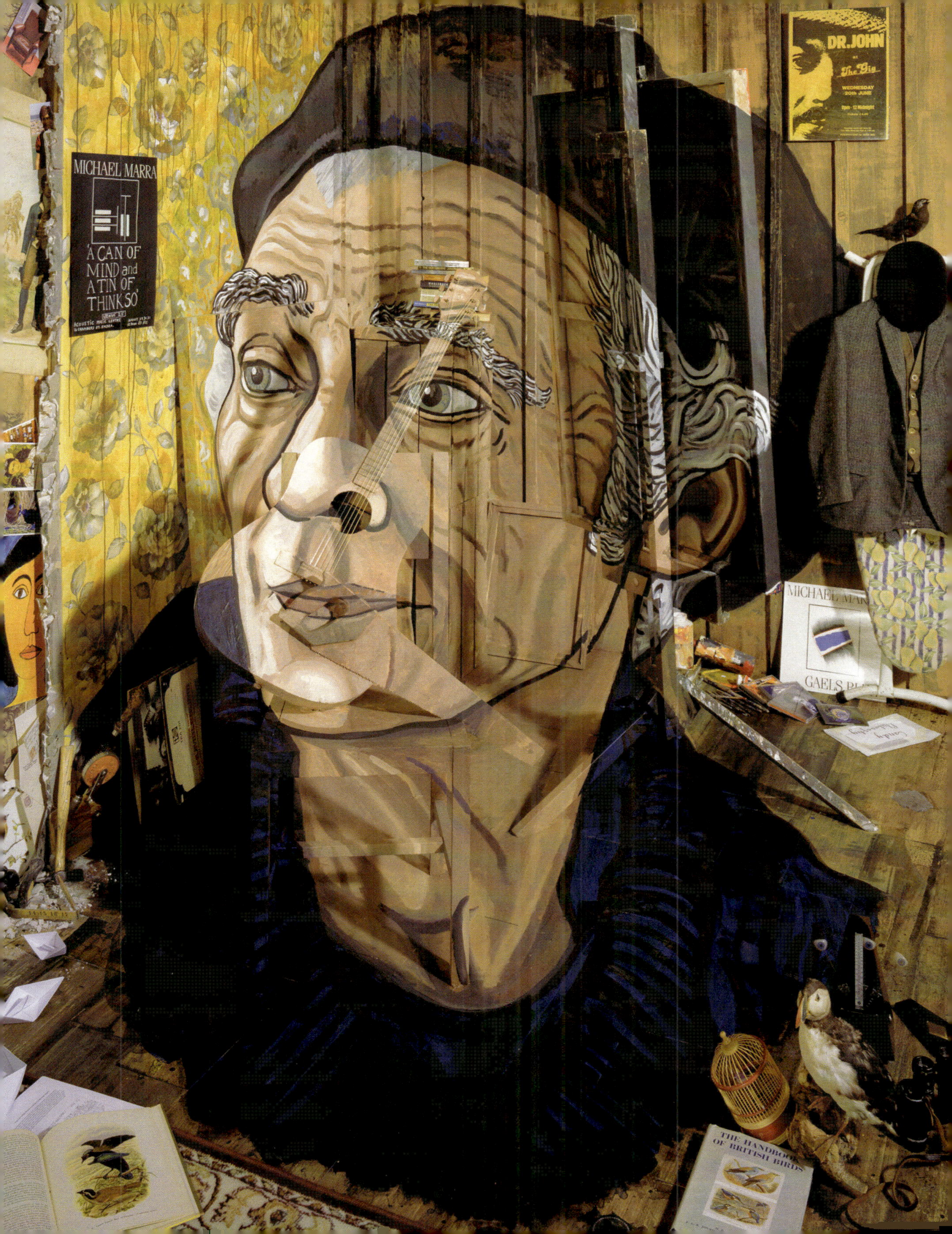

MICHAEL MARRA
'A CAN OF MIND and A TIN OF THINK SO'
DR. JOHN
MICHAEL MARRA
GAELS
THE HANDBOOK OF BRITISH BIRDS

a carpenter's saw can just be identified, a play on Marra's inimitable rasping voice. Marra is seen dressed in a rough jumper and wearing a beret. Forever the bohemian.

Surrounding this portrait is a host of references that distill the talents and interests of the sitter. *The Handbook of British Birds* is placed in the lower right corner of the image, and this interest in ornithology is reprised throughout the work. An assembly of tools (a hammer, a drill and a joiner's rule) creates an association with Marra's respect for everyday labour and working people. Over the left shoulder of the 'sitter' is his neatly folded tweed suit and waistcoat, with his beret. These are hung across an ironing board, so often used as the makeshift stand for his keyboard, and, atop the beret, a stuffed blackbird appears to sing.

The seemingly arbitrary paraphernalia throughout the work directly references the works of Marra, both his songs and his painting. To the left, a brightly painted woman's head, half-seen, is attached to the wall. This is one of Marra's own paintings. Above this, a postcard image of the artist Frida Kahlo is presented and indeed, Marra wrote a touching song to Kahlo reflecting on her unequal association with the dominant and dominating figure of the muralist, Diego Rivera. Likewise, a poster advertising a concert for Dr John, the cult New Orleans musician, echoes Marra's association with the singer and performer. Naturally, Marra's own records, albums and CDs are scattered across the set, with highlights including *Gaels Blue* and a reference to his 1996 work *Candy Philosophy*, the artwork for this latter being created by Colvin.

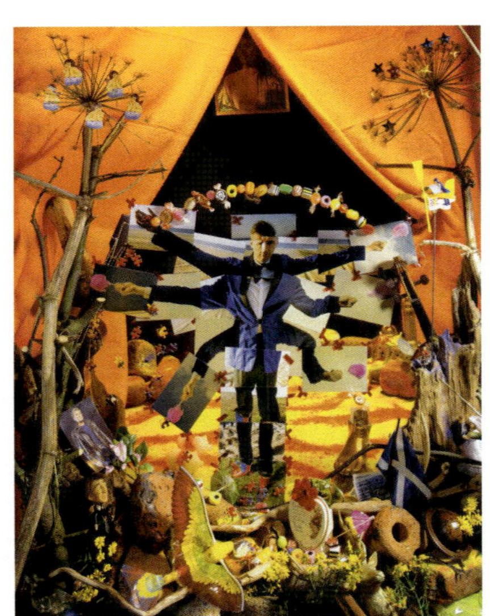

Michael Marra, 'Candy Philosophy'
artwork by Calum Colvin

The *Portrait of Michael Marra* is something of a *tour-de-force* and here the maturity of Colvin's work as a portraitist can be recognised. It also signalled a desire to celebrate and memorialise those individuals who were significant to, and for, his world-view. These might be acclaimed artists, like Michael Marra, or ordinary people whose talents and personality spoke to the wonder of the human spirit.

Colvin's *Portrait of Colin McLuckie* from 2011 remains a fascinating example of his more reflective portraiture. Colin McLuckie was a figure from Colvin's childhood and early adolescence. He had been a pitman, a miner, in the town of Haddington but had succumbed to the curse of pneumoconiosis. Sent to the east coast to recuperate, he had married and settled. In his new environment and still suffering from the debilitating lung disease, he would declaim the poetry of Robert Burns throughout the village. These performances were done from memory, with every theatrical flourish. Colvin was intrigued by these spontaneous recitations, and by the native culture to which it attested. When he began to develop his *Burnsiana* project, beginning in circa 2011, the figure of McLuckie came to represent the power of Burns and his poetry within the common culture.

The *Portrait of Colin McLuckie* is a powerful and evocative vision of human fortitude. Set inside a rough wooden shed, the subject is painted as a head and shoulders rising from the detritus of his outhouse site. The tools of a miner's labour are scattered to right and left: a pickaxe, hammer, brush and Davy Lamp. Interspersed with these emblems are various publications of the works of Robert Burns and memorabilia relating to the poet. The two central props are a short step ladder and a distressed wheelbarrow, upright and leaning against the wall. It is across these objects that the figure of McLuckie is painted. He is in old age, he appears feverish and fragile, and is dressed in a tartan dressing gown with pyjamas. But, he also appears to be in the process of an oration. He is both recalling the lyric and rhythm of

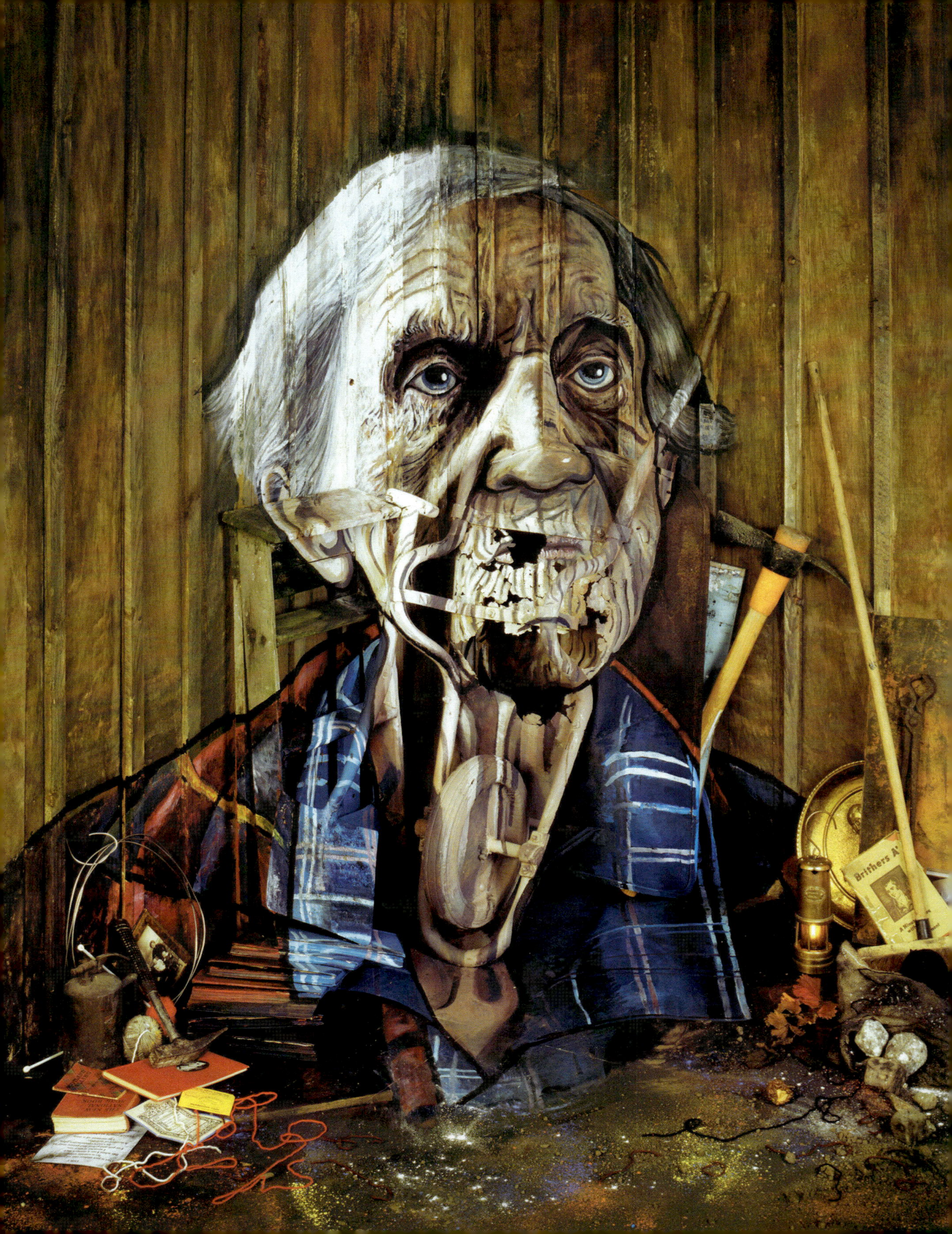
Brithers A'

Burns' poetry and experiencing the ecstasy of recitation. The rusted and broken shards of the wheelbarrow's floor describe the mouth of the orator and his fractured voice.

These portraits have all been important within Colvin's body of work. Many were commissioned, some volunteered. In the majority, these were people known to the artist, a number of whom he regarded as close friends. If they did not formally 'sit' for the portraits then they were available to him through photographs and through memory. They were, for the most part, his contemporaries.

But Colvin has also engaged in a kind of 'imagined' portraiture. In these works, he has resurrected influential and compelling individuals from history and re-visioned these using his unique approach. These likenesses have often been gleaned from photographs or from canonical works of fine art and, always, they are allowed to reflect on the contemporary world and modern culture.

In 2017, Colvin undertook a *Portrait of Hugh MacDiarmid*. MacDiarmid had, of course, died in 1978 but his reputation remained resonant in Scotland's culture. He had, from the 1920s, been a champion of Scottish vernacular poetry in a style labelled 'synthetic Scots'; he forged the Scottish Literary Renaissance in that period, and sustained it through generations of change. A poet of international renown, he was also an essayist, polemicist, journalist and politician (of sorts). MacDiarmid had been instrumental in founding the National Party of Scotland in 1928, but was also a member of the Communist Party of Great Britain; he was, at different times, expelled from both parties. Self-consciously a *provocateur,* MacDiarmid chose always to stand 'whaur extremes meet'.

MacDiarmid, it happens, had also been an Honorary Member of the Royal Scottish Academy of Art and, in 2017, Colvin was invited, as an Academician, to contribute to the *Ages of Wonder* exhibition within the

Academy. *Ages of Wonder* was a landmark exhibition that surveyed the history of the Academy through the presentation of its historic and contemporary collections. And so, throughout the winter months of 2017–8, in excess of 60,000 visitors would journey to the Academy rooms and explore the wild treasure-house of the academy's art world.

Within the Clifford Room, on the Academy's lower floor, these visitors would encounter a space where Colvin was preparing the set for his MacDiarmid portrait, and they would witness the various stages of its painting and production up until the final photograph. Here, the performative aspect of Colvin's practice, evidenced in his *Portrait of Janice Galloway*, was opened out on a grand scale, but this also involved a significant dimension of interactivity. Colvin was publically available to speak of his techniques, decision-making, and the inevitable hesitations and changes within the *mise-en-scène*.

The final portrait, for all its challenges, is a powerful presentation of the poet. Colvin set MacDiarmid as if in a 'life class'. His representation is surrounded by easels, with paint stands and the accoutrements of the painter's trade scattered in the scene. The central cast of furniture is a desk and a chair, raised on a plinth. These are decorated with the papers, books and ornaments of the subject's world. Across this scene, the likeness of MacDiarmid is painted; a representation from late in his life, but still with that sense of haughty confidence and visionary command that embodied his character. A head and shoulders portrait, the poet fills out the picture plane and dominates the space beyond the image.

A fascinating counterpoint to the portrayal of the imperious MacDiarmid is the 2017 portrait of William McGonagall. Another 'imagined' piece, this was undertaken for the *Museography* exhibition at Dundee's McManus Gallery. The Victorian celebrity performer William Topaz McGonagall is oftentimes regarded as Dundee's own poet. He has also been universally traduced as the worst poet in the English language. He had a real sense

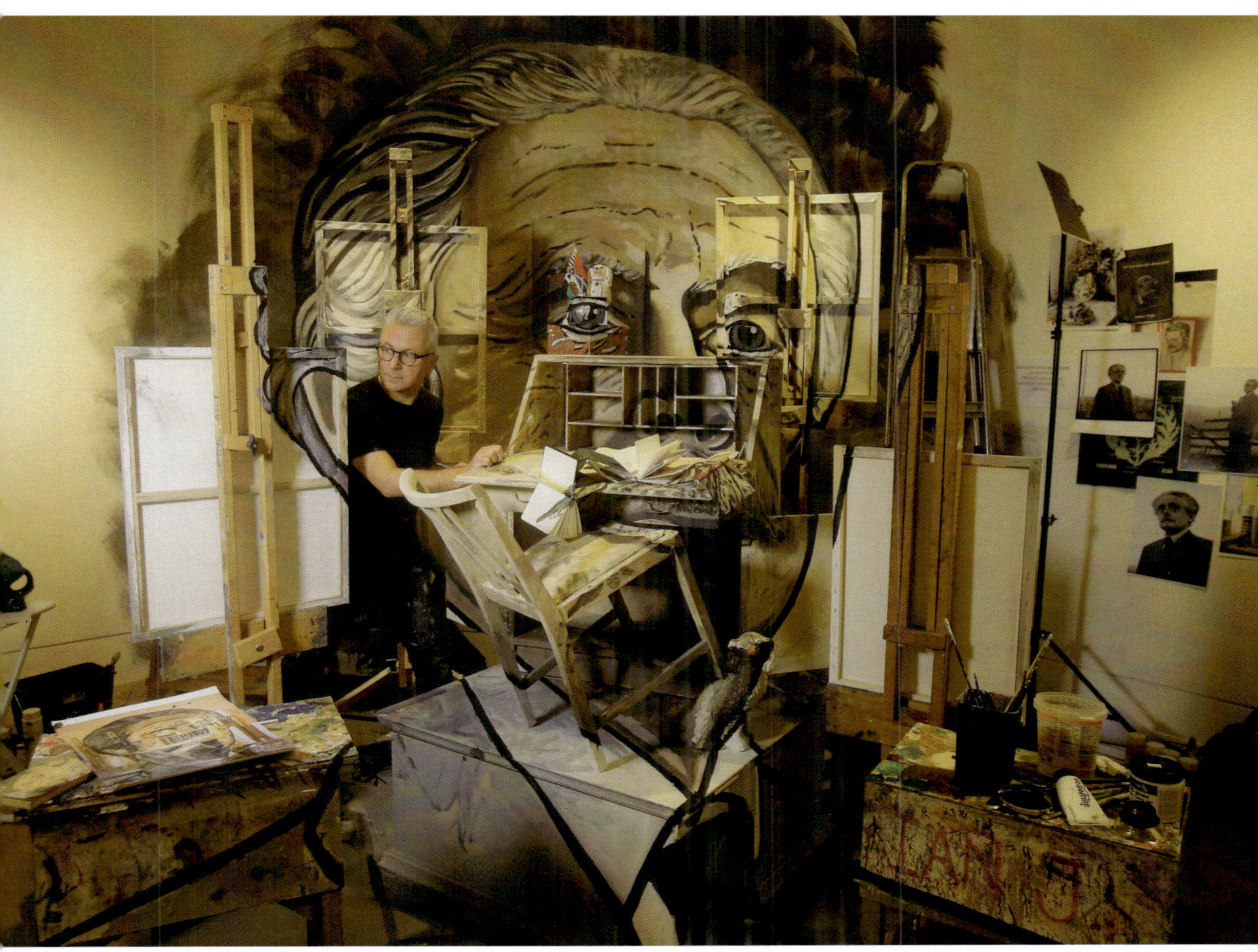

Calum Colvin preparing the set for the Portrait of Hugh MacDiarmid, Royal Scottish Academy, 2017

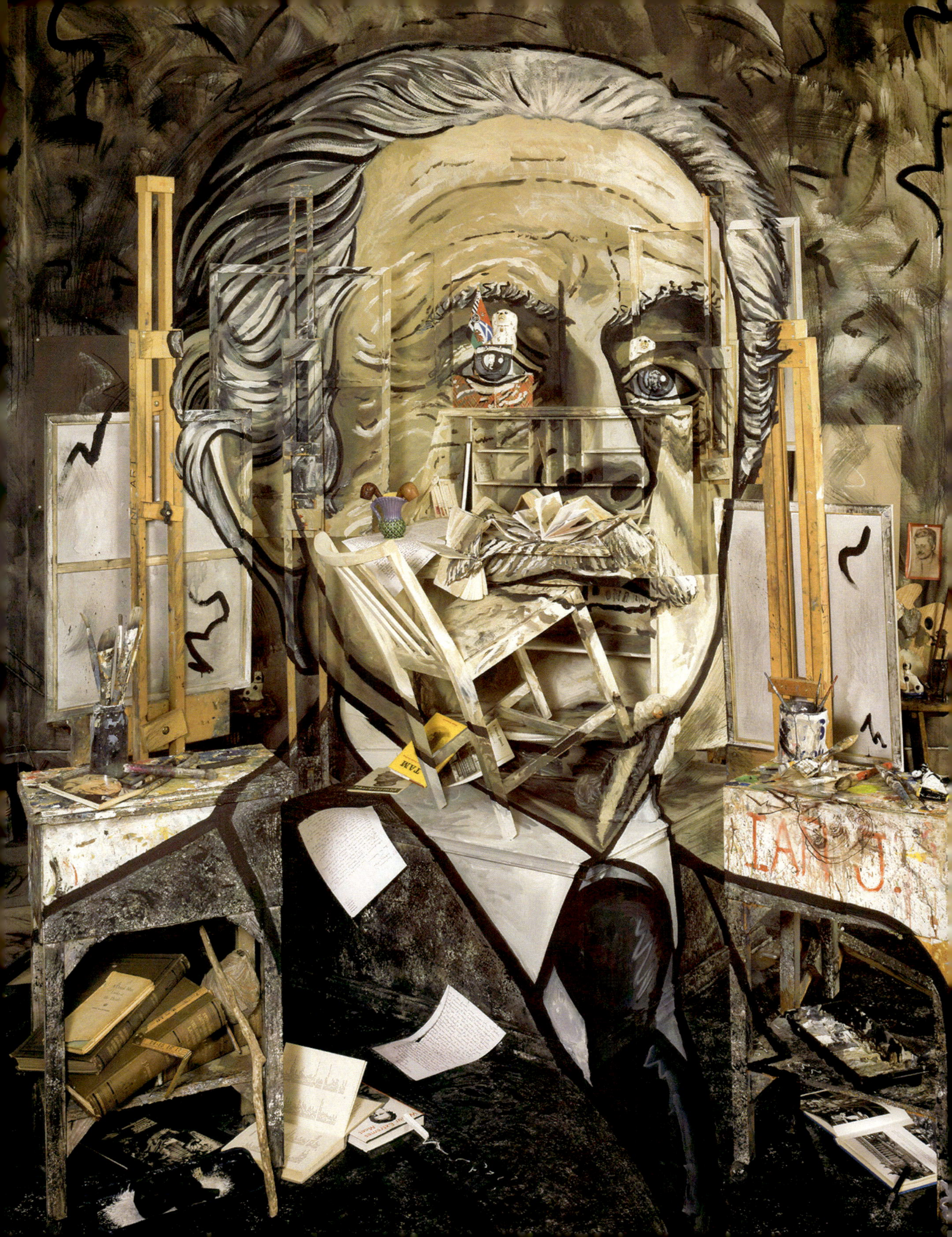

of his own worth and an unswerving commitment to his 'art'. This led to him abandoning his work as a weaver and styling himself a poet and performer. Famously, he wrote of *The Tay Bridge Disaster* and *The Famous Tay Whale*. and his recitations of these works were often treated as a comic music hall performance, though the poet himself was insensitive to these cruel appraisals.

Colvin's portrait of McGonagall is created as a three-dimensional stereoscopic image and properly titled *William McGonagall, Anaglyph*. The portrait places the head of the poet in an artist's studio, painted against an easel. In the background, a distressed

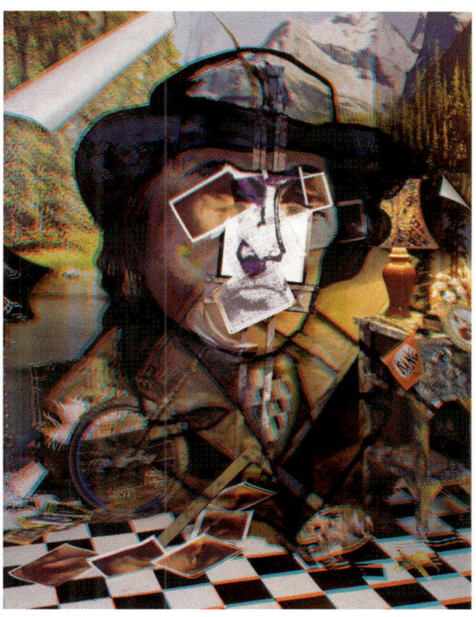

William McGonagall, Anaglyph, 2017

wallpaper shows a panorama of mountains, forest and a flowing river, surely the 'silvery Tay'. Amongst the paraphernalia in the foreground, there is a banana skin, a toy gun and a monocycle. This is the poet as variety performer. The elements of kitsch comedy and the trappings of throwaway novelty trinkets are the emblems of his melodramatic bathos. Yet Colvin's image of McGonagall has a certain resilience, and even a dignity. His *William McGonagall, Anaglyph*, for all the comic absurdity of its subject, is redeemed by an odd sense of grace. Colvin, as a champion of the liminal space between 'high' and 'low' culture, celebrates McGonagall's eccentric triumph.

In fact, the *Museography* exhibition produced a full cargo of portrait studies, largely as a response to the ethos of honouring Dundee's contribution to world affairs through the recognition of its citizens and their related

Portrait of
Hugh MacDiarmid,
2017-18

achievements and, of course, Dundee is 'The City of Discovery'. In which case, Colvin explored the achievements of both Robert Falcon Scott and his nemesis Roald Amundsen.

Colvin's *Portrait of Robert Falcon Scott* presents the commander of the British National Antarctic Expedition of 1901–4. The expedition was a mixed success; it provided scientific insight and helped map the Antarctic region. However, it might be suggested that the real hero of this expedition was the RSS *Discovery*, built by the Dundee Shipbuilders Company. This ship was modelled on the whaling ships that had been built in Dundee for decades, and it was launched into the River Tay in 1901.

The portrait head of Scott is painted onto the interior of his base-camp depot. The wooden hut contains all the apparatus of his mission: ski poles, binoculars, a microscope, a paraffin lamp, even warm socks. Around him the regalia of the British adventurer is displayed: the ship's ensign, the mission flags and the Union Jack; the emblematic symbols of imperial exploration. Scott's rank as a naval officer is given expression in the epaulettes and buttons of his uniform casually placed on a wooden crate, while a copy of *The Daily Mirror* heralds his adventure. The explorer himself is viewed with his seaman's polo-neck jumper a transposed wicker basket and with his chin, nose and left eye painted across an old gramophone, that singular entertainment on the polar expedition.

In contrast, the *Portrait of Roald Amundsen* is a subtle counterpoint to his study of Robert Falcon Scott. Following Scott's partially successful expedition to Antarctica in 1904, the race to reach the South Pole became a fixation amongst explorers. Famously, the Norwegian Amundsen was first to reach the South Pole, arriving there in December 1911, more than a month before Scott's own ill-fated expedition where he and his company would perish early in 1912.

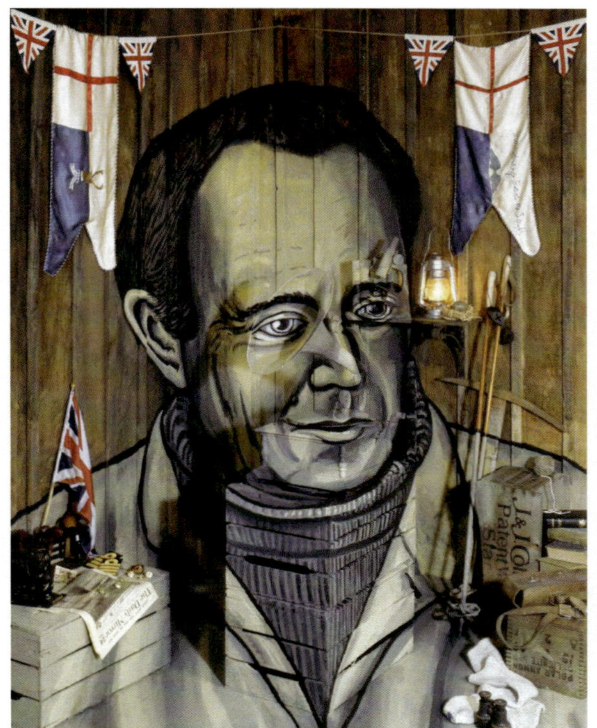

Portrait of Robert Falcon Scott,
2012

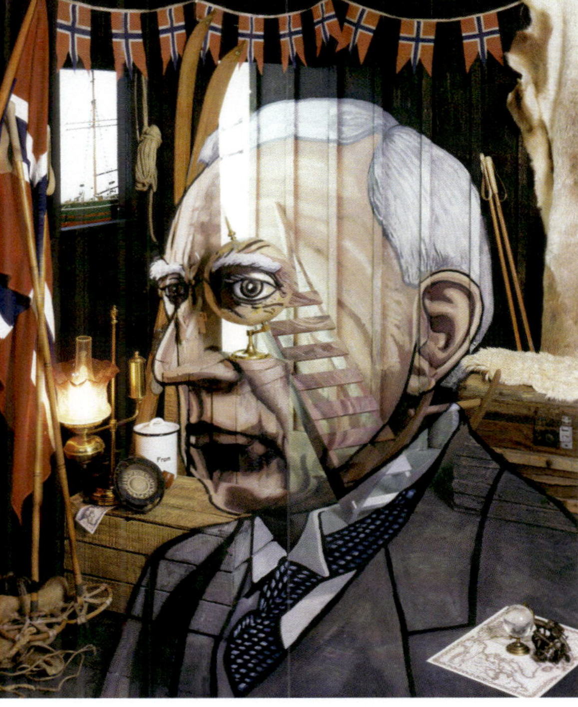

Portrait of Roald Amundsen,
2017

Colvin's Amundsen is again a portrait head and is situated in a cabin-depot,
presumably in transit to the South Pole. Here, incongruously, the austere
Amundsen is shown suited, in a wing-collar shirt and tie. Around him,
the Norwegian flags echo the British flags of the Scott portrait, but surely
signal his triumph in the race to the Pole. Likewise, his right eye morphs
from a globe and so announces his single-minded determination to conquer
the Antarctic. Around him, the scattered paraphernalia of ship and sled
and ski poles recall the instruments of his victory in this extraordinary,
if heroically vainglorious, race.

As an opus, this dimension of Colvin's photography encompasses commissioned work, portraits of friends and associates, and portrait studies of those figures he deemed worthy of representation and reflection. There are, however, very few self-portraits within his oeuvre. A fascinating exception is his *Self-portrait 04* from 2004. Here is his head only, and in profile. He does not turn to face the viewer in the manner of so many self-conscious artists, demanding recognition of their ingenuity and challenging their audience. Rather, this is almost a silhouette, a ghost image.

Within the work, the profile is repeated in two smaller likenesses: a representational black and white photograph, viewed as the frontispiece in an open book; and as a colour image seen reflected in a round mirror. Besides the colour in this last iteration of Colvin's profile, the only other coloured aspects of the photograph are a red book jacket, replete with rounded holes in the shape of a question mark, and a small card decorously emblazoned with the legend 'walk a mile in my shoes'. The rest of the portrait and its background are monochromatic, in shades of grey.

Whereas the convention in Colvin's portraiture was to paint his subjects, this particular photograph evidently references the art of drawing. Although the medium is applied with a brush, the line, the 'mark' and the shading imply a drawn image. Likewise, the setting for the image delineates the characteristic black-and-white-squared-pattern of an artist's studio floor. More tellingly, the squared surface on to which the portrait is created echoes the glass plate on the back of Colvin's large format camera. The platform on which he draws the outline of each subject and artwork.

In some part, Colvin is reflecting on his practice. Indeed, the spectral context for the profile head includes an easel with stretched canvas, a table holding a still-life of goblets and pitcher and a barely discernible cuckoo-clock reprised to right and left of the main subject. These objects function so often as the props of his constructed works. But the whole piece interrogates his manner and his creativity. The frontispiece in the open book on the floor in this image juxtaposes the black and white photograph of Colvin on the verso page with a simple word 'TRUTH' on the recto. Tellingly, this is posed against the book jacket with the question mark glyph, resting to the right of the revealed image and title. In some sense then, this self-portrait is manifestly self-reflexive, and even critical. Certainly, it challenges the nature of creative insight.

Perhaps the key to this self-interrogation is the page of text half-hidden to the right of the photograph, a page of writing that the artist's profile seems to face and to evaluate. The text reads, 'I exist and all that is Not-I is mere phenomena dissolving into phenomenal connections'. This may appear to be a particular kind of solipsism but it is, in fact, a quotation from Edmund Husserl's *The Idea of Phenomenology*, as published in the English language edition of 1964. The German philosopher Husserl had developed his work on Phenomenology from the late 19th century, and his philosophy has remained profoundly influential into the contemporary period. The core insight, that the world does not exist as material and object but is read inside the consciousness of the individual as phenomena, is surely a paradigm for Colvin's fluid vision and mercurial imagination. Just as powerfully it recognises the deceptive nature of the camera, and the photograph, as a purveyor of 'objective reality'.

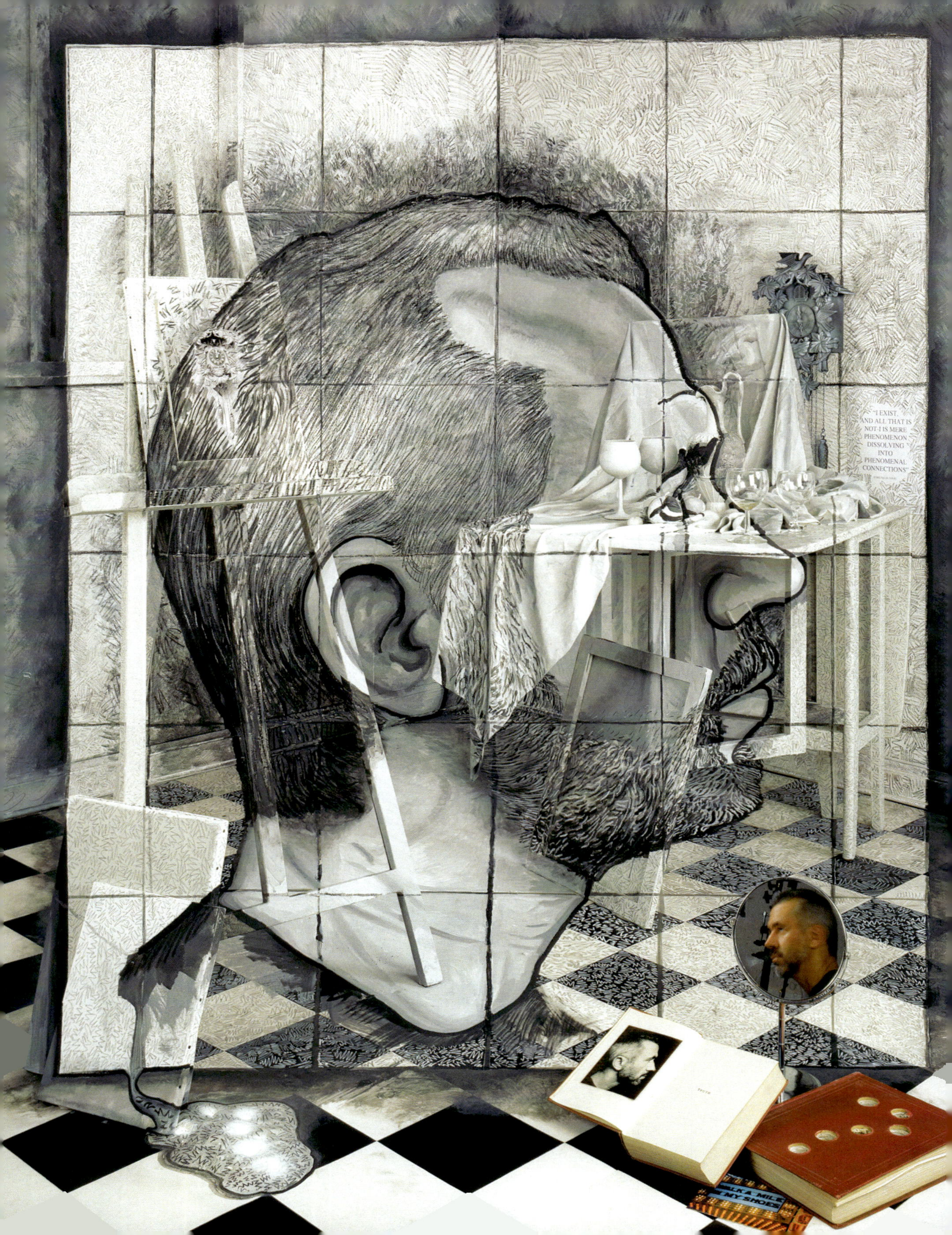

"I EXIST, AND ALL THAT IS NOT-I IS MERE PHENOMENON DISSOLVING INTO PHENOMENAL CONNECTIONS"

Self-portrait 04,
2004

Calum Colvin's *Self-portrait 04* was printed and exhibited as a conventional photograph and as an 'anaglyph'. The anaglyph is the creation of a particular kind of stereoscopic image. This is produced by generating two views of the subject each with a different colour filter, most usually red and cyan. When these images are overlain, the one atop the other, and viewed through the appropriate coloured glasses, then the photograph appears in a startling three dimensions. The experimentation that Colvin was engaging in when producing this work was typical of the fascination that he has consistently shown in the technologies of the camera and the creation of the photograph. This interest reached forward into digital technologies, and stretched back into the early history of photography as an art and science. In each case, he looked to explore the means by which the photograph both projects a reality and offers a kind of fiction. And so, photography's aspiration towards 'truth' was consistently undermined by its editorial and interpretative capacities. This, Colvin understood, was the chimera of the medium, it longed to capture the world in all its objective materiality but inevitably fell into a capricious illusion.

Of course, Colvin had engaged in experiment with the medium for most of his career. His 'constructed narratives' were created in the liminal space between painting, sculpture and the photograph. But, from the late 1980s, and with the rapid changes in the nature of photographic technologies, his interest in diverse forms of generating photographic images intensified. Characteristically, Colvin reached deep into this brave new world with an extraordinary creative enthusiasm.

Colvin's first foray into computer image-making was occasioned by an invitation from The Photographers' Gallery in London. In 1989, as the celebrations for the 150th anniversary of the invention of photography were underway, The Photographers' Gallery was preparing an exhibition to be titled *Machine Dreams*. As part of this project, Colvin was given the opportunity to make works using the new computerised technologies that

Self-portrait 04,
Anaglyph
2004

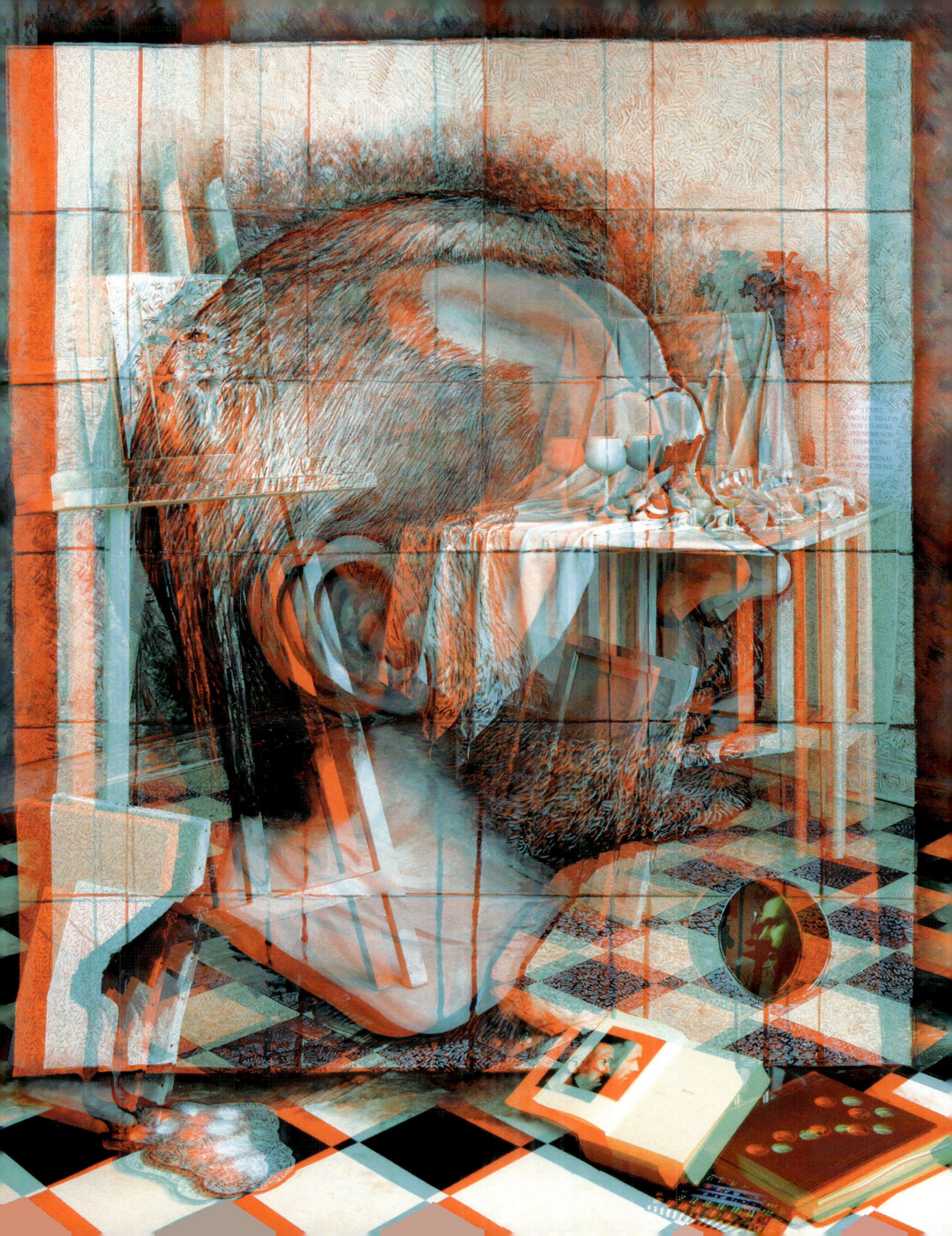

were then becoming available. In the event, he was provided with the facilities of a major electronics company in Hemel Hempstead and began to experiment with computer-manipulated imagery.

Colvin created three photographs using these still fairly rudimentary technologies. These were *Jacob's Ladder*, *Flying a Kite* and *Icarus*, all completed in 1989. Technically, each photograph takes the form of a montaged scenario in a framed background landscape within which a kind of drama unfolds. These episodes are set against a black background and each has a brief quote gleaned from an *Oor Wullie* cartoon, that deity of Scottish popular culture, that acts as a kind of commentary. Each image exists in three spatial planes, and this renders the photographs relatively flat, so exposing the artifice of their making. Equally, the primitive nature of the technology generated a pixelated image, one that is not immediately obvious in the finished works but gives a quite distinct 'feel' to these photographs, a feel that contrasts with his more conventional work completed in the studio.

In this period, the technology was certainly challenging but Colvin explored its potential and produced works that focussed upon its aspirations. He undertook this by uploading and deploying the symbolism that had become familiar in his photographs of the mid-1980s. Chief amongst these was the mobilisation of his kilted Action Man figure. In *Jacob's Ladder*, the figure ascends the eponymous ladder, each rung emblazoned with a legend that illustrates developing insight; the senses, the imagination, the intelligence. As the avatar moves towards a graphic depiction of enlightenment, Oor Wullie offers the warning, 'There's danger on the Whinny Braes – or so oor climbing hero says!'

Jacob's Ladder,
1989

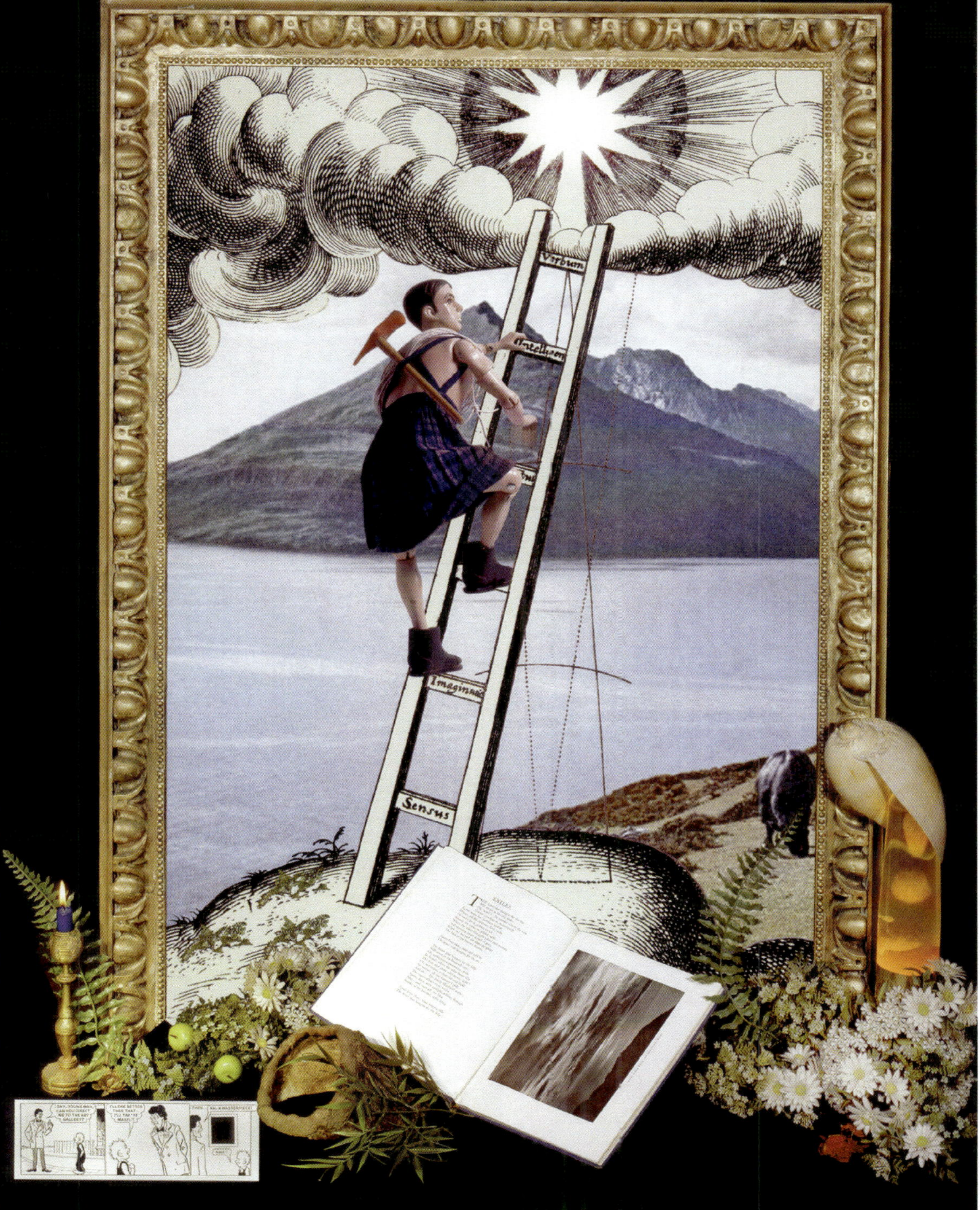
Verbum
Intellect
Imaginatio
Sensus
SAY, YOUNG MAN, CAN YOU DIRECT ME TO THE ART GALLERY?
I'LL DAE BETTER THAN THAT! I'LL TAK' YE MASEL'!
THEN...
AH, A MASTERPIECE!

This aspirational endeavour is extended in *Flying a Kite* where the Action Man doll accompanies a plaster mannequin, holding the string of a flying kite and dressed in Highland regalia. This is apposite, for the background motif consists of a scenic Highland Games against a landscape of hills and sky. The legend here intones that 'Oor Wullie's life is never boring – Here he is awa' exploring!' This notion of 'flying a kite' does speak to the experiment with the new technologies in combination with the sense of a kind of spiritual ascension, as afforded by the rise into the ethereal realm.

Though this dramatic fiction appears to have an aspirational goal, it becomes grounded in the subject of *Icarus*. Here the Action Man figure, complete with feathered wings, is seen to have fallen to earth. Judged unequal in the ambition for creative and spiritual flight, and evidenced in the tipped scales behind the fallen figure, the hero is, quite literally, grounded. He is saved, however, by the mixed foliage into which he falls and, reflecting on this redemption, Oor Wullie declares, 'Just when it seems disaster looms – Up come Wullie's quick grown blooms!'

These three works do not strictly compose a triptych, though evidently the narrative interlinks and offers something of a morality tale. Colvin was certainly conscious of the adventure entailed in exploring the new technology, and presented something of a commentary on the potential of these innovations. But the core issue in these works is the idea of creativity and creative ambitions. The recurring motifs, apart from the omnipresent Action Man figure, are nature, foliage, an open book that references the links between poetry and landscape, the comic interventions of Oor Wullie and the montaged elements of graphic illustration.

Indeed, throughout these works, Colvin used graphic illustrations appropriated from the works of the 17th century scientist and occultist Robert Fludd. Fludd was a complex individual but he did believe in a tripartite division of life; nature, human being, and the magical spiritual dimension. These themes appear everywhere in Colvin's first series of

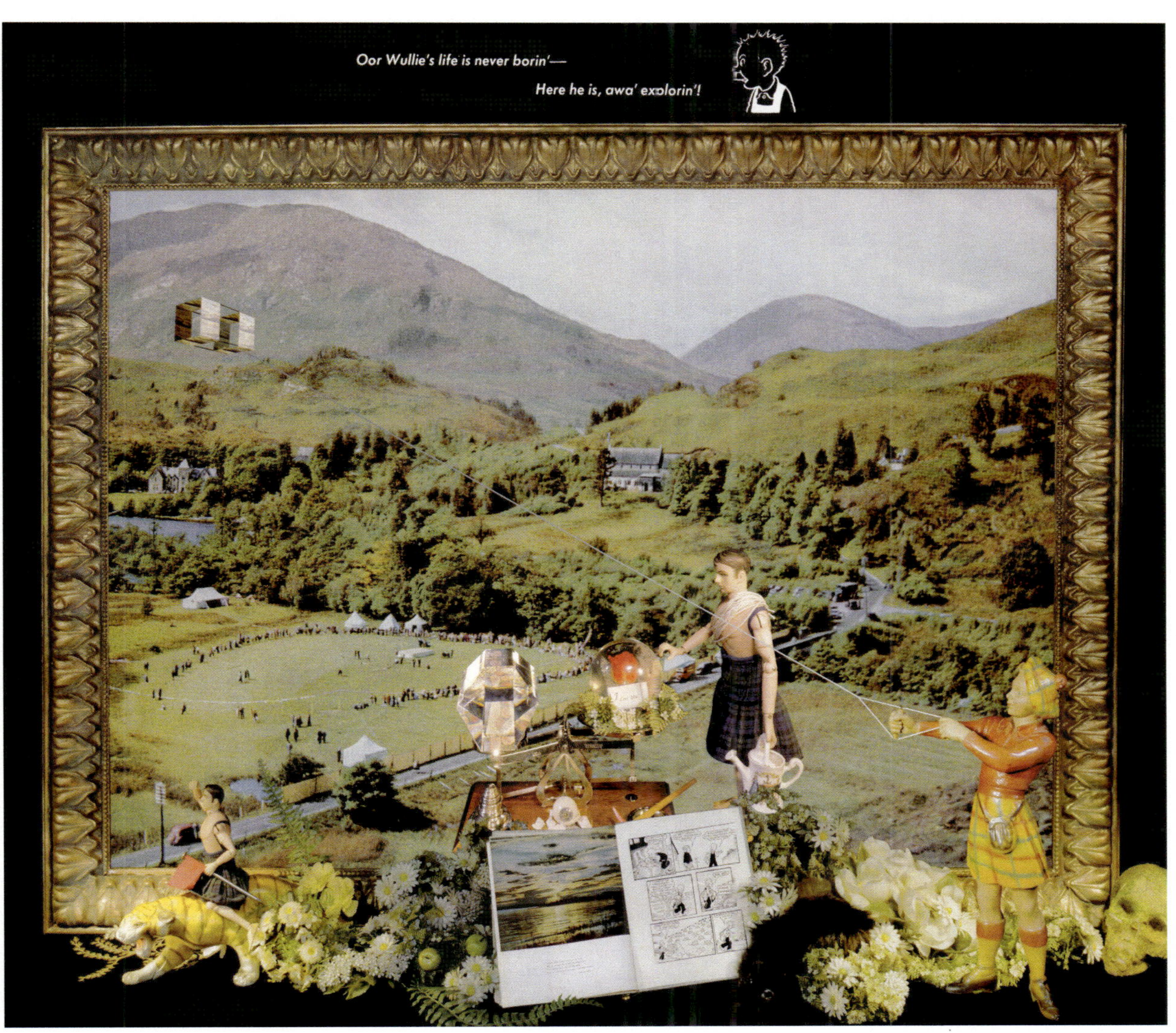

Flying a Kite,
1989

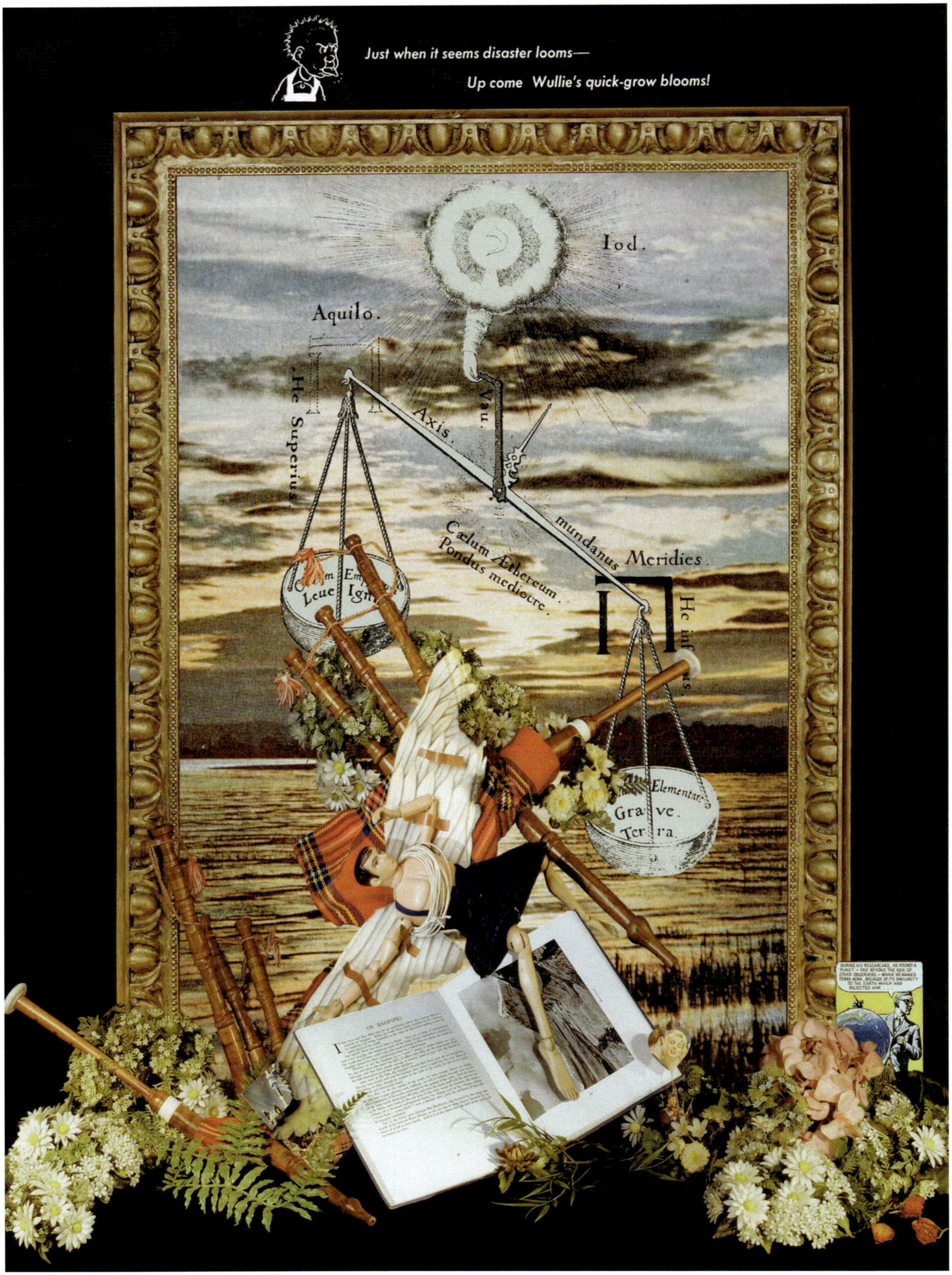

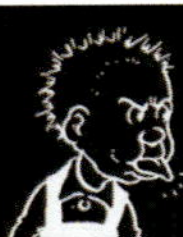

Just when it seems disaster looms—
Up come Wullie's quick-grow blooms!

computer-generated photographs. They exist, discretely, in the form of the photographs where the threefold separation of the montaged layers is the building block of the narrative. Moreover, they are presented also in the runic, Latinate, inscriptions and instructions written through the images. Fundamentally, they are present in the mystical view of creative endeavour that remains the core of these images.

Colvin would develop his engagement with computer-manipulated photographs at the point where the technology became more sophisticated, and its potential more dynamic. In 1993, he approached a subject that had come into his orbit following a visit to The Prado in Madrid. There, he had studied Hieronymus Bosch's remarkable work titled *The Seven Deadly Sins and the Four Last Things*, dated to the period around 1500. Bosch, the Early Netherlandish painter of grotesque parables peopled with terrifying monster-machines and macabre incidents, produced this work in his middle period and, indeed, it may be substantially the work of his studio. Certainly it is less fantastical than some of his more lurid images, but its subject chimed with Colvin's thinking in this period.

Bosch's work is an oil painting on wooden panels constructed to form a table-top. The core motif is a large human 'eye' with, at the centre, an image of Christ above the written warning, 'Beware, Beware, God Sees'. A circular 'iris' displays episodes exposing the Seven Deadly Sins: Gluttony, Sloth, Lust, Pride, Anger, Envy and Greed. In each corner of the table-top, the 'Four Last Things' are revealed: The Death of a Sinner, The Last Judgement, Hell and, for the chosen few, Heaven. Colvin adapted this morality tale and made it relevant to the contemporary world.

The principal work is a large composite photograph of the 'Seven Deadly Sins' and 'Four Last Things' that echoes the manner of Bosch's presentation. Each episode is powerfully constructed and afforded its separate image. Some of these are comic, and some darkly tragic. The representation titled

Icarus,
1989

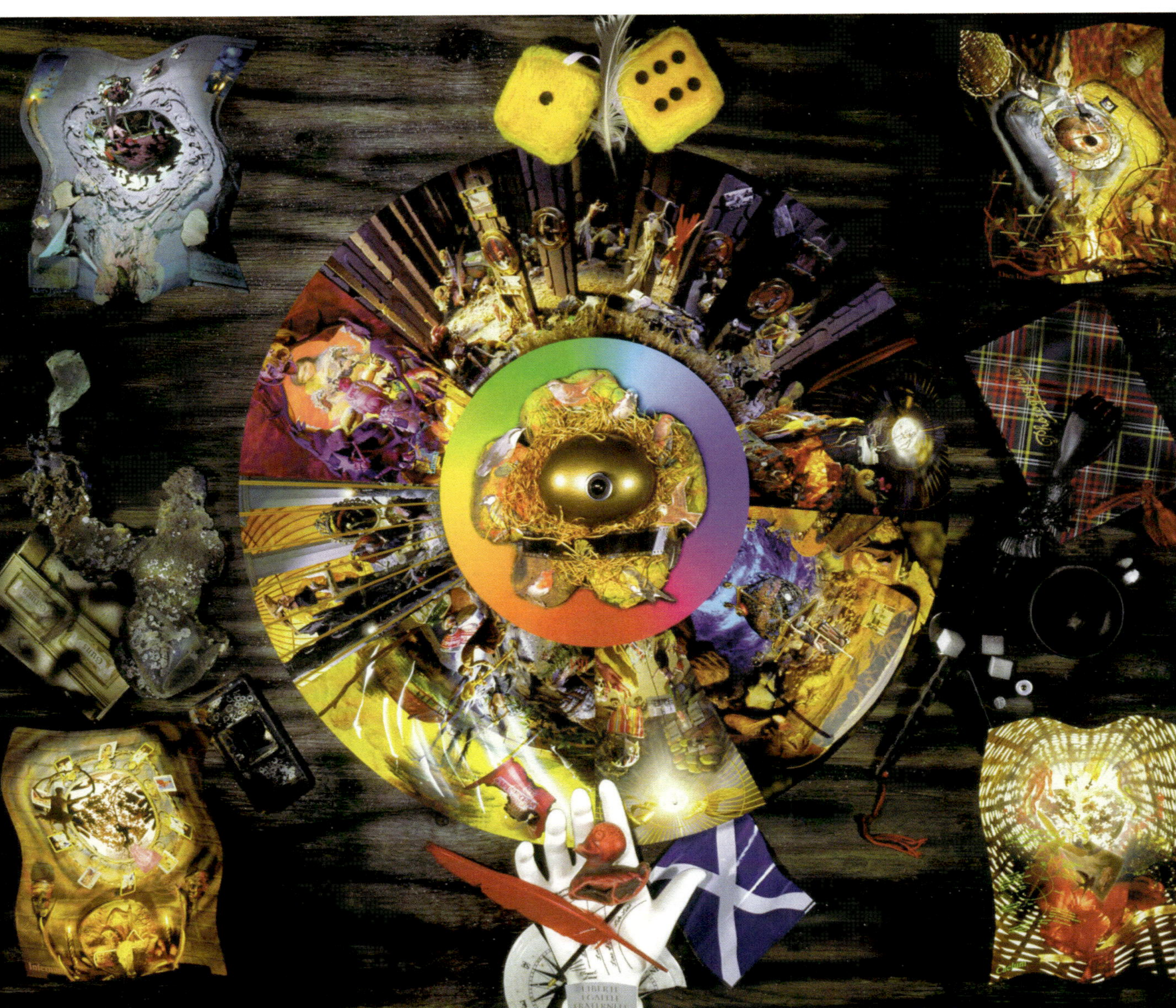

The Seven Deadly Sins and the Four Last Things,
1993

Anger is telling. Colvin has generated an extraordinary incident in which two figures appear in combat. One is the kilted Action Man doll seen wielding a claymore. The other is a manipulated photograph of Colvin himself, with bare torso and in a kilt, seen defending himself from this onslaught with an absurd toy coat-stand or perhaps a cocktail stirrer.

This scenario is set against a kitsch landscape of yellow sky and an indeterminate dwelling-house, but the notion of 'anger' is amplified in the related associations and symbolism presented in the context.

A junk shop ornament, made from shells, is set in the scene. It shows a predatory fish with smaller fish caught in its mouth, a subtle reference to the Netherlandish proverb, 'Big fish eat little fish'. This sense of enmity and fury is further accented in the background banner which consists of a scorched McDonald's wrapper and logo. This is juxtaposed in the lower left corner of the image with some crushed Campbell's soup cans. The clear reference to the Glencoe Massacre of 1692 is accented by the juxtaposition of a Clan Lager tin discreetly placed in the foreground of the image.

The photograph, then, is a layered meditation on ideas of anger and injustice. Indeed, Colvin skilfully includes a shadow portrait of James Lock at the feet of his warring protagonists. Lock was the agent for the Duke of Sutherland and was infamous for his participation in enacting the Highland Clearances in the early part of the nineteenth century. Subtly, then, this meditation on 'anger' offers reflections of Scottish history. It also expands this concept into the economic 'wars' of globalised corporations. While the inclusion of the Latin text used by Bosch to identify this particular sin 'IRA' presents another layer of thought and insight.

The idea of global expansion and neo-imperialist ambitions is developed in Colvin's image relating to the sin of greed, titled *Avarice*. Here, Action Man is seen sailing on a twee hostess-trolley. Between its lower and upper

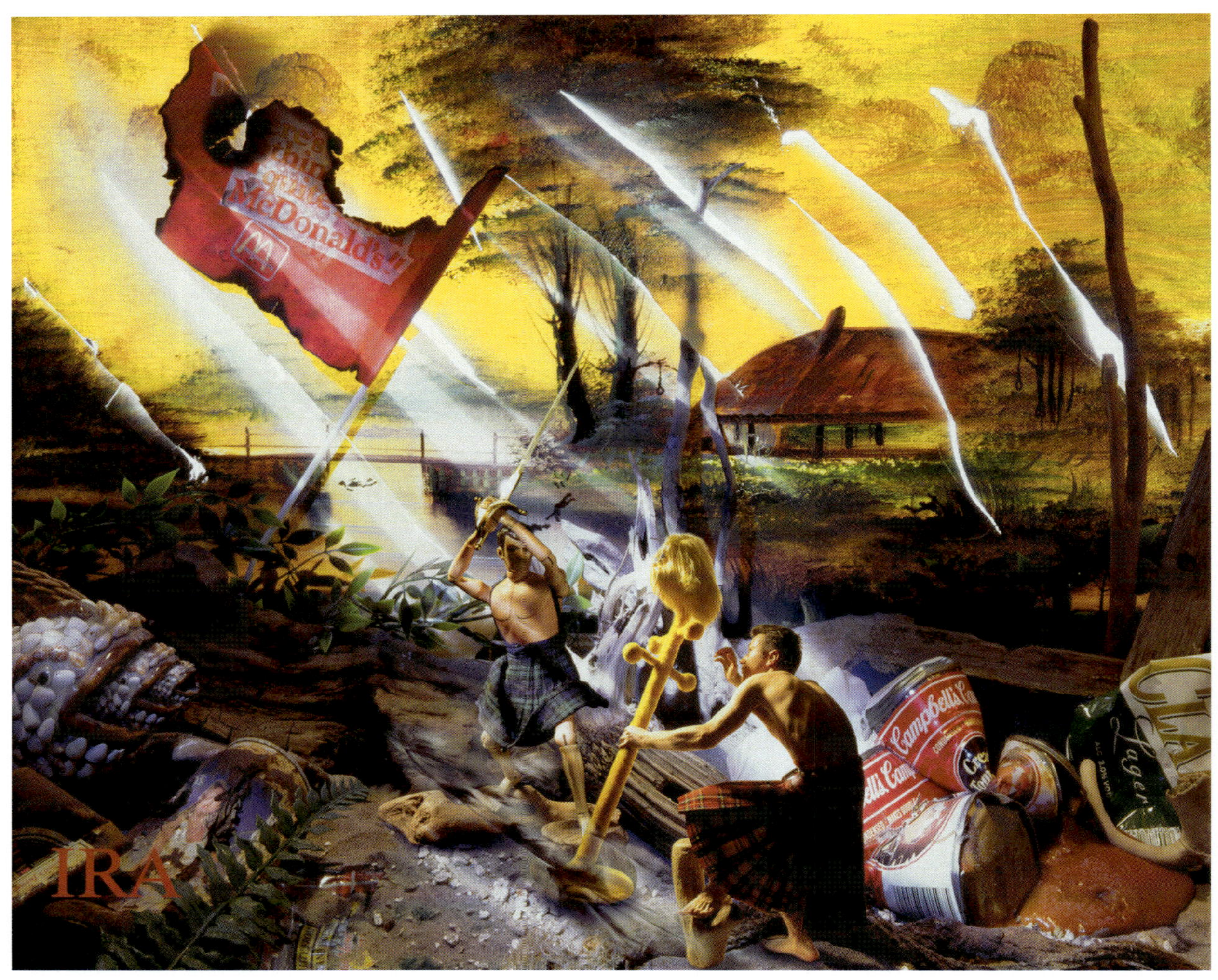

Anger,
1993

platforms an inflated beach ball is shown, decorated with a map of the
cosmos. The figure sails this 'ship' with the aid of a toy mast decorated
with geometric symbols; those symbolic representations of logic and
reason. But the 'ship' sails towards an untouched landscape, in fact
a decorated tea-tray, picturing land, hills and sky. Notably, at the foot

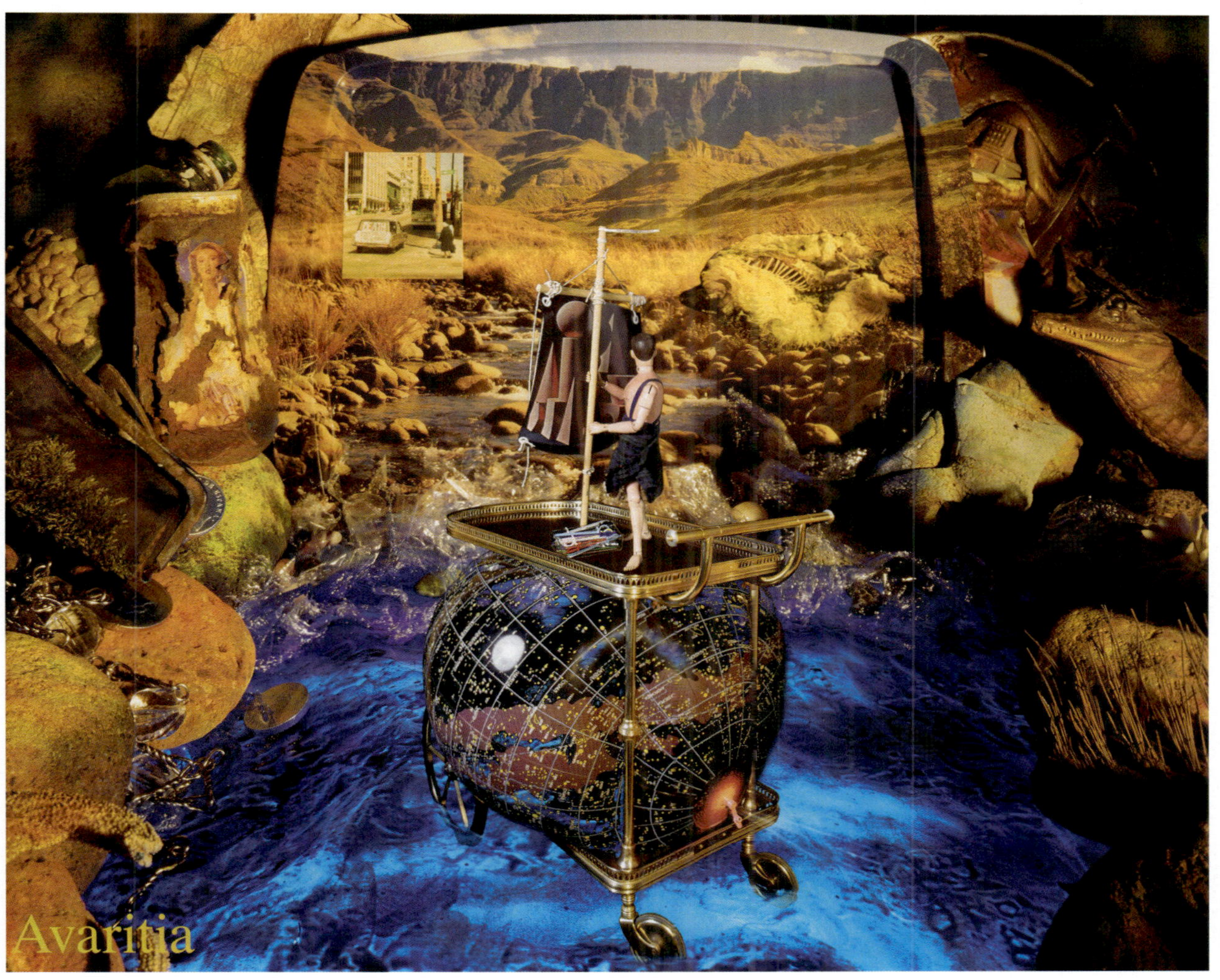

Avarice,
1993

of the doll there is an array of toy swords representing the tools of
persuasion, while a purse, with coins and jewels, falls open to the lower
left of the image. This 'treasure' is the fruits of conquest. The avarice
referenced here applies to the invasion and occupation of foreign lands
and, indeed, the potential subjugation of the cosmos itself.

Evidently these are serious issues, though half-hidden within an absurdist fantasy drama. The fullest example of this revelatory comedy is presented in his exposition on the theme of lust. In *Lust,* Colvin allows his protagonists to perform an odd ritual of mechanistic craving and meaningless gratification. The central motif is a joke-shop 'Mr Bum' figure, a pneumatic toy that will drop his trousers when manipulated, and expose his rear. He faces towards a postcard image of a young woman, ever the voyeur. To the left of the photograph, the Action Man doll fires an arrow from a toy bow, piercing the absurd Mr Bum; the avatar is, in this iteration, a toyshop 'cupid'. Mr Bum reacts to these stimuli by exposing himself, while a toy water-pistol, in the shape of a tiger, jets a stream of fluid across the scene. *Lust,* then, offers a ludicrous parody of human desire and the most callous representation of human passion. It speaks to the emptiness of this atavistic appetite.

Of course, the sins of human kind would inevitably be appraised and atoned for in the Four Last Things: death, judgement and the afterlife. Colvin's vision of these things was startling, and secular. In *The Last Judgement,* the omniscient Action Man doll is compelled to walk a convoluted bamboo tightrope. Behind him, the 'eye of God', in fact the eye of a dead turkey, judges his life in the balance. In the foreground, a multitude of birds reflect on the value of this human life. To left and to right, options of paradise, and of hell, are presented as light and shade. In this proposition, it is Nature itself that will judge the import of human actions on Earth.

The entirety of *The Seven Deadly Sins and the Four Last Things* was commissioned by Gloria Chalmers, the visionary director of The Portfolio Gallery, a dedicated photography space in Edinburgh, and was exhibited in the early summer of 1993. This was an ambitious foray for the gallery into the exhibition of computer-generated images, but the quality of these works as photographs was undisputed. And, briefly, Colvin was identified as having left the studio, with its associated processes of construction and painting, and so being committed to the new technologies.

Lust,
1993

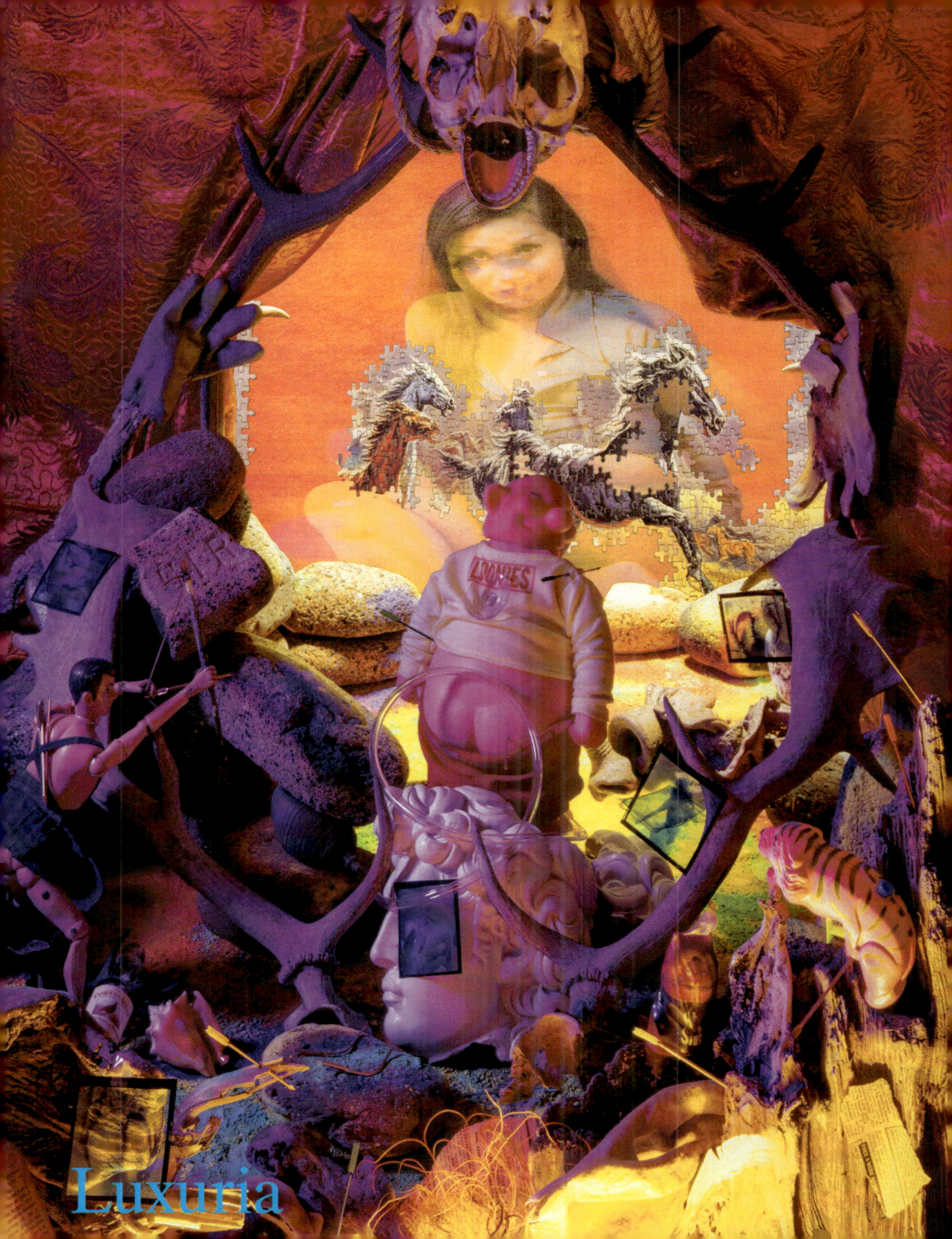
Luxuria

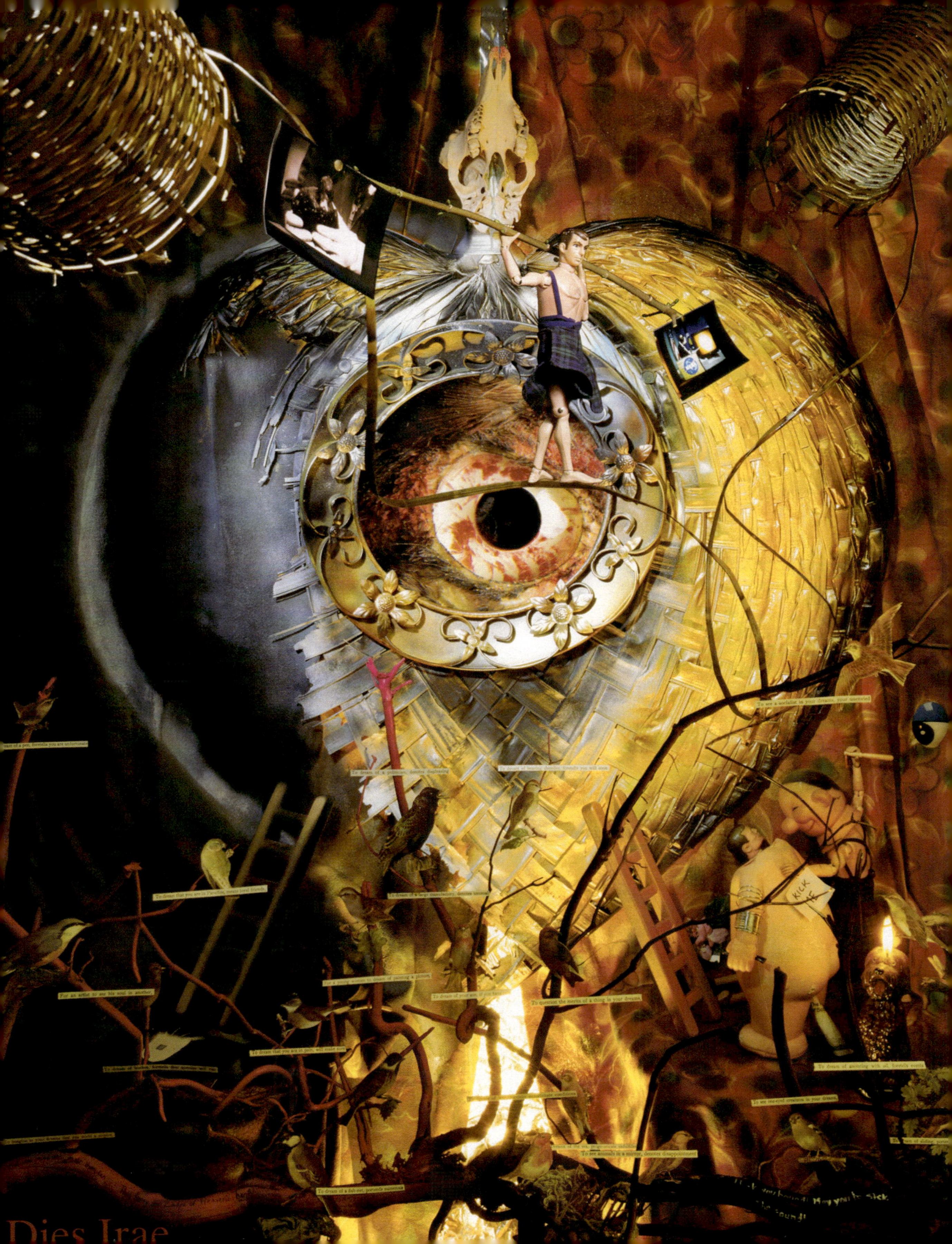

Dies Irae
KICK ME

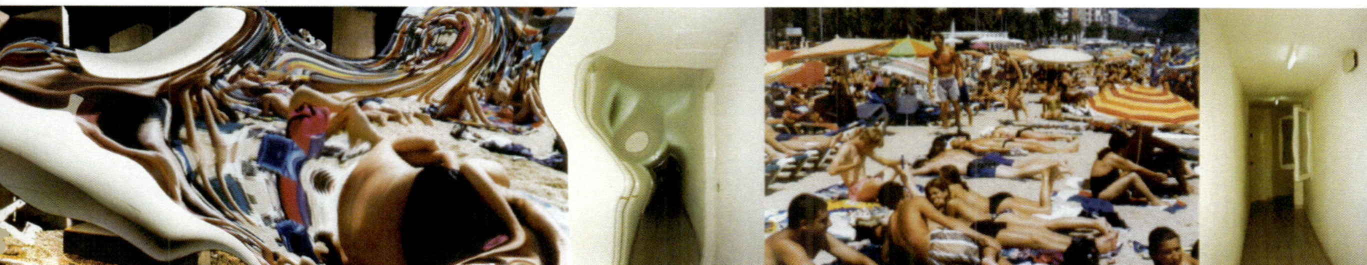

Untitled – Triptychs 1, 2, 3, & 4, (detail),
1996

While Colvin would return to studio-based practice, he remained fascinated by the ways in which computer technology might expand and contest the 'truth value' of the photographic image. In 1996, Colvin was invited to work as a Senior Research Fellow at Northumbria University. This opportunity was supported by the Impressions Gallery in the City of York and resulted in a series of works collectively titled *Pseudologica Fantastica*. The Portfolio Gallery would exhibit these works as the gallery's Edinburgh Festival exhibition in August 1997.

The works in *Pseudologica Fantastica* represented something of a departure in Colvin's computer-generated imagery. The avatar of the Action Man was largely absent; the single exception being in the black and white photograph titled *Mundus Subterraneus v*. The principal body of works was shaped as long, panoramic triptychs that melded snapshot images with surreal, mercurial landscapes. The snapshots were taken by Colvin on a visit to the Spanish resort of Lloret de Mar. Images of tourists sunbathing became the catalyst for an extended threnody on vanity and dissipation. In which case, the snapshot of a sun-drenched beach peopled by sun-worshipping holiday-makers segues into a melting hotel corridor, and on into a liquefied quasi-abstract scene of molten bodies.

The Last Judgement,
1993

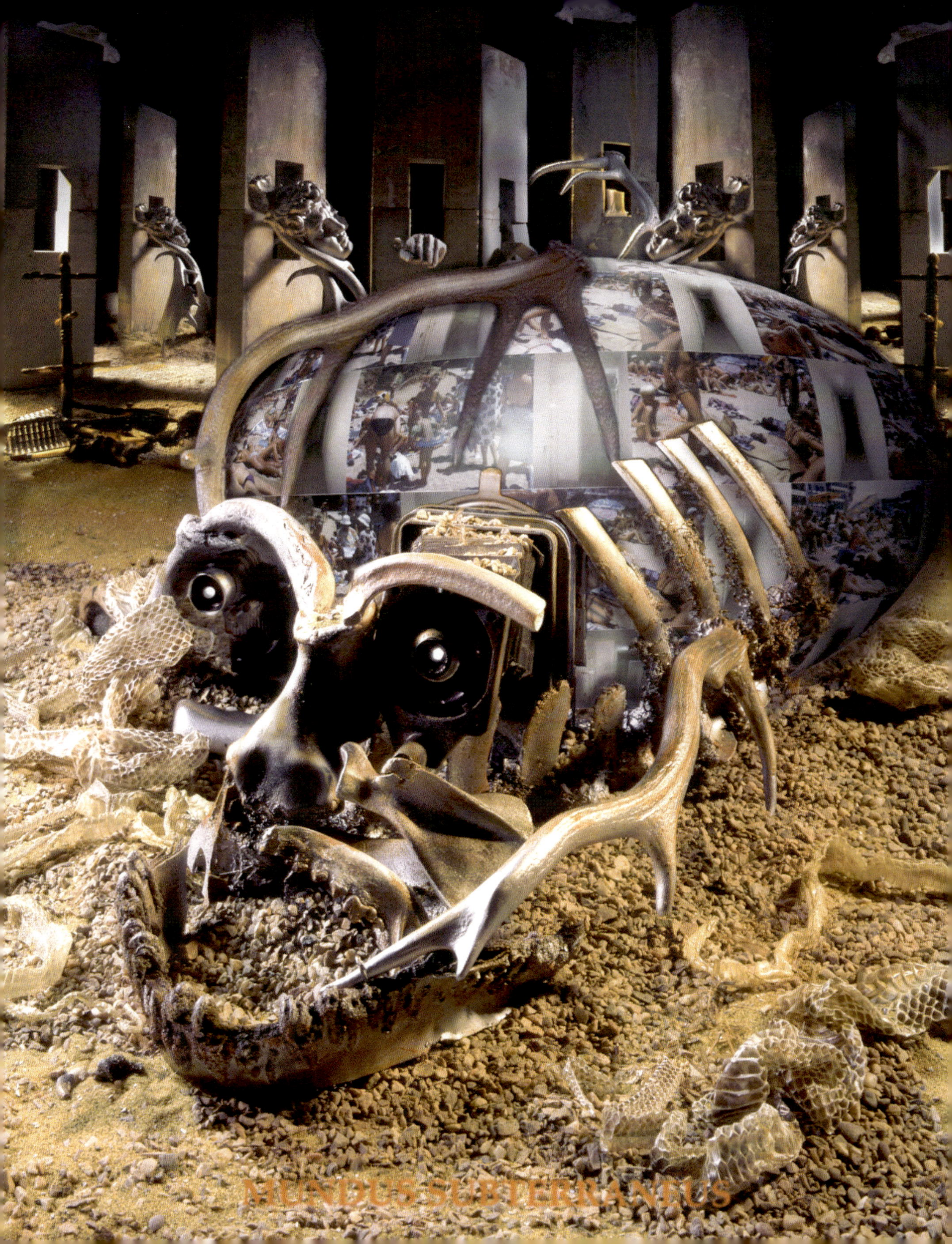
MUNDUS SUBTERRANEUS

David Alan Mellor has written on these astonishing works, noting that

> ...there is a reversal of expectation about the legibility and
> substantiality of different forms of imaging; his terminal and
> indeterminable beaches, actual and recorded on film, become
> de-realised by pixilation and digitisation – turned into teardrop
> reliquaries of our desired images of consumer leisure.[6]

And this is surely the tenor of these photographs where all that is solid melts into a surreal igneous magma.

The sense of a scorched underworld comes to dominate this series of images. Partly, this was determined by Colvin's interest in alchemy and, during this project, he was in thrall to the works of Athanasius Kircher, the 17th century German scholar. Kircher was a Jesuit and a polymath whose diverse scholarship remains impressive; indeed, he was, amongst a wealth of interests, fascinated with lens technology. His studies also touched upon a critique of alchemy as a practice and this was partly expressed in his work, *The Subterranean World*, from 1664. This publication, properly titled *Mundus Subterraneous*, and so providing the title for Colvin's project, also explored issues in geology and the earth's 'internal fires'. By these subtle pathways, it is evident Colvin's project may be read as a discourse on the contemporary effects of global climate change.

The apotheosis of these concerns can be viewed in the scorched underworld scenes in *Pseudologica Fantastica*, and perhaps most clearly in *Mundus Subterraneus 1*. In this photograph, a charred human skull, partly composed of antlers, sits in a cavernous grotto. The interior space of the skull is filled with the snapshot images of sunbathing bodies, while all around are the charred remains of a burned landscape. Intriguingly, the 'eyes' of the skull are constructed from two camera lenses. They stare out as witness on to the desolate and blighted netherworld.

Mundus Subterraneus I,
1996

Pseudologica Fantastica was a radical development in Colvin's computer-manipulated photography. The 'look' and the level of experiment in the works was distinctive. Moreover, the sense of symbolism, and even allegory, was overlain by a Surrealist vision of melting forms and transforming shapes. At its core, however, there remained that singular investigation of the ways in which the camera records and interprets the material world, a world that was increasingly overdetermined by the new technology of the computer.

This project would be the terminating scheme in Colvin's engagement with the most contemporary of technologies, for he became increasingly interested in the early history of photography and its experimental modes. Before moving to that place, however, he would exploit one other aspect of the computer's wizardry. This was his *Portrait of James Macpherson*, completed for his exhibition titled *Ossian: Fragments of Ancient Poetry* which was displayed at the Scottish National Portrait Gallery in Edinburgh during the winter months of 2002 and 2003.

James Macpherson was the author, or 'translator', of the poetical works of Ossian. Ossian was projected as a 3rd century Gaelic bard. In the early 1760s, Macpherson published a number of popular poetry books styled as having been discovered, as fragments and orations, in the Gàidhealtachd. The authenticity of these works was hotly disputed, and Macpherson was sometimes regarded as having constructed rather than translated these epic poems. In which case he was, for all his international recognition, sometimes regarded as a skilled counterfeiter by eminent contemporary figures.

Colvin's extended meditation on the implications of this phenomenon has been one of his most intriguing projects and it was completed as a constructed and painted narrative photography. However, the concluding image in his narrative was his work titled *Portrait of James Macpherson.*

Portrait of
James Macpherson,
2002

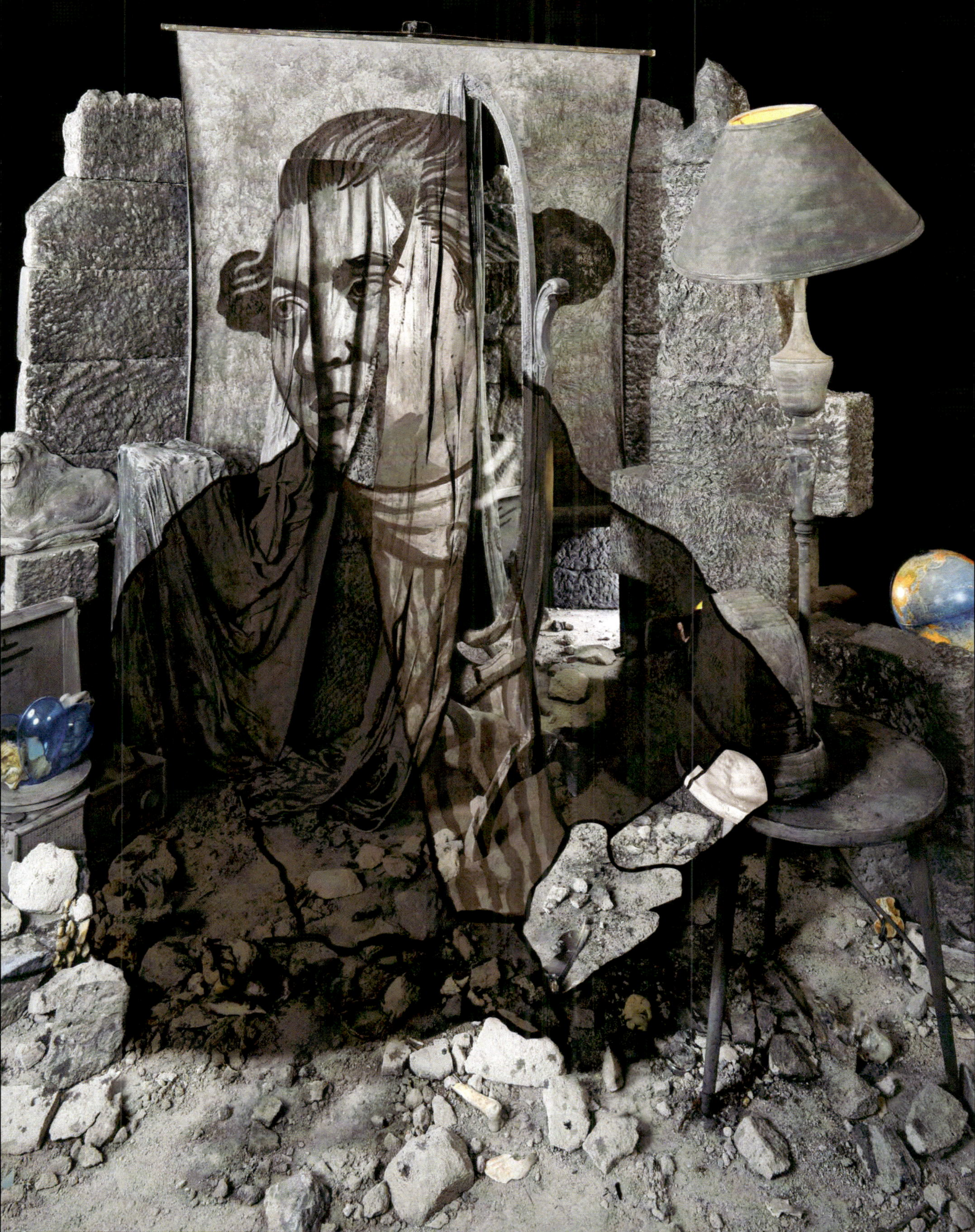

For this photograph, he decided to emulate the conceit of Macpherson. He appropriated the *Portrait of James Macpherson* held in the Scottish National Portrait Gallery and painted in the 18th century by an unknown hand, but after Joshua Reynolds. This image he projected onto his *Ossian* tableau and then used Photoshop to edit the painting so that it was revealed in the style of Calum Colvin. Here, the presumed fraud in Macpherson's practice was echoed in the deception of Colvin's invention. And Photoshop, that arch manipulator of the authentic image, was recognised as a tool in the creation of those multiple fictions that constitute contemporary life.

Evidently, towards the end of the millennium, Colvin recognised the nature of the new computer technologies and their implications for photography. But, as the new century dawned, he began to focus on the qualities of the camera, and the photograph, as these were developed in the early history of the medium. Here, too, he opened out a discussion on the fabricated character of this 'scientific' search for veracity to nature. Indeed, his subject became the history of photography as this was developed in the British Isles, and especially in Scotland, in which case the exacting figure of Sir David Brewster came sharply into focus.

David Brewster was a distinguished 19th century academic whose discipline was Natural Philosophy. This polymathic study has its modern parallel in physics but traditionally incorporated the entire study of the natural world. Brewster would ably fulfil this expansive bailiwick with research in everything from astronomy to the history of science. His core engagement, however, was the science of optics. Here, he would experiment in refraction and developed a multitude of scientific instruments, or 'new philosophical instruments' as he would call them, that explored the distant horizons of human vision.

In the 1830s, and beyond, this would naturally lead Brewster into experiments with various types of lens, the early forms of the camera and the development of the photograph. Moreover, as an eminent scientist and Principal of the University of St Andrews, Brewster was a confidant of William Henry Fox Talbot, the English inventor of the paper negative Calotype method of producing photographs. This process was announced in the period circa 1840, as a response to Louis Daguerre's publication of the Daguerreotype technology in 1839. It happens that Talbot had heavily copyrighted his Calotype but Brewster was instrumental in securing the patent-free use of the Calotype process in Scotland, in this way securing a preeminent place for Scotland in the early history of photography.

Following from Brewster's correspondence with Talbot, in which his experiments and the subsequent developments were freely discussed, he would promote these innovations within the St Andrews Literary and Philosophical Society. Here, local academics and professionals would experiment with the new medium. It was from this group that Brewster selected the photographer Robert Adamson and introduced him to the painter David Octavius Hill, thus establishing the most significant photographic partnership in the historical canon.

Brewster, however, remains most notable for two key inventions that might best be described as scientific toys: the kaleidoscope and the stereoscope. With both these inventions, as elsewhere in his life, Brewster generated more controversy than celebration. The kaleidoscope, surely one of the most popular and charming of optical playthings, was invented by Brewster after his optical experiments of 1816 and was patented in 1817. Controversy followed as it was noted that the principles of the kaleidoscope had been known to science for centuries, and so Brewster's patent was undermined. The ensuing public squabbles continued for over 50 years with Brewster publishing his self-justifying *Treatise on the Kaleidoscope* as late as 1858.

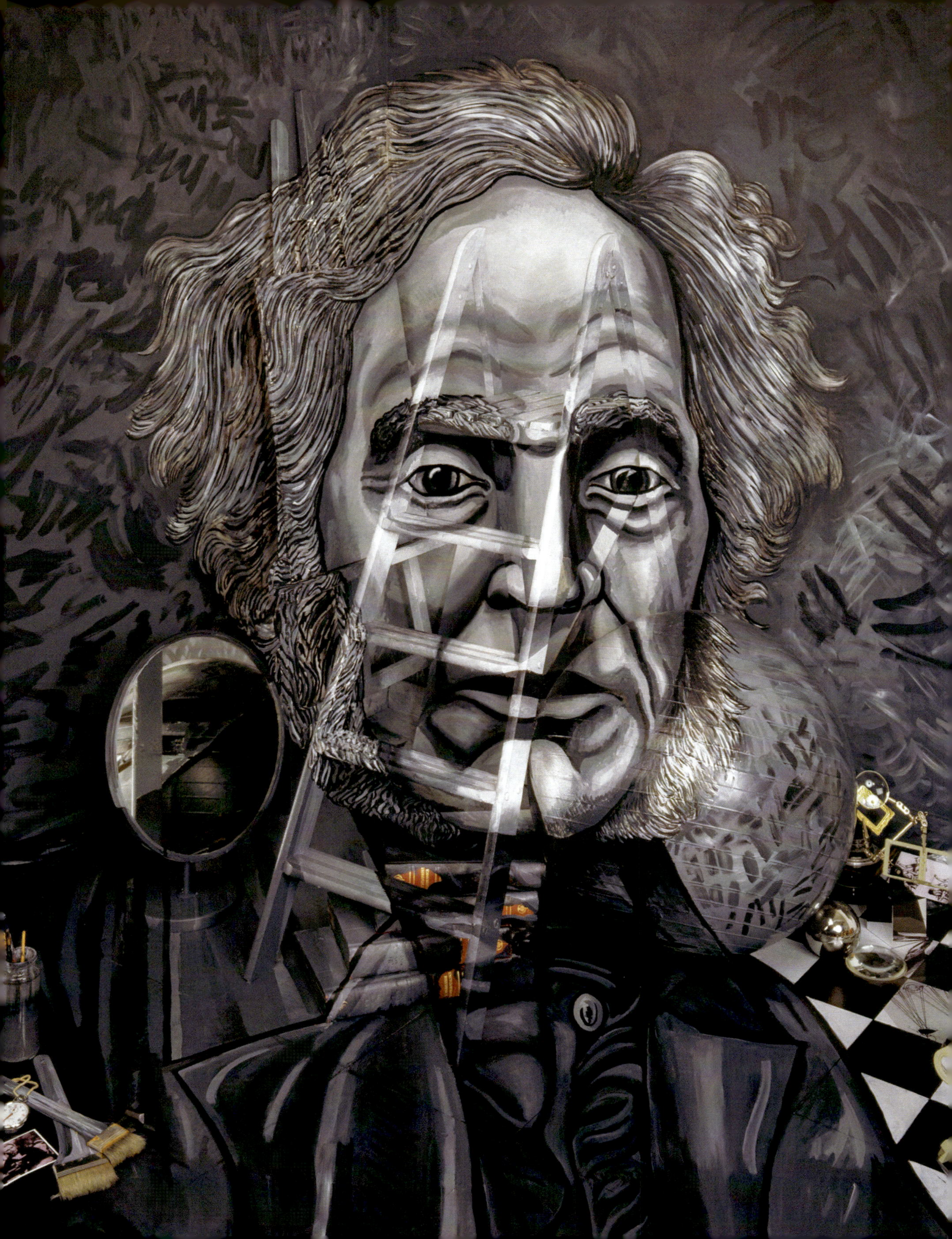

A parallel controversy followed his invention of the stereoscope, which Brewster announced in 1849. In fact, this device was a development of the mirror stereoscope invented by Charles Wheatstone as early as 1832, but it was Brewster's lens-based 'lenticular stereoscope' that would be demonstrated at The Great Exhibition in 1851. From this point his model, accompanied by his binocular camera, would become the market leader in what was a popular obsession. But, typically, Brewster remained mired in dispute on the issue of the 'priority' of this invention for the remainder of his life.

It is this last issue, and the accompanying controversy, that has intrigued Colvin and became the core subject of his work in the middle years of the first decade of the 21st century. In consequence, and through a series of stereoscopic images, he explored the problematic of Brewster's inventions, and the contingency of his interest in vision and the photographic image, to offer an imaginative survey of this disputed terrain. In this project, he has developed all the nuanced tropes of his oeuvre.

Within this context, the portrait study became the vehicle for Colvin's discourse on Brewster's world, and it was Brewster who became his first subject. His epic study of the irascible Brewster is recognisably fashioned on the scientist's *carte-de-visite*. The elderly, whiskered Victorian is presented with all the paraphernalia of the stereoscope in his orbit. There are models of stereoscopes to his left and a prime example of a stereoscopic print to the right of the subject. In the latter case, this is an image of the chemist and photographer Dr John Adamson, the brother of Robert Adamson who most probably took this image circa 1845. The mirror, again to the left of the portrait head, plays upon the idea of the camera lens and references also the dialectic between the mirror and lenticular stereoscopes.

The set itself is composed of a desk with piled books, the evidence of Brewster's research and, laid into this space, a ladder, the coded symbol

Portrait of
Sir David Brewster,
2008

of the Enlightenment and of intellectual progress. The palette of the image is tones of grey, while the background is described in a pattern of flecked strokes and cross-hatchings. Evidently this alludes to the monochrome of the early photographic experiments and the grained surface of the photographic print. In juxtaposition to this the desk holds some painter's brushes while, propped against the back wall, there rests an artist's easel. Colvin is carefully echoing his own practice as artist and photographer but is also revisiting that core debate of the 19th century; the relationship of the photograph to the parallel realms of art and science.

This photographic portrait is a *tour-de-force* of Colvin's complex art: it is replete with metaphor and symbol, citation and suggestion, quotation and contradiction. Moreover, it is designed to be viewed stereoscopically. Colvin has created two pictures of the set, each from a slightly different angle to the image and so, when viewed through a stereoscopic apparatus, it is perceived in three dimensions. Hence, Brewster's toy captures Brewster's portrait in a reflexive and ironical prism.

Echoing this dialectic of the stereoscopic image, Colvin has created a corresponding portrait of the London-based experimental scientist Charles Wheatstone. Wheatstone is best remembered for his role in developing telegraphy but, like Brewster, he was a multitalented physicist. He certainly invented a form of kaleidoscope in the 1820s and was an originator of the stereoscope in the period after 1832. Though Brewster certainly adapted and popularised the stereoscope, the debate on its 'invention' and origin became a feature of scientific discourse in the 1850s. Brewster was intensely vocal in claiming his authorship. This dispute is mirrored in Colvin's portrait of Wheatstone. Placing the depiction of Wheatstone in the same set as his image of Brewster, replete with desk, books, ladder, easel and mirror, Colvin decorates the Wheatstone tableau with small circular images of Brewster to the right of the principal subject. These are accompanied by diagrams of Wheatstone's symbolic notations concerning

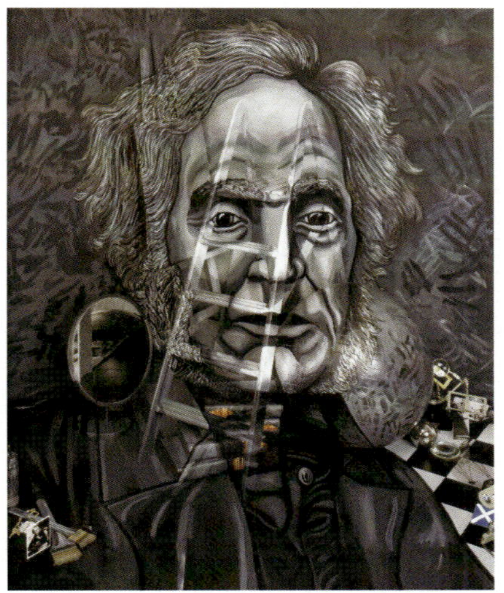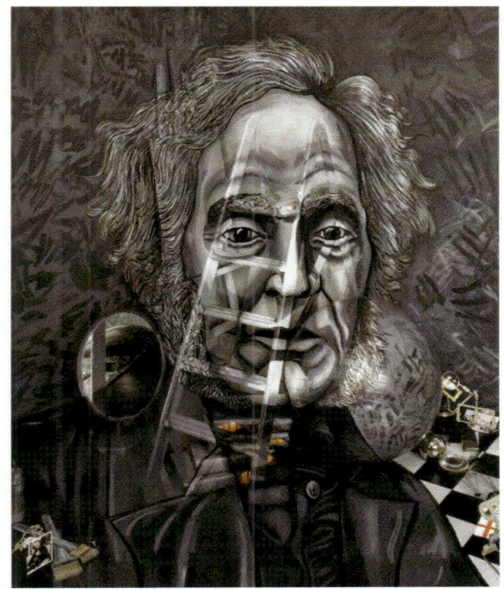

Portrait of Sir David Brewster, stereoscopic photograph,
2008

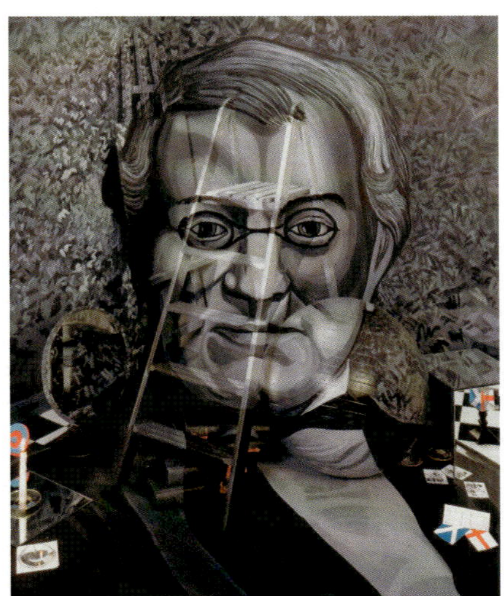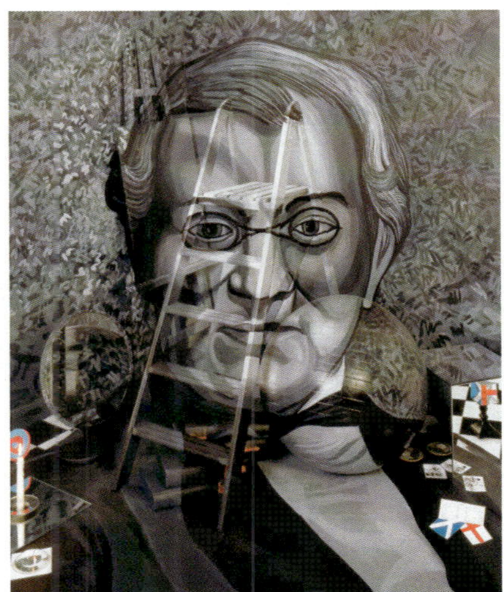

Portrait of Sir Charles Wheatstone, stereoscopic photograph,
2008

the nature of stereoscopic vision, and totemic representations of the flags
of St Andrew and St George. Already the debate is projected into one of
competitive national history and subtle national identities.

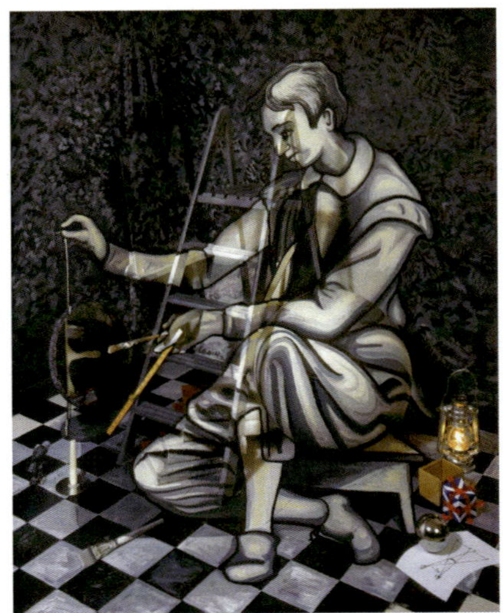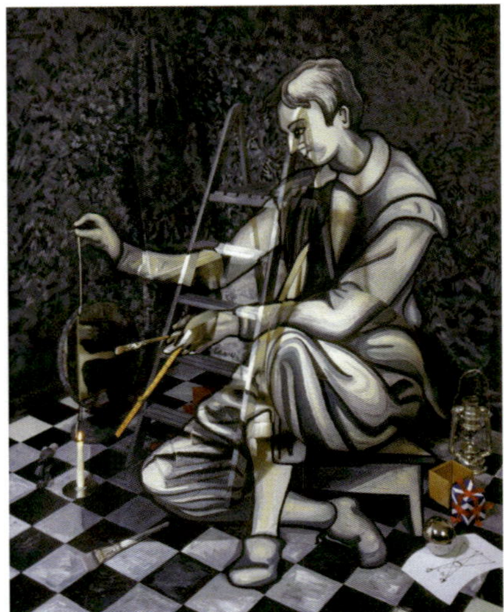

Chimenti I + II,
2008

If the debate concerning priority is here morphed into a discourse on
national identity then the problematic, perhaps even the absurdity, of this
construct is referenced in a further symbolic figure lying to the right of the
Wheatstone portrait. A scrap of drawing, repeated and mirrored, has been
placed within the *mise-en-scène*. This is the renowned sketch, or rather
sketches, by the seventeenth-century Italian artist Jacopo Chimenti.
Chimenti's drawing shows a young man holding those essential instruments
of mathematics and perspective, a compass and a plumb-line. In the fiery
debate between Brewster and Wheatstone, these sketches became crucial
for they seemed to indicate a knowledge of the stereoscopic process extant
in the period circa 1600. Evidently, these drawings, set alongside each other,
presented the possibility of a reading in three dimensions. This offered to
Brewster the opportunity to undermine Wheatstone's undeniable claim
to 'priority', though, intriguingly, Chimenti's drawings were subject to
the closest scrutiny by nineteenth-century scientists and shown to fall short
of a true stereoscopic intent. In which case Colvin's *Chimenti I + II* offers

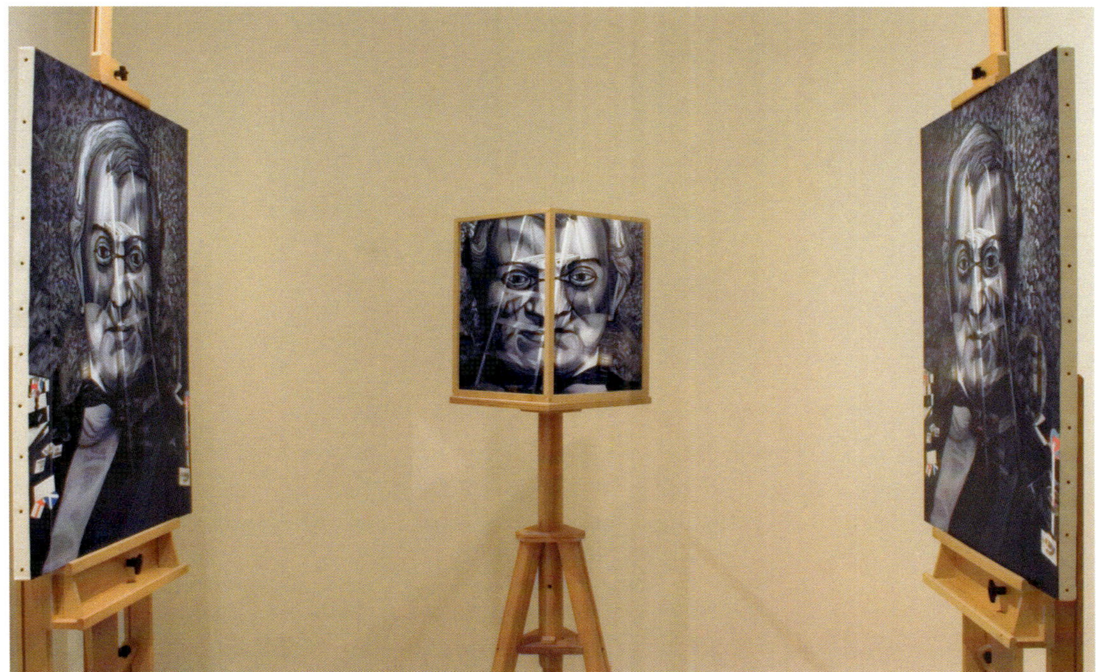

Installation view, *Natural Magic,*
featuring the Portrait of Charles Wheatstone as a stereoscopic presentation,
Royal Scottish Academy, Edinburgh,
2009

an ironical commentary upon the delusional clamour of this very public
altercation between two of the 19th century's most distinguished scientists.

Colvin presented these works in the exhibition titled *Natural Magic* held
at the Royal Scottish Academy in Edinburgh during the spring of 2009.
Many of the photographs were featured as large-scale stereoscopic displays.
The element of audience participation and a physical involvement with
the exhibition was encouraged. Besides the portrait representations, Colvin
also prepared a number of stereoscopic images that explored the impetus
towards the kinds of visual alchemy that had fashioned the pre-history
of the photograph.

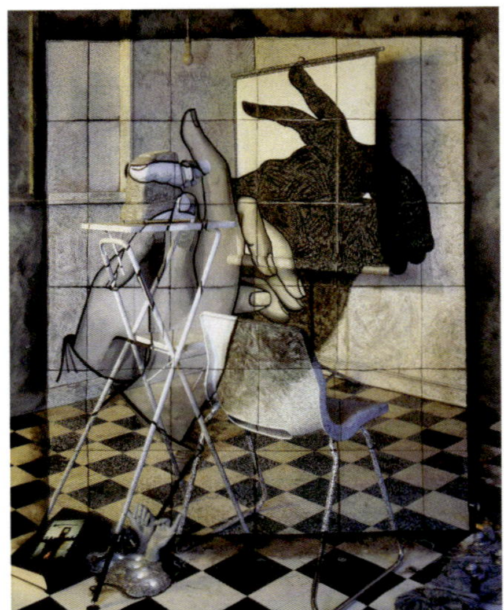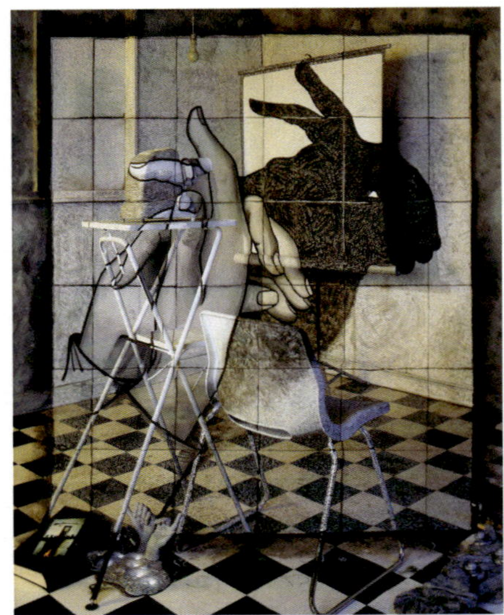

Hand/Rabbit,
2008

Among these subject pictures is the fascinating *Hand/Rabbit* photograph. This references the ancient art of creating shadow puppets; manipulated images of birds, dogs, rabbits, et. al. In the 19th century, this kind of visual 'play' was a feature of most Victorian parlours, requiring as it did only candle light, a blank wall and the dextrous manipulation of hands and fingers to cast a shadow outline of animals, and even human faces.

Colvin's *Hand/Rabbit* is a playful reflection on these illusions, while recognising that such experiments properly belong to the pre-history of photography. A chair rests besides a slide-projector stand where the knotted hands of the illusionist cast a shadow image of a rabbit onto a screen. The work, moreover, was created as a stereoscopic photograph and so accents the link to Brewster's experiments in the visual field.

Indeed, there is a further, if obscure, relation to Brewster's interests. In her book, *Phantasmagoria*, Marina Warner has commented on how

David Brewster... attended phantasmagorias and gave highly

> detailed descriptions of the moving eyes and lips of the spectres,
> of the dissolves, fades, and other proto-cinematic effects....[7]

Brewster, like many Victorians was in thrall to the popular entertainments that promised magic and illusion and every variety of fantastic excitement. His interest, however, was in the scientific investigation of these deceptions principally because their success depended upon trickeries that related to the science of vision. Moreover, in 1832, he would publish his *Letters on Natural Magic addressed to Sir Walter Scott, Bart.* Scott was ever the discreet presence in the early history of photography, but Brewster's letters were created to explain the myriad enchantments that masqueraded as 'supernatural'. Importantly, it was these 'philosophical toys', these visual entertainments and light-based playthings, that provided the antecedents for the invention of photography and so captivated Colvin's fascination with the bewildering enchantment of the photograph.

This sense of experiment as 'play' continued and expanded in Colvin's work. Most especially where it allowed for the photographic image to conspire in an antic of animation and deception. In exploring these tricks of visuality and perception, he moved deeper into the early history of transformative configurations.

Two works from the period circa 2014 highlight this intriguing illusionism. The first is *Lochaber No More, Anamorphosis* and, in juxtaposition, the second is *Mirror Anamorphosis, Portrait of Charles Edward Stuart (after Liotard)*. Evidently the technique used in both works is 'anamorphosis', but this is a complicated and varied format. Developed and deployed by artists from the 16th century varieties of anamorphosis were utilised to create puzzles, or more often to disguise risqué subject matter. It may be that the subject matter was deemed 'improper' for political reasons or for reasons of taste. In essence, anamorphosis allowed for an image to be distorted in ordinary view but to be reconstituted by the adept viewer.

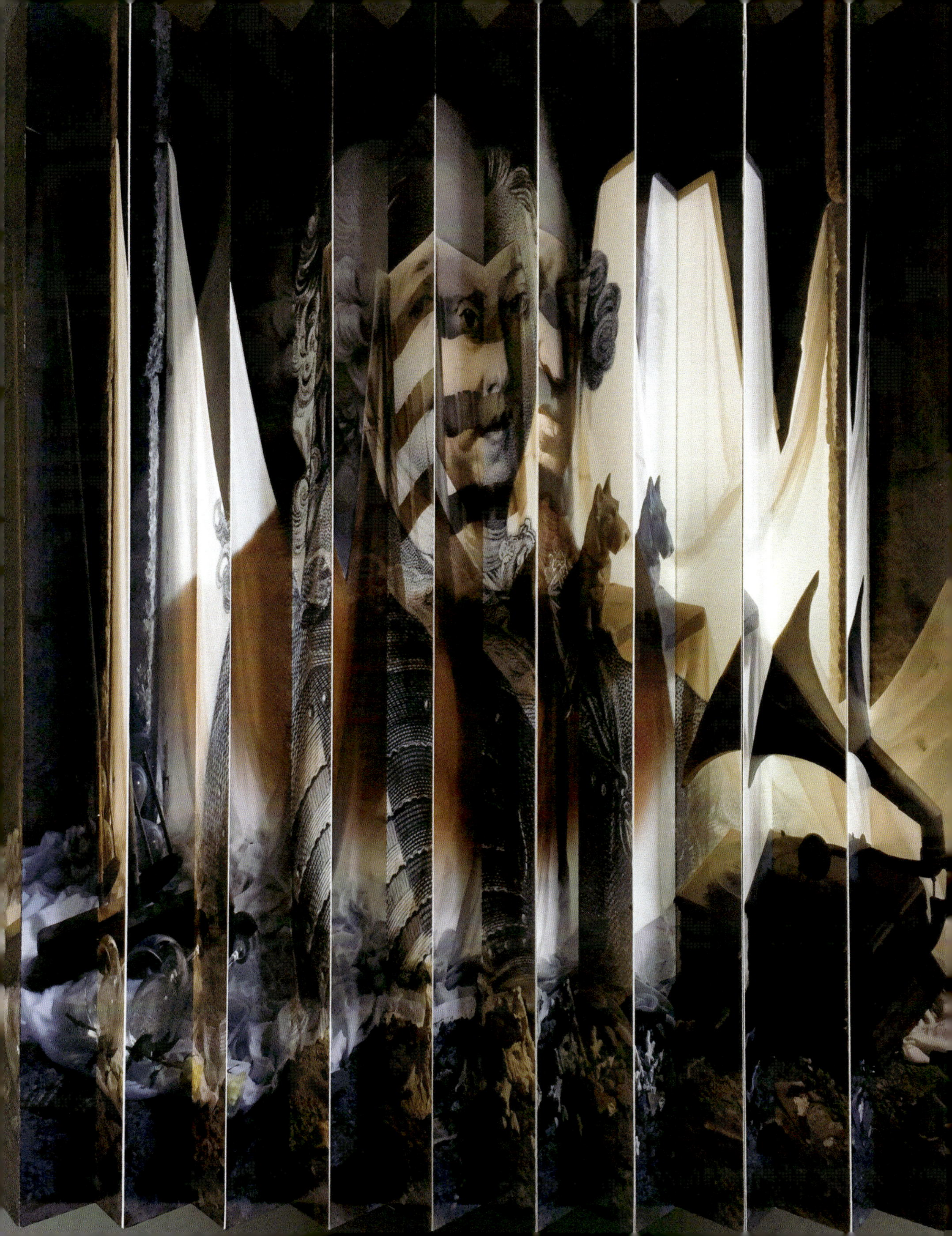

Two fundamental types of anamorphosis have been specially prized by artists, 'channel anamorphosis' and 'mirror anamorphosis'. *In Lochaber No More, Anamorphosis,* Colvin has deployed a channel anamorphosis. This format would be particularly celebrated in Scotland for the Scottish National Portrait Gallery holds a remarkable *Portrait of Mary Queen of Scots,* by an unknown hand, created as a channel anamorphosis. Viewed from one angle the image shows a sensitive portrait of the tragic queen, from another it transforms into a skull. Colvin has taken this form and applied it to a study of Charles Edward Stuart. An image that moves between the young Prince and the old exile. The 'turning portrait' consequently reflects the sense of time, history and change in the representation of this much mythologised subject.

The *Mirror Anamorphosis, Portrait of Charles Edward Stuart (after Liotard)* presents a contrasting conundrum. Colvin had previously created a fine photographic construction titled *Portrait of Charles Edward Stuart (after Liotard),* and this was certainly a stellar image of the Prince in his pomp. But Colvin was also aware that, following the rebellion of 1745, images and paraphernalia relating to the Prince were outlawed, in which case the 'secret' portrait became a sign of loyalty and commitment to the Jacobite cause. Moreover, it became a form that captured Colvin's febrile imagination. In *Mirror Anamorphosis, Portrait of Charles Edward Stuart (after Liotard),* Colvin has stretched his portrait of the Prince on a flattened surface such that it exists only in a hidden and a distorted form. In the centre of this horizontal board he has placed, vertically, a cylindrical mirror. Magically, viewed in the mirror, the secret image is revealed.

In working with these formats, Colvin was exploring the practices of art and photography as they responded to changing technologies, new and old. Digitisation and computer manipulation, the anaglyph, the stereoscopic image, channelled and mirrored anamorphosis, even the reductive graphic manipulation of Photoshop, all were arenas wherein the constructed

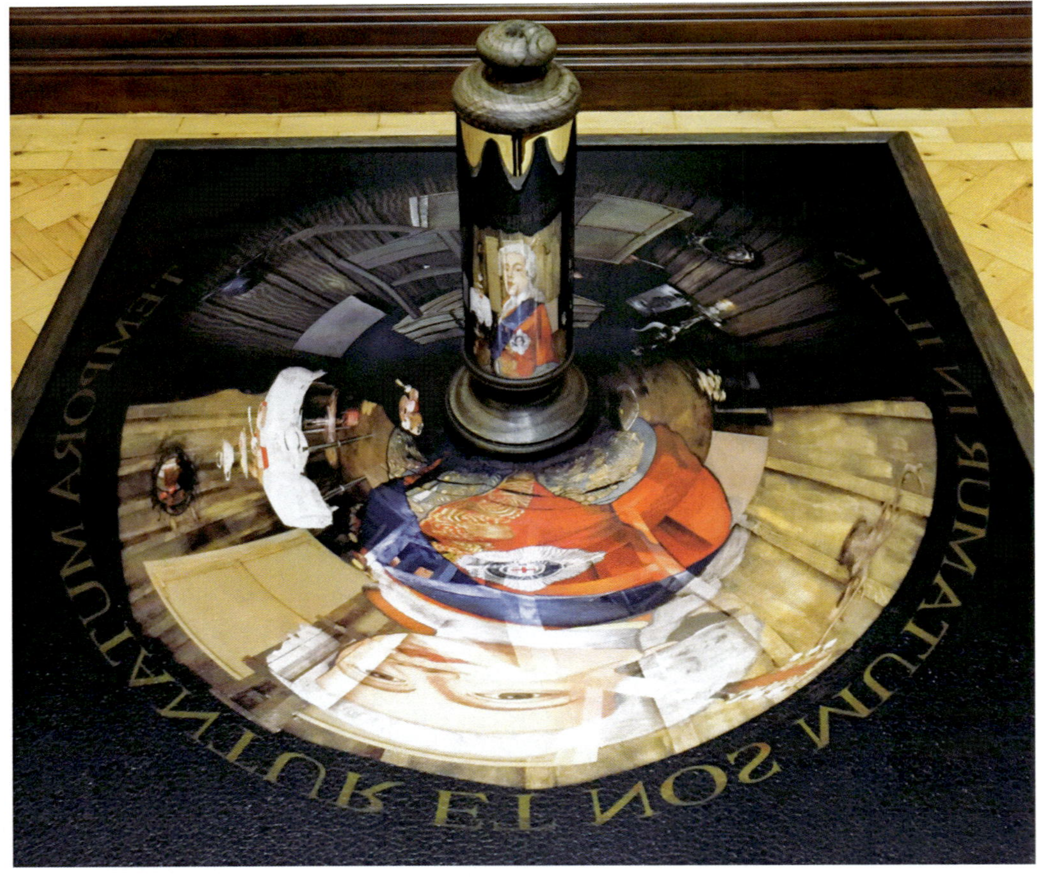

Mirror Anamorphosis,
Portrait of Charles Edward Stuart (after Liotard),
2014

photograph might prospect. In these experiments he was recognising the relationship of his art to science and its many innovations. He was, moreover, acknowledging the fragility of that odd illusion that has haunted photography from its invention, the sense that it might capture nature in an unmediated and wholly authentic manner. Recording and reflecting upon this chimera, he was able to authenticate the creative flights of his personal imaginary, a form of wild fantasy that broke out from the constraints of prudence and conservatism.

Hybridity: themes and variations

The experiments in art and science were a natural accord for Calum
Colvin for they chimed with the broader dimensions of his interests and
practice. But this was not the only association, or correspondence, that he
developed in his work. Indeed, he has consistently moved across borders
and broken down fences. In the current terminology, this approach has
generally been conceptualised as 'hybridity', and Colvin has previously
confessed that

> The concept of 'hybridity' has been a fundamental aspect of
> my practice since I formulated my working methods.[8]

The concept itself applies to Colvin's photography in two senses. In the
first instance, his work is hybrid in that it has traversed a number of
approaches in the fine art tradition. Popularly, he is a photographer and
this is the product of his work. But, in order for the photograph to exist,
he has behaved as a collector and assembler, a sculptor and a painter. It might
be added that he occupies the space of the installation artist, the performance
artist and the public artist. All of these contemporary art practices combine
in his productions. There is, however, a further dimension to his hybrid
output. Colvin has consistently moved outside the world of fine art practice
into the realms of parallel art forms. His work engages with music, with
literature and poetry, and more generally with text. Moreover, at the
broader level, it embodies an association with philosophy and with politics.

The world of music and sound has been a constant in Colvin's constructions.
Most obviously, there is the medieval shawm in the central panel of *Deaf
Man's Villa*, but also an accordion in the right-hand panel of this
inexhaustible triptych. Not surprisingly, Colvin has included a violin and
music stand in the *Portrait of James MacMillan* and a guitar in *Portrait
of Michael Marra*. There are bagpipes evident in *Icarus* and other works,
and a gramophone in his *Portrait of Robert Falcon Scott*. Record sleeves,
and vinyl records abound in Colvin's compositions, notably the album

Round at Calum's set like a surrogate signature in the bottom corner of *Philoctetes Left on the Isle of Lemnos by the Greeks*. In fact, looking deeply into most of Colvin's photographs will reveal a hidden world of sound.

A fine example of this trope is the delicate image titled *Siren* from 1991. The model for this work, revealed as a collaged element in the top right-hand corner of the photograph, is Tintoretto's *Susanna and the Elders* painted in 1556. Tintoretto's masterpiece shows Susanna about to bathe and spied upon by the elderly voyeurs. Around her the artist has placed symbolic jewels, silver jugs and silken shawls. Colvin has taken this image of Susanna and rededicated her as a Siren, whose beauty and singing lure sailors to their destruction. In Colvin's work, the Siren is painted across a coloured background, but her breasts are painted on an accordion and a guitar mirrors the curves of her body. These musical notations reference her irresistible mantra; and so, she dries her feet on the rocks that wreck the seafarers as they are drawn, fatally, to her beguiling song.

Siren was part of a larger suite of seven photographs that would be titled *The Two Ways of Life*. This project travelled as an exhibition to the Art Institute of Chicago in 1991, and subsequently to venues throughout North America. The title for the exhibition was gleaned from the acclaimed photograph by Oscar Rejlander, *The Two Ways of Life*. This landmark photograph, taken in 1857, was an image created as a series of some 30 negatives then combined into a single panoramic scene. Famously, it depicts a sage-like figure who guides two youthful neophytes into a scenario representing the world of opportunities. To the left of the combine, the 'sinister' side, there is a life of debauchery and sinfulness. To the right, a world of hard work and fulfilment. The young tyros are tempted in opposite directions.

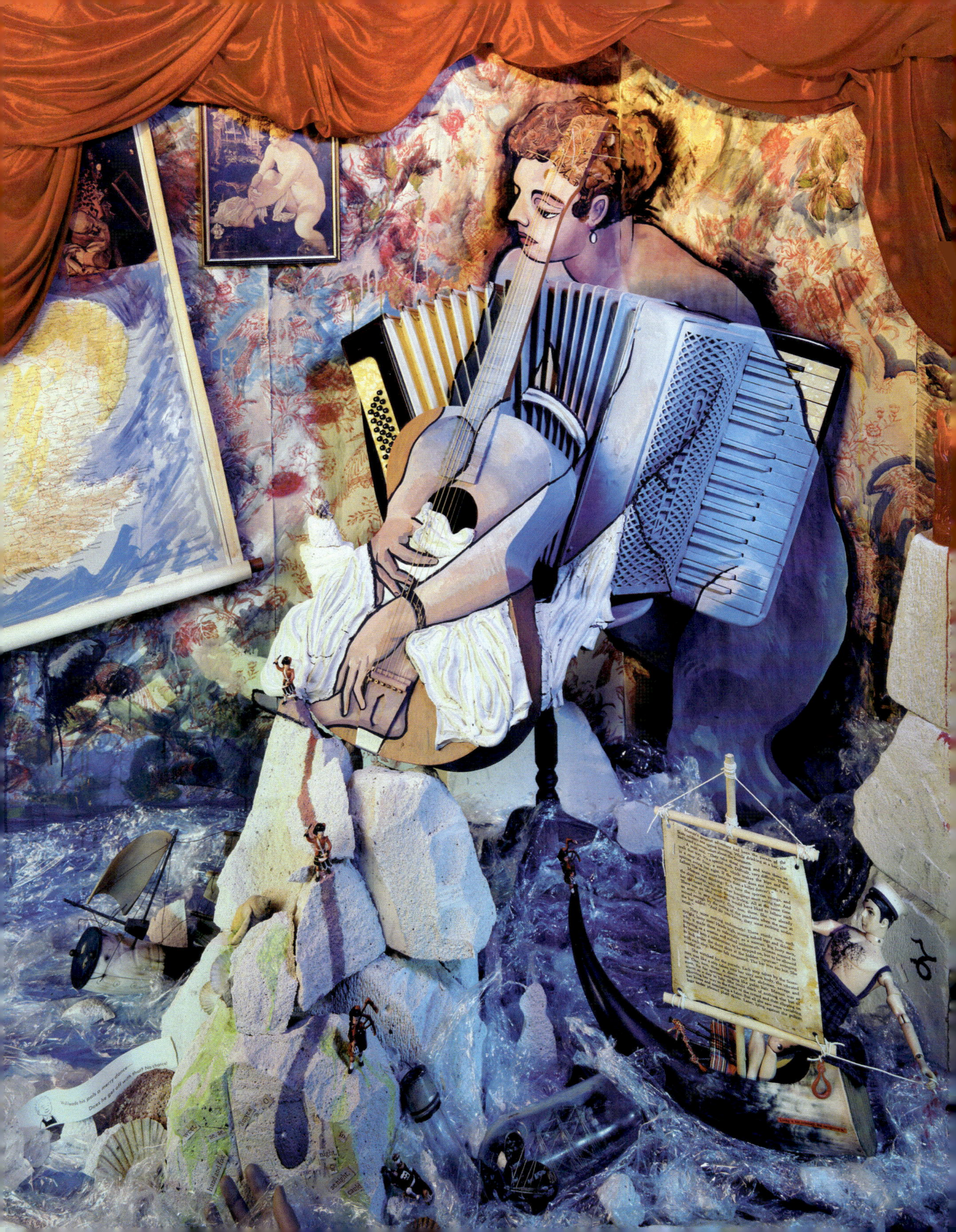

Evidently, this is an allegorical tale but its success was assured when Queen Victoria bought the work for the collection of her consort, Prince Albert. With this gift, the photograph was given the royal imprimatur and so became a canonical work. This is surprising, in part, because the image embraces an astonishing display of nudity. The left-hand side, depicting a life of depravity, is replete with naked women and, in the centre of the photograph, a veiled nude woman, symbolically representing 'remorse', is made available to the male gaze. Significantly, the representation of this figure within the 'real' ambit of the photograph has pushed it into the realm of a suspect erotica. Naturally then, in Scotland, the work was displayed with the left-hand side tastefully covered by a heavy curtain.

The key work in Colvin's appraisal of this subject area was, appropriately, titled *The Two Ways of Life*. It is a complicated construction, but the central figure is modelled on the painting of *John the Baptist Preaching in the Wilderness* by the German artist, Anton Mengs. This work, from circa 1760, is held in the Museum of Fine Art in Houston. Colvin's pastiche of John the Baptist seems to occupy a hunting lodge, replete with antlers and skulls. There is also, prominently displayed, a set of bagpipes. But surrounding the central figure is an array of magazines, and cushions and objects that relate to Elvis Presley. On one side of the prophet, we see the young, raw Elvis and, on the other, the dissolute Elvis, fallen into the corporate world. Colvin has spoken, eloquently, on this subject

> Elvis…is a modern deity with a complex iconography that surrounds him; Elvis magazines, Elvis pop-up books, Elvis dolls. He even has his relics like bits of hair and toe-nails. In this sense he's been sanctified in our culture. So Elvis becomes an archetype and a cultural presence. He's also a martyr to his fame and celebrity and myth and this makes him a tragic figure. There is also his gospel story, moving from the young Rockabilly hero…through his later fall from grace and death….to the rumours that he is alive so we have a kind of resurrection.[9]

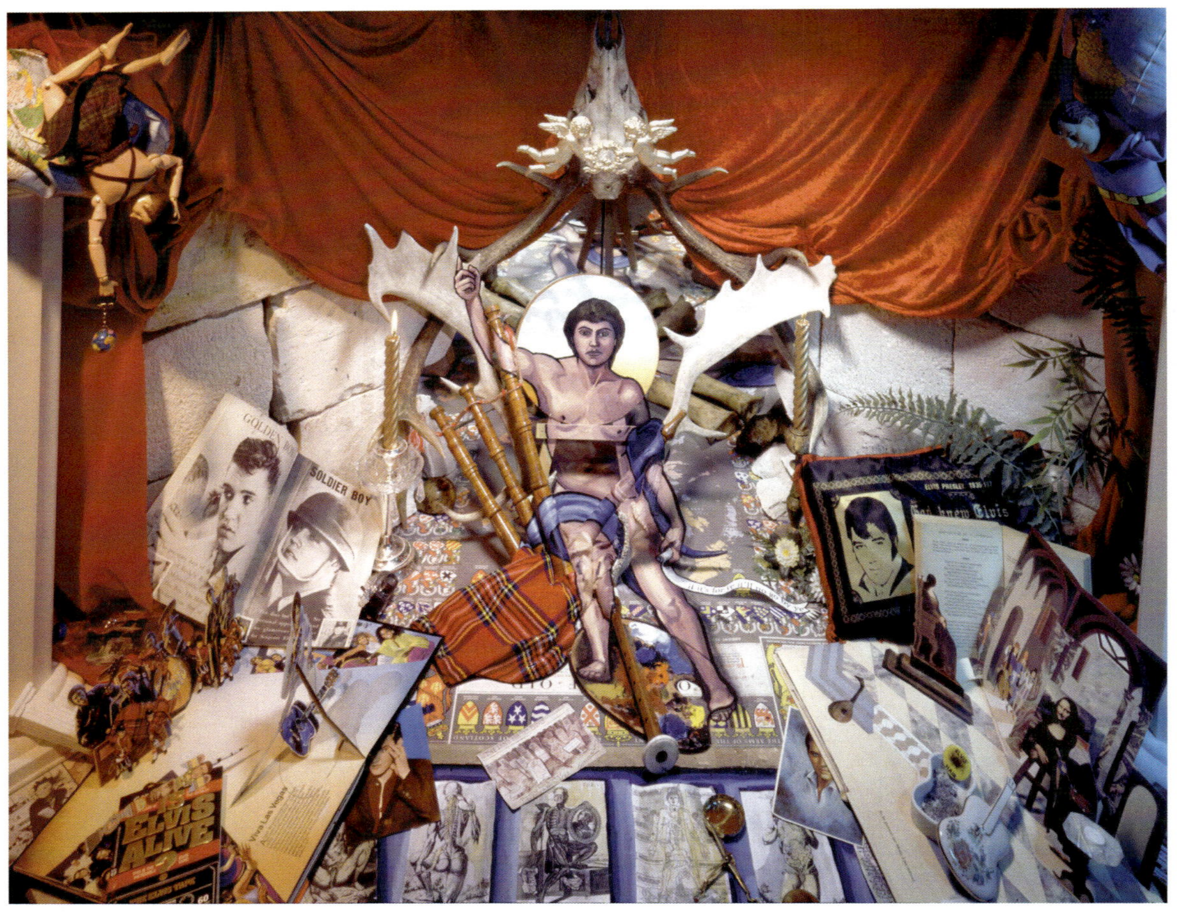

The Two Ways of Life,
1991

The life of Elvis Presley, then, represents a parable, and one that was an echo of Rejlander's allegorical photograph.

Colvin would extend this idea and incorporate in it the biography of his Action Man avatar. In *Crying in the Chapel*, from *The Two Ways of Life* series, this doppelganger can be seen, collapsed, in the foreground of the photograph. A gramophone plays its melancholy song at his shoulder, while the 'god' of Elvis can be viewed in the distant altar, a wreathed set of bagpipes above his sacred head.

Crying in the Chapel,
1991

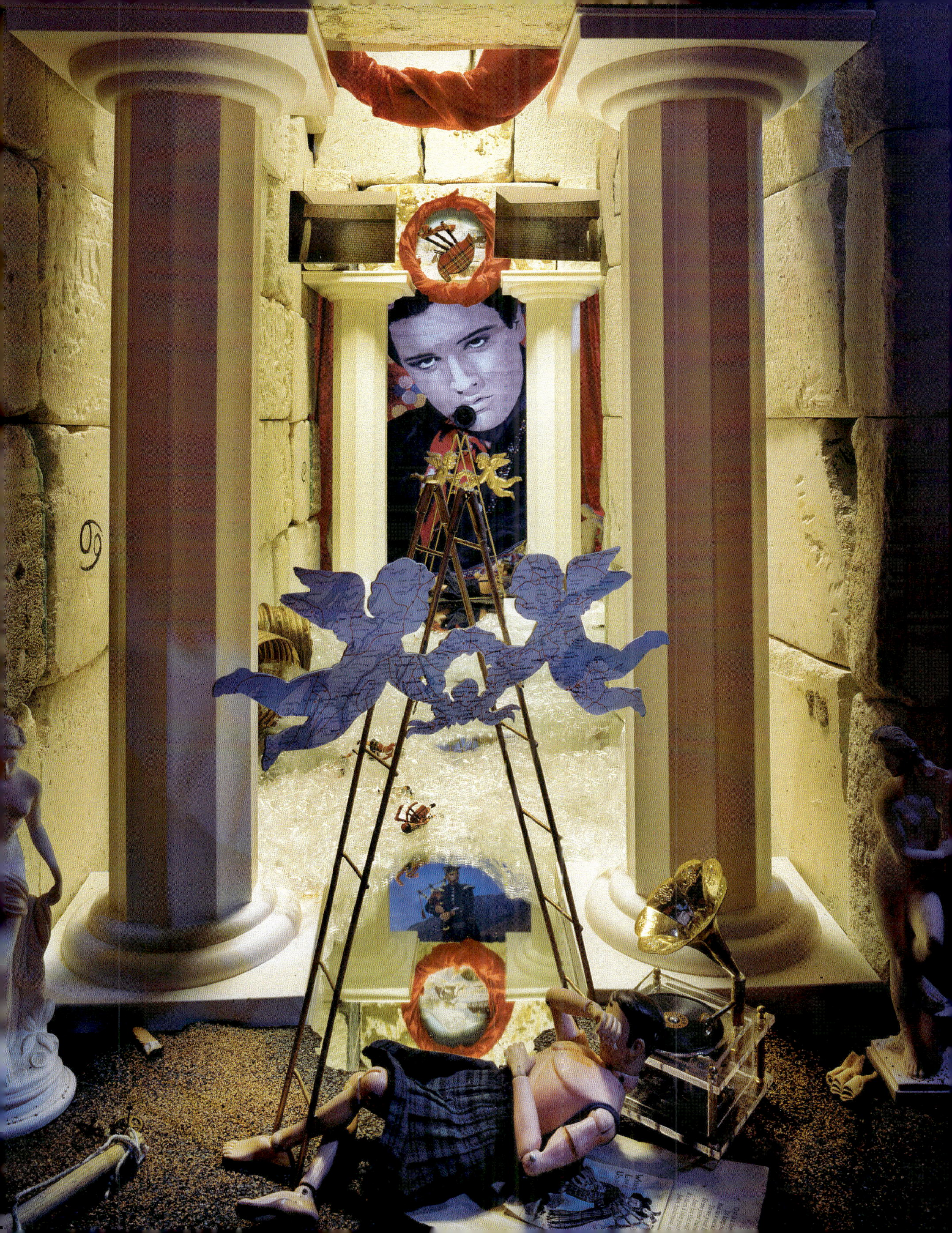

Though these musical themes and metaphors are ubiquitous in Colvin's work, this is not the only way in which he references corresponding art forms. Conspicuously, Colvin has cited literature, poetry and text in his photographs. Books are frequently used as significant props and can be seen in *Natural Magick* (2009), in his group portrait of writers and poets, *The Kelvingrove Eight* (2000) and in his *Portrait of Sir David Brewster* (2008). Most often, these books directly reference the key works relating to the protagonists, and signal their character. In *Narcissus* (1986), Magnus Hirschfield's *Sexual Anomalies and Perversions* lays open in order to provide the viewer with some insight into the photographic construction. Less provocatively, in *Jacob's Ladder* (1989), the poetry book *Unto the Hills*, with verse by Brenda G. MacRow and photographic illustrations by the esteemed Scottish landscape photographer Robert Moyes Adam, decorates the foreground. The open page speaks to the language and romance of landscape, an idea reflected in Colvin's whimsical narrative. It should also be recognised that newspapers, magazines and popular comics abound in Colvin's photographs. An early work like *Untitled (Head and Room)* (1985), is littered with journals and comic strips, while his *Diana and Acteon* (1998), includes a magazine titled *Naked Truth*, a journal called *Score* and a newspaper with the headline 'Stalkers'.

The cross-referencing of text and image provides a further level of narrative in Colvin's photographs, but this also allows for an explosion of puns and metaphors that highlight the vernacular protest in his fine art productions. His *The Three Graces (after Antonio Canova)*, a singular photograph from his *Sacred and Profane* series of 1998, sets the bountiful allegorical figures beside a hospital bed and, prominently displayed, there is an edition of the popular weekly magazine, *The People's Friend*. This, coupled with an open book on the bed, draws the refined sentiment of Canova's sculpture into an everyday world of storytelling. Consistently, text is used to complement and contest the dominant narrative in Colvin's profoundly layered constructions.

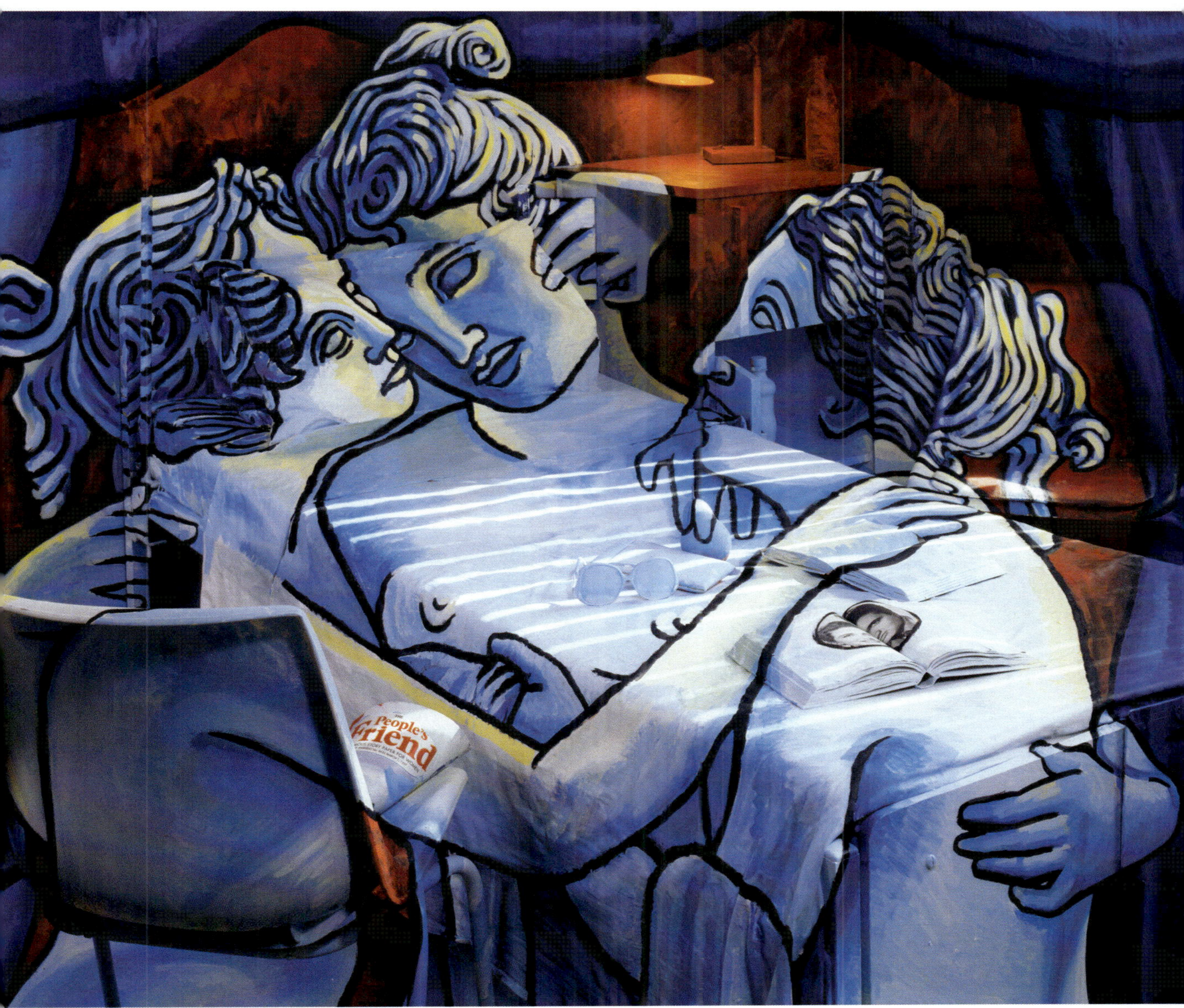

The Three Graces (after Antonio Canova),
1998

A remarkable example of this quality can be found in *Untitled (Sum Quod Eris, Quod es Olim Fui)*, from *The Seven Deadly Sins and the Four Last Things* series of 1993. The photograph is uncharacteristic of Colvin's output in that an open book becomes the 'set' for the photograph. The text is open at a chapter that is titled 'The Religion of the Savages near the Isthmus of Darien'. The book is, comically, attended by three-dimensional specs emblazoned with the logo of *The Sun* newspaper. Two candles light the altar of painted reliquary objects, joined together by a string of snapshot photographs. As a banner, above the open text, the motto 'Sum Quod Eris, Quod es Olim Fui' is presented.

This phrase refers to the notion of death, and is a reminder to the living that all will pass. Naturally, this chimes with the remonstrations of the Seven Deadly Sins and their dire warnings. But this particular image picks up on the threads of Colvin's *Avarice* photograph from the series. Darien was, of course, the scene of a distinctively Scottish imperial adventure, and it was calamitous. Indeed, it led directly to the Act of Union of 1707 and so the dissolution of the Scottish nation. Consequently, in *Untitled (Sum Quod Eris, Quod es Olim Fui)* Colvin takes the viewer into history and politics through the inclusion of narrative and text. This quality extends the wild refractions in the prism of his hybrid aesthetic.

Whereas music and text exemplify the character of Colvin's hybridity, they do combine in a form that intensifies the implications of his photography. A close study of his *The Last Judgement*, also from *The Seven Deadly Sins and the Four Last Things* series, reveals an esoteric communion between text, song and image. In this work, the soul of the sinner has been placed in the balance and he will be judged. But he is to be judged by his posture towards the natural world, specifically, in relation to the magnificent populations of the world's bird-life.

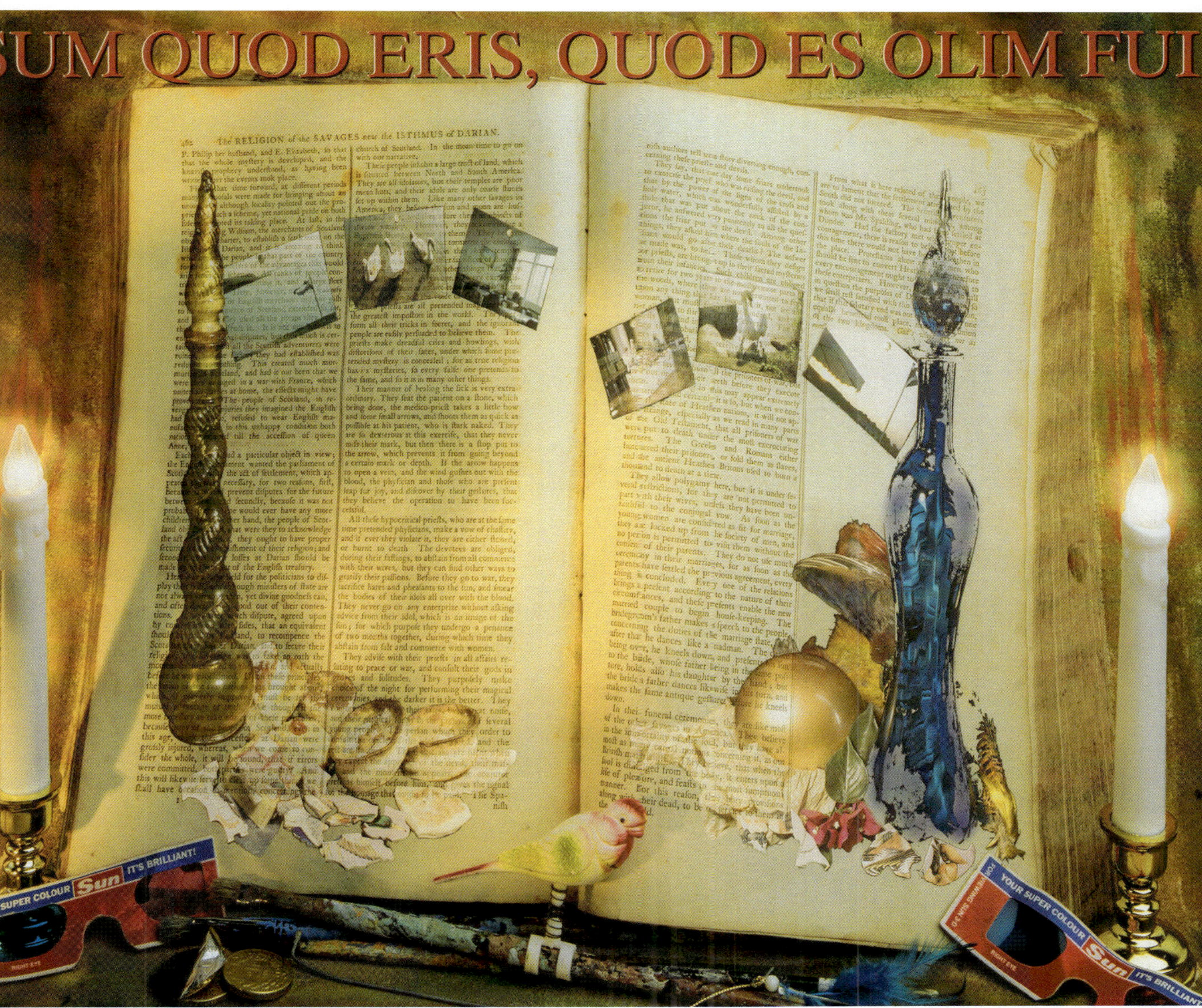

Untitled (Sum Quod Eris, Quod es Olim Fui),
1993

In *The Last Judgement*, while the sinner balances precariously on his high-wire between Heaven and Hell, he is judged in the background by 'the eye of God', noted, already, as the scarred eye of a dead turkey.

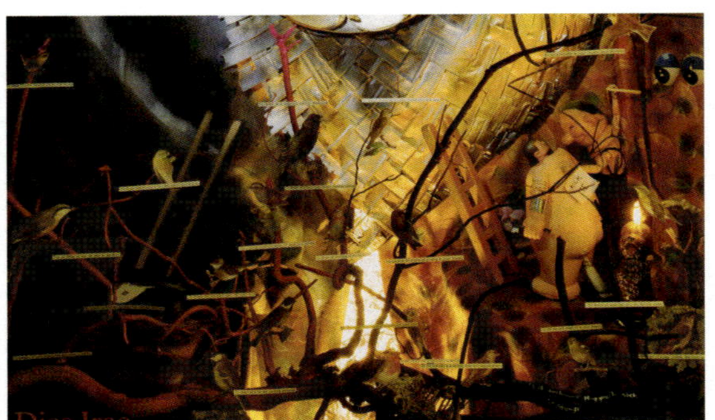
The Last Judgement (detail),
1993

But the foreground is filled with beautiful illustrations of small birds appropriated from decorated children's books. Each bird is complemented by a banner of text. These, in turn, present obscure aphorisms from a dictionary of dreams. Patently, in this work, it is Nature that will judge this sinner, and by extension all of human kind, in which case Colvin's hybrid aesthetic presses on into ecology and environmentalism.

It is the case that Colvin had presaged this thought in *Deaf Man's Villa*; a photograph that overflows with images of birds. Above the shoulder of the 'Nude Youth with a Shawm', there is a delicate vignette of a song thrush. It rejoices in its chant and aria. In the image, a stream of notes and texts flow from the bird into the photograph. These are the written transcription of its song, its individual musical notation expressed as onomatopoeia. Colvin has appropriated these from the Ladybird book of *Song Birds*.

Moreover, he has cut them and pasted them into the scene in an arbitrary manner, in the fashion of Dada collage. The bird, here, offers its comment on the 'noise of the world', so eloquently captured in this epic triptych.

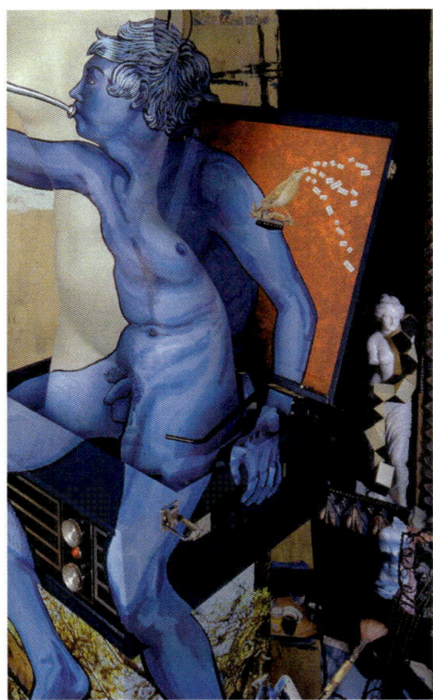
Deaf Man's Villa (detail),
1989

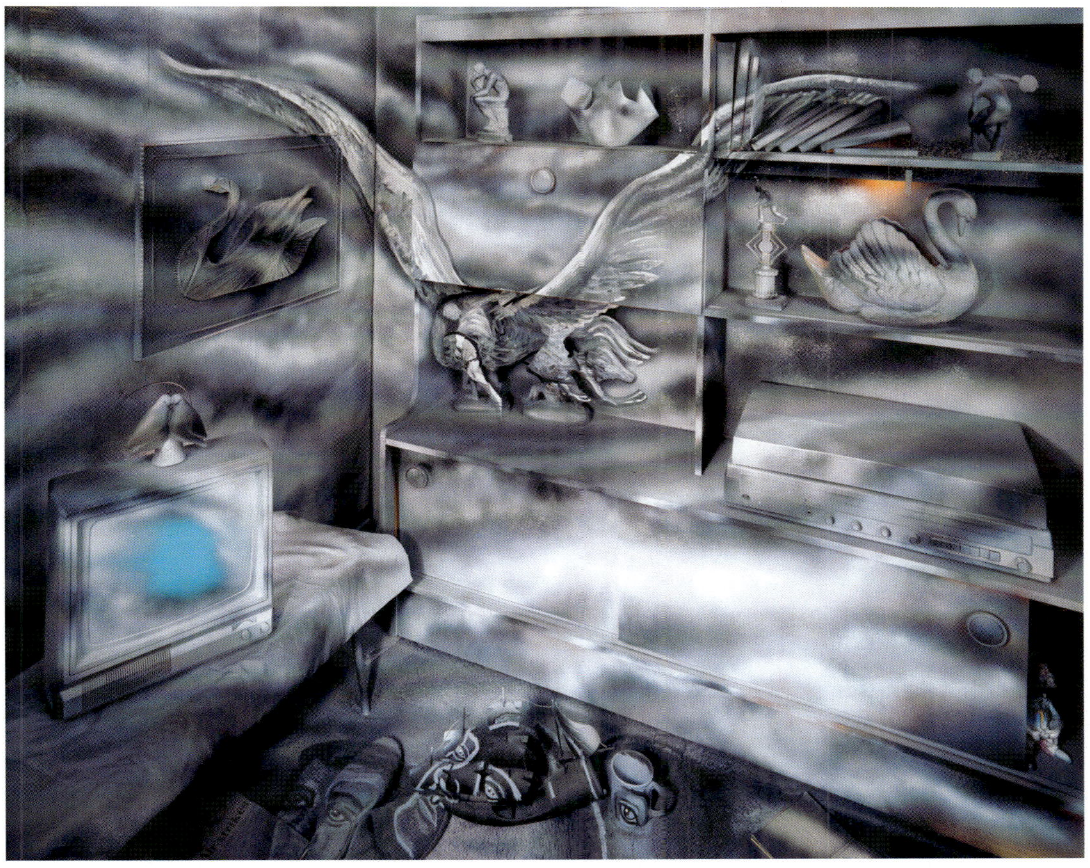

Unidentified Aircraft,
1994

These political dimensions to Colvin's fascination with birds began to find
expression in an ongoing series of works titled *Ornithology*. An early example
of this trope was the photograph titled *Unidentified Aircraft*, completed in
1994. This work has its source in a mysterious painting by the Montrose
artist, Edward Baird. Baird's image of *Unidentified Aircraft* was painted in
1943 and reflected anxieties concerning bombing raids in World War II.
In Baird's surrealist work, three partial heads, seen acutely and in profile
on the lower horizon of the painting, search the sky for enemy bombers.
The middle distance of the painting is a topography of the town of Montrose.

Colvin has repeated this context in the three portrait heads that rest in the bottom section of his photograph. However, his locus is a sitting-room with television, display cabinet and assembled ornaments. The whole is over-painted in the grey-blue of a clouded, seemingly contaminated sky. In this domestic space, an albatross, with arching wings, soars and glides across the scene observed by the onlookers. Surrounding this display are pictures and ornaments of swans and other birds. The underlying theme, and feel, of the photograph explores the idea of threat and apprehension; as befits the mythic reputation of the albatross as a dark portent. Colvin has noted that the work is concerned with 'atmospheric pollution'. In which case, the anguish of implied warfare in Baird's work is rechannelled into a disquiet concerning ecological disaster and social perils in this evocative photograph.

The pattern of this thread is extended in *The Magnificent Frigate Bird*, an image from 1995 that seems to reflect upon calamity but actually speaks of resilience and hope. The core of the photograph is the frigate bird that lies prone in the centre of the work. Examined closely, it is evident that this is the young bird emerging from its egg and about to embark upon a life's journey, a feature given emphasis by the child's tricycle that forms the bird's torso.

The setting is a dilapidated living room, a scene of carnage with a sense of loss. The losses are multiple. Stuffed birds signify environmental loss; landscape images reference ecological harm; the broken bricks proclaim social decline and fracture; and, to accent all this menace, an abandoned book in the bottom right of the photograph displays the title *A Passage Perilous*.

Nevertheless, manifestly, this bird will grow and, like its kin, it will fly around the tropical waters of the Americas making a display of its long, forked tail. Likewise, the paraphernalia of the living-room context

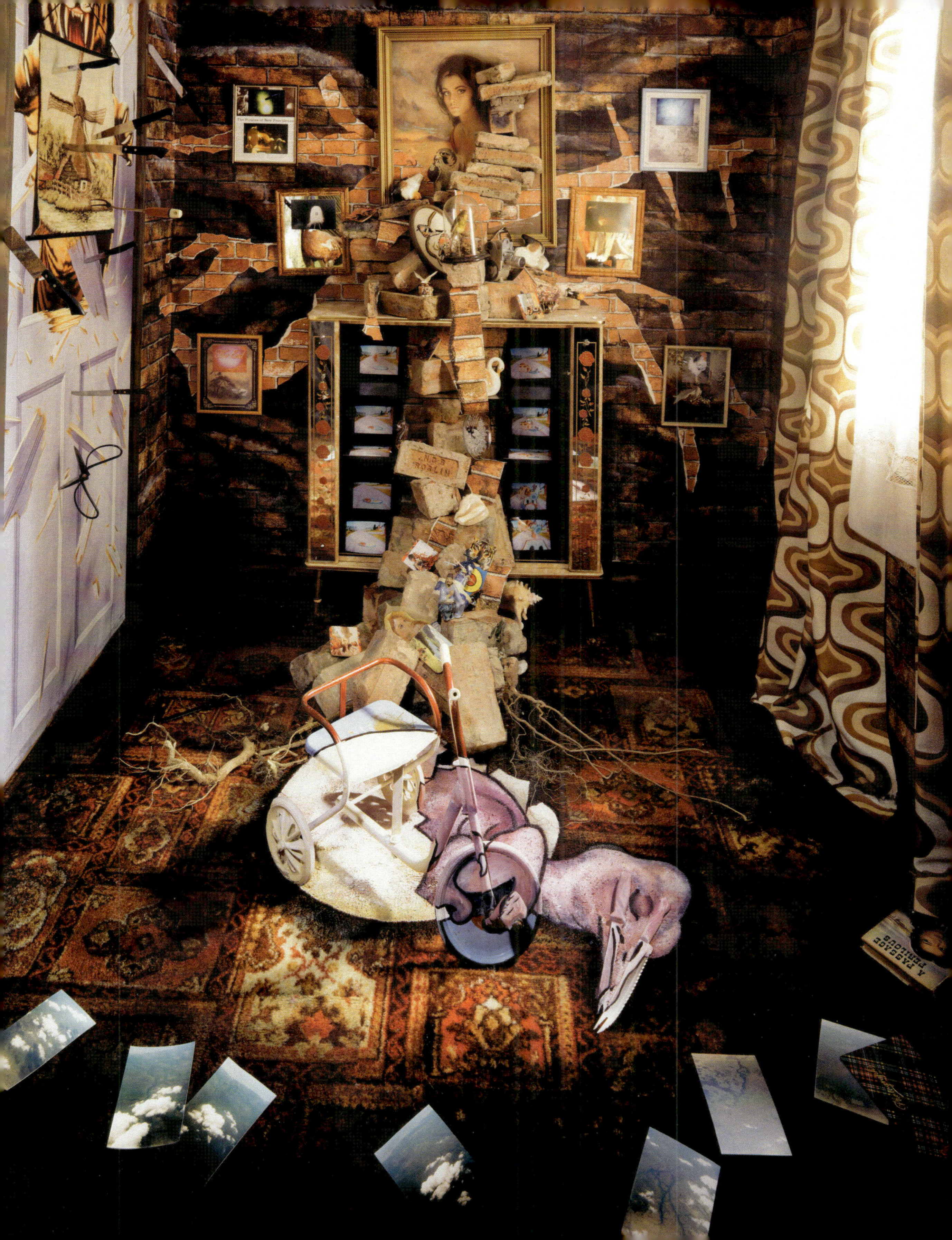
A PASSAGE
PERILOUS

discreetly connotes this sense of optimism. The bricks in the set spread into a 'tree of life' drawn on the wall, while everywhere the insignia of creativity promises a potential for growth and change.

In developing these ideas, Colvin's *A Caucus Race* (1999), is a meditation on a scene from Lewis Carroll's *Alice's Adventures in Wonderland*. Here, Alice speaks with the dodo. They and their associates, all represented as differing kinds of birds, are looking to get dry after a swim. They decide to run a 'caucus race'; a race with no starting point nor any end in which everyone 'wins' and each gets a prize. In Carroll's work, this represented something of a political satire, and these associations would not be lost on Colvin.

The dodo, of course, is an extinct bird. A large flightless bird that was resident on the Island of Mauritius, its resemblance to a turkey sealed its fate after the colonisation of the island by European settlers. In this photograph, an added dimension concerns the destiny of the dodo, for this is an augury that signals the death of analogue photography in the digital age. So, the detritus of analogue film stock, film reels and flash bulbs is strewn across the floor of this homely interior and, the dodo gifts Alice a digital microchip as her prize for the race.

Again, in 1999, Colvin continued his reflections on birds with *The Common Runt*. This is a comic and appealing work, its subject being the common pigeon that occupies the streets of every modern city. In this photograph, the birds are seen indoors, in a sitting-room that seems to have been created from a second-hand furniture store, with a stock from the 1970s. The birds roost and perch throughout the set. They watch television, reflect on the various kitsch prints on the walls and stumble through the books, magazines and photographs that litter the room. In the magazine rack, a copy of *The Courier* is prominent.

The comic invention is rife in this image. The set references the idea of a 'home' and so the association with the 'Homing Pigeon', beloved of bird-fanciers and hobbyists everywhere, while the inset of *The Courier* recalls the idea of the 'Courier Pigeon'; that earliest form of social media and the preferred messenger service in both World War I and II. In every instance, these common birds are revealed to be quite uncommon, and even heroic, in which case the image as a whole may be understood as a homage to the ordinary and the everyday.

Evidently, taken as a whole, *Ornithology* is a complicated series of works, for the references and the symbolism in the photographs are diverse and varied. At one level, the birds signify changes in our environment and the human impact on nature. At another, they stand as metaphors for human aspirations and human failures and always, they comment, with wit and insight, on the social world that we create.

This diversity is evident in the photograph, *Mute Swan*, an early example of this trope from 1994. Here, the elegant white bird with its unfolding wings and curved neck occupies the entire centre of the photograph. The image, painted on a set with a coloured background and various decorations of fans, pictures and ornaments, is framed by scarlet curtains; like a bedroom space with something quite private revealed. The swan is painted across a dressing table with open drawers and mirror. From the drawers, various pieces of jewellery and underwear spill onto the floor. Notably, in a further reference to Colvin's concern with hybridity, there lies abandoned, in the right foreground, a book titled *The Missing Dimension in Sex*.

This is a story of love, and perhaps of misfortune. *The Mute Swan*, alone and seemingly constrained in its tiny space, twists its neck into a shape resembling a heart. In this contorted pose, the bird, for all its vibrancy, presents a tragic figure.

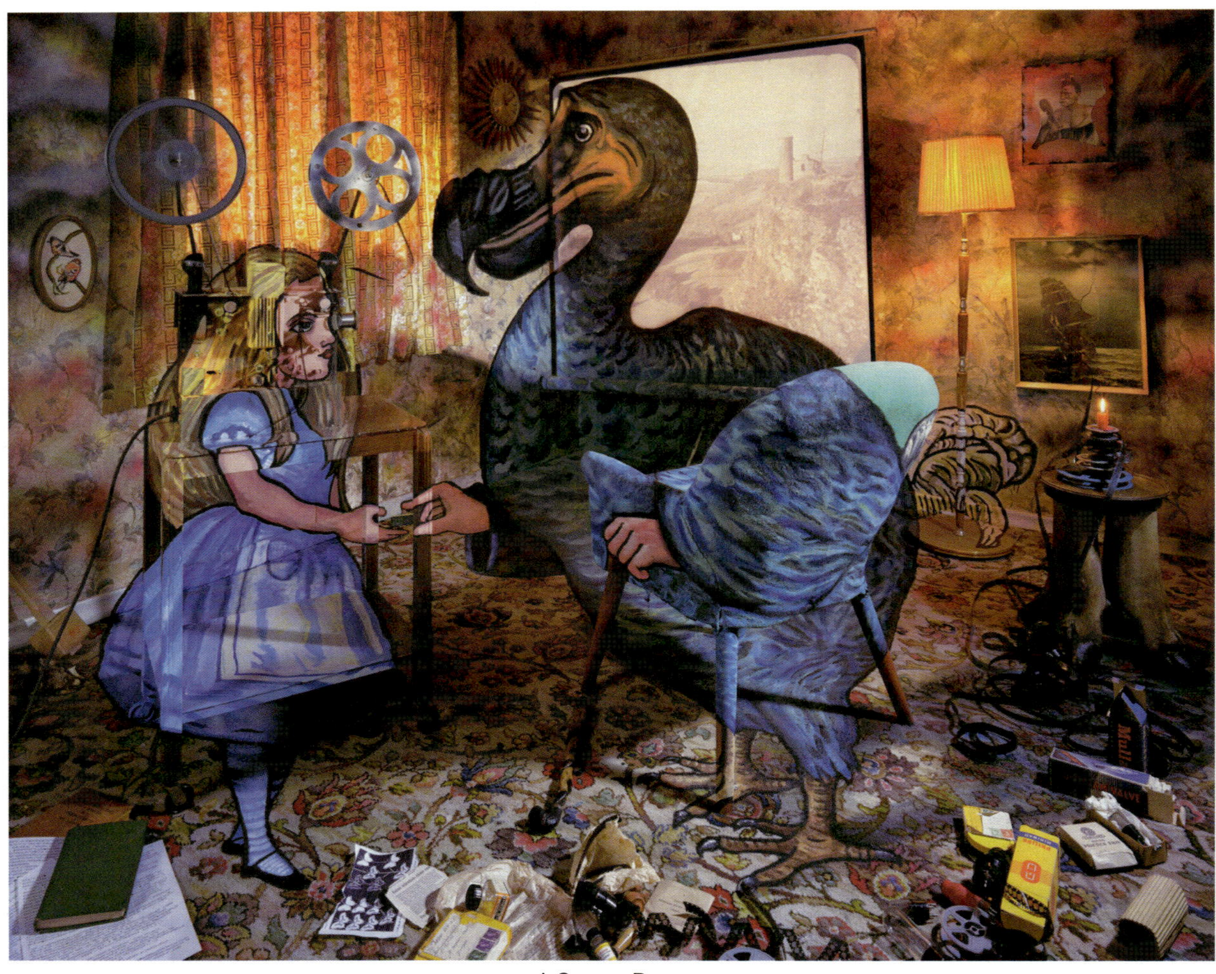

A Caucus Race,
1999

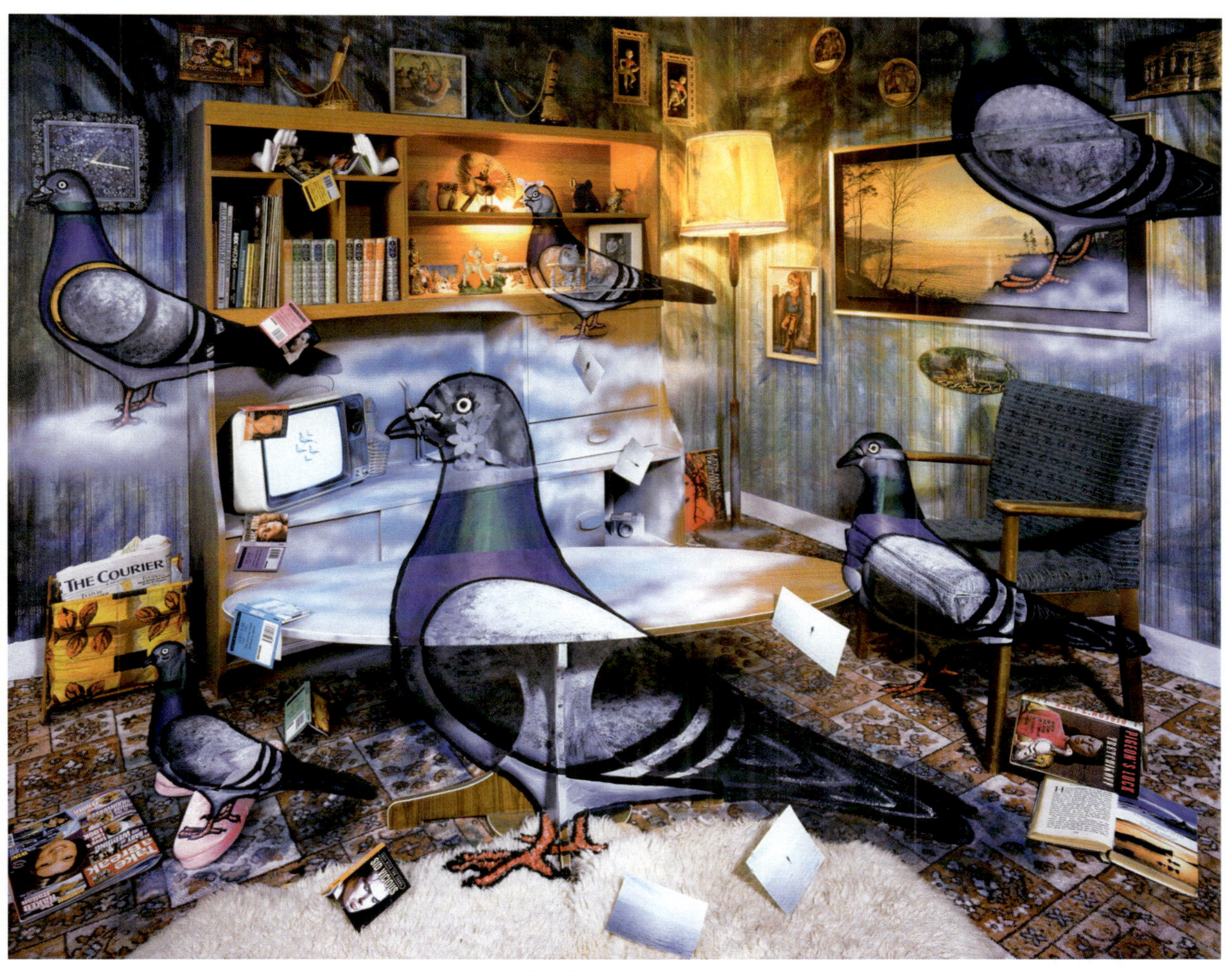

The Common Runt,
1999

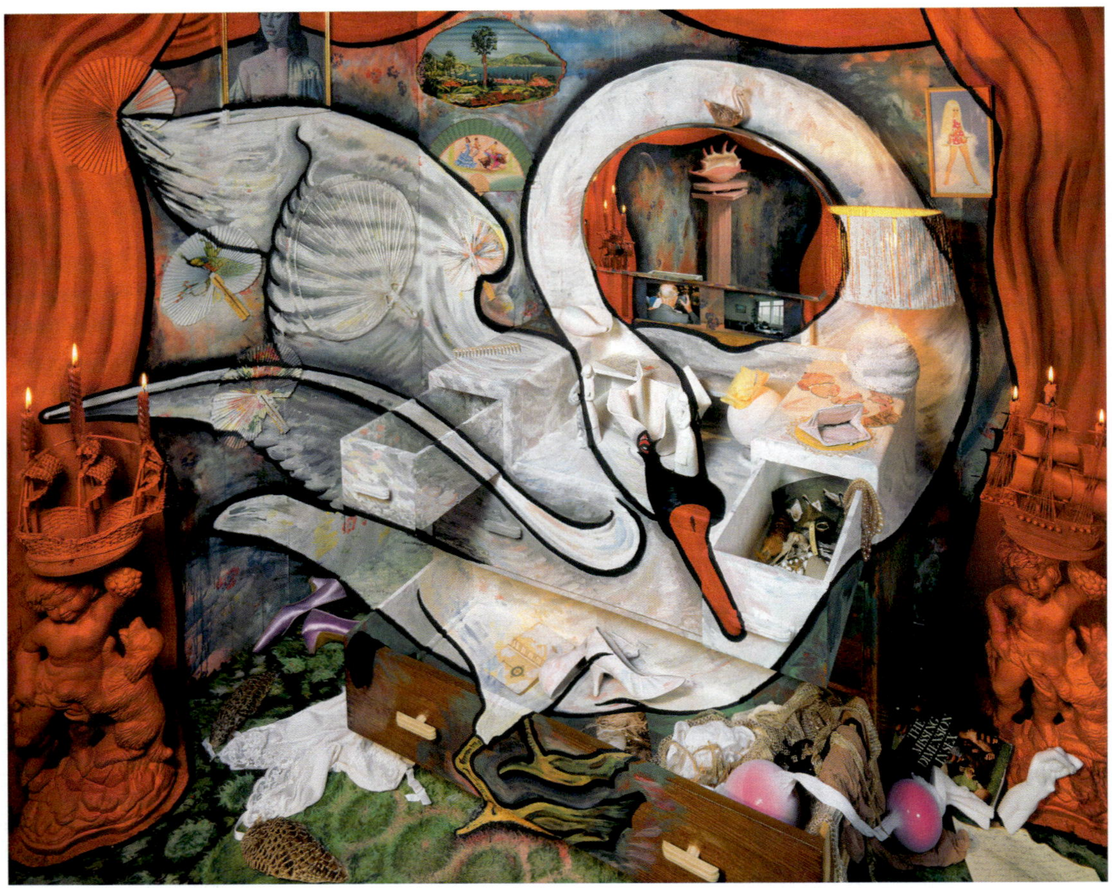

Mute Swan,
1994

Throughout these works, there is an implied sound, most especially of bird song, and this is underscored by reference to texts of every kind. This fascination with layers of thought and meaning is typical of Colvin's aesthetic. Whereas this may be conceptualised as an interest in 'hybridity', it remains fundamental to his creative thought process at a more intuitive level. As an artist, he is constantly visualising correspondences and associations, selecting themes and recognising their infinite variety, moving between the rarefied and the familiar. In consequence, there is an element of playful inventiveness in all these photographic constructions, but also an aspect of profound insight.

Scotland and beyond: culture, history and myth

Calum Colvin had returned to Scotland in 1992. This was following a stellar career based in London, where he established himself as an artist of international renown. In some degree, his status as an exile had shaped his work. The world he had envisioned was one of shifting landscapes, colliding values, dislocated identities, uncertain alliances, broken and aberrant entanglements. He codified these transitions in his intricate, labyrinthine photographs. They presented a mosaic of modernity, replete with mutable meanings and fluid associations.

The embodiment of this estrangement was surely the kilted Action Man doll. This doppelganger acted as a surrogate. Here was the exile, here the alien and here the wandering Scot. This traveller looked in wonder, and in disbelief, at the disruption in the contemporary world. From this position as observer, he might recognise the folly and hubris of the present reality.

Returning to Scotland, this emissary would gradually fade from the lexicon of symbols in Colvin's work. Approaching the millennium, his vision would come to focus upon the ways in which a culture might come to understand its history, most especially on the ways in which that history may be constructed as myth; so that issues of nationhood, identity and civic 'character' might be imagined within totemic representations. In respect of this, from the year 2000, he began to embark upon a series of projects that explored the meanings and significations of key figures from Scottish history. His chosen subjects were established archetypes: James Macpherson's construction of Ossian, the 'Celtic Homer'; the national bard, Robert Burns; and the 'Bonnie Prince', Charles Edward Stuart.

The first of these projects was realised in an exhibition created for the Scottish National Portrait Gallery in 2002. *Ossian: Fragments of Ancient Poetry* would be a landmark presentation that offered a nuanced reflection on an epic saga. Such was its import that it travelled throughout Scotland, and was the subject of a special exhibition and conference at UNESCO in Paris.

The story of Ossian intrigued Colvin, in part, because the nature of its 'construction' and cultural significance held parallels with his own creative methods. Ossian was 'discovered', or created, by the eighteenth-century poet and writer James Macpherson. Macpherson claimed to have come upon collections, fragments, of ancient verse while travelling in the Highlands of Scotland. These, he affirmed, he had rescued and 'translated' from their presentation in the original Gaelic and Erse languages. Moreover, he asserted that these epic works originated in the lyric chronicles of the Celtic bard, Ossian, the blind son of the legendary warrior hero, Fionn mac Cumhaill, Finn McCool. And so, in 1760, he published *Fragments of Ancient Poetry, collected in the Highlands of Scotland*. This was followed by *Fingal* in 1762 and *Temora* in 1763. These epics would be gathered together as a collected edition in 1765 and published as *The Poems of Ossian*.

The reception afforded these works was extraordinary. They were generally hailed as startling evidence of a classical culture of the north, and as witness to a heroic and virtuous civilisation amongst Gaelic-speaking peoples. Their cultural import was such that they were championed in Scotland by Robert Burns and Sir Walter Scott; in England by Lord Byron and William Wordsworth; on the continent by Johann Goethe and Denis Diderot; and in America by James Fenimore Cooper and Henry Wadsworth Longfellow. They would become the source for musical compositions by Beethoven and Mendelssohn, amongst others, and a host of canonical Neo-classical and Romantic paintings. Famously, Ossian was presented as the 'Celtic Homer', and Napoleon would carry these verses throughout his many campaigns.

Naturally, these triumphs were met with some resistance. The authenticity of these 'discoveries' and 'translations' became contested, most notably by the most celebrated of eighteenth-century writers, Samuel Johnson. In 1775, Johnson declared the Ossian poems fraudulent and a mere pastiche of classical verse. There followed a controversy that lasted for decades and continued after Macpherson's death in 1796.

Colvin, of course, recognised the fault-lines in this discourse. Macpherson may have discovered some fragments of original Gaelic story telling, but these he embroidered to create a 'constructed narrative'. Here, 'truth' and 'authenticity' was a will-o'-the-wisp, fleetingly glimpsed in a landscape of fantasy and dream-like apparitions. The intriguing element was the way in which these phenomena might move from cultural forms into attested history and on towards myth. This dynamic became the subject of his *Ossian: Fragments of Ancient Poetry*.

The leitmotif of Colvin's project was an engraving of Ossian from the frontispiece of the 1807 publication of *The Poems of Ossian*. This work is often ascribed to the Scottish painter, Alexander Runciman, though, tellingly, even this attribution is disputed. Colvin created a fractured and broken landscape. It resembles a ruined temple or the fragments of a monolithic monument. Across this he has presented the head of Ossian, with tangled flowing hair and beard. Like the original engraving, this Ossian is seen in the ecstasy of a creative flight. He appears to recite his epic verse that is revealed from somewhere deep in his psyche. Around him the broken landscape contains shreds and remnants of a culture in decay. The scene is melancholic, tragic and romantic.

Colvin created a suite of nine images: *Blind Ossian 1–ix*. They are characterised by a gradual degeneration, a sense of disintegration and loss. *Blind Ossian 1* presents a near complete image, with the 'seer' bathed in a blue aura, his curling hair and beard describing the patterns of Celtic design and written across the broken monoliths of his surroundings. In *Blind Ossian vii,* the palette has shifted. The blue tones have become umber and creeping shadows begin to obscure the scene. In *Blind Ossian ix,* the figure has all but disappeared. Only the ruin of a monolithic landscape remains.

Through the series of nine images, the substance of Ossian is dissolved, as are the symbolic motifs that lay around him, half-hidden in the ruins. To the lower left of the scene, a seared photograph of a Maori head is shown, his facial tattoos an echo of the Celtic design revealed by Ossian's hair and beard. In the lower right portion sit some stag's antlers, a subtle reflection on the fate of Celtic Scotland in the period of the Highland Clearances.

The sense of 'fragment' is replete in these images. Colvin speaks of a culture and history that is revealed, then lost. Its mythic elements remain, but only as shadow. This reflected the fate of Macpherson's Ossian, but it also speaks to the destiny of Highland life and civilisation in the modern period. Macpherson's Ossian may be viewed as an attempt to restore the dignity of Celtic culture following the compound defeats of a failed Jacobite uprising, the insult of the Clearances, and the grievance of induced emigration. The presentation of this desire as a fraud was a final insult.

Colvin offers an elegy to this history, but he also reflects upon the complexity of its manifestation. Certainly, the romantic elements in the *Blind Ossian* series embody ideas of tragedy and melancholy. But the extension of this project spreads outwards to envisage issues relating to identity and the construction of belief systems. Indeed, the corresponding images in this project reflected upon the ways in which a nation and culture might 'imagine' its character in a complicated and heterogeneous world.

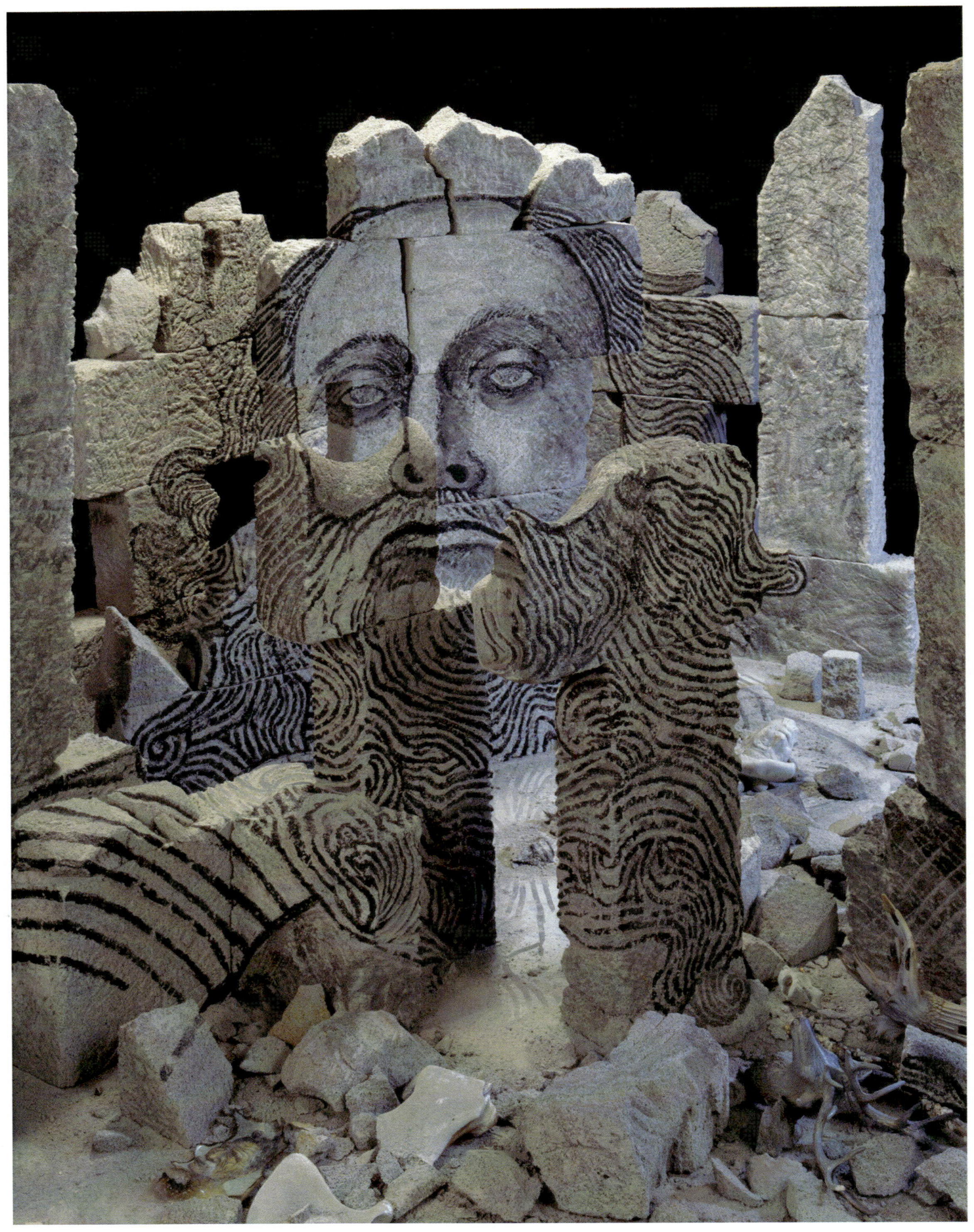

Blind Ossian I,
2002

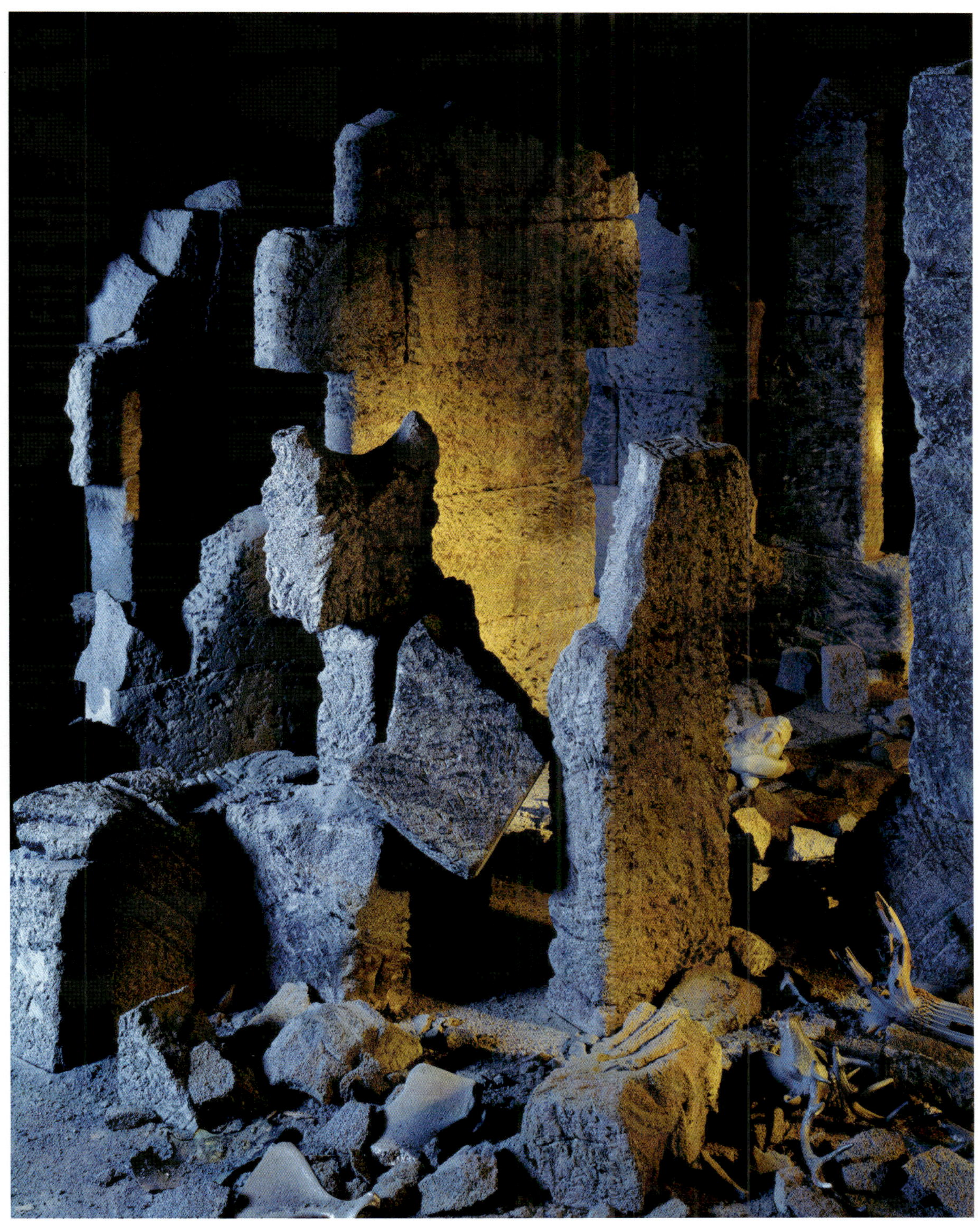

Blind Ossian IX,
2002

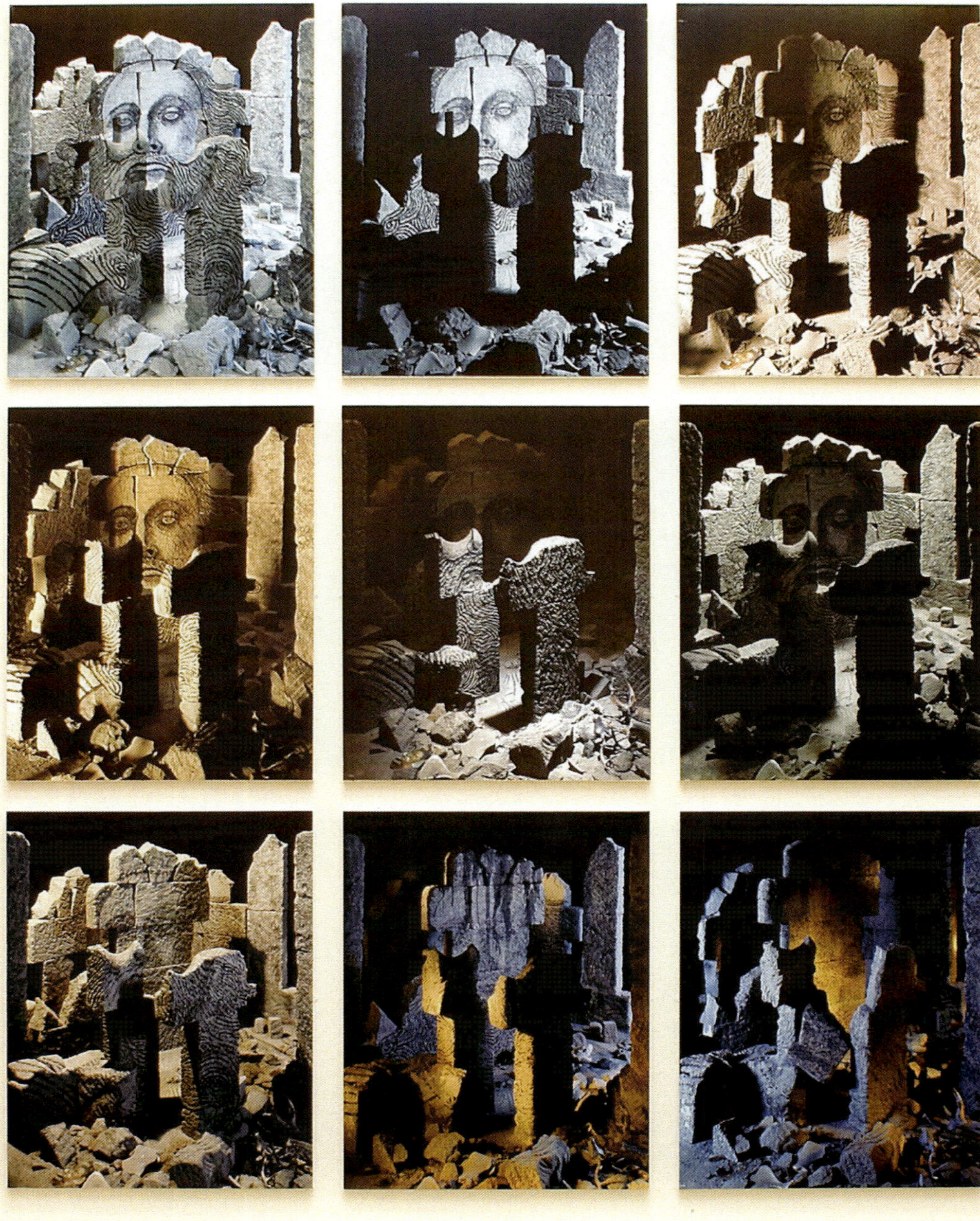

The fundamental building-blocks of this construction were, elliptically, explored in the triptych, *Cruthni 1; Cruthni 11; Cruthni 111*, from 2002. Whereas *Blind Ossian* was a meditation on the mythic nature of identity construction, the *Cruthni* series spoke to the idea that science might establish the core characteristics of a people. The Cruthni, it is understood, were an early medieval Irish people sometimes associated with the Picts. They have been presented as an early manifestation of a 'Scottish' tribal community. Typical of these 'foundation myths', the history is obscure and disputed but it is argued that this group occupied the area sometimes known as Dalriada, in the west of Scotland, while the Picts were essentially an east of Scotland dynasty. The combination of these groups developed, through manifold complications, into something that might be described as a 'Scottish' people.

In reflecting upon this foundation myth, Colvin offers *Cruthni 1* which presents a few broken standing stones in a dark and tempestuous landscape. Scattered in the foreground are fragments of tribal cultures with memorial objects (a wicker barrow, a landscape photograph) that recall the detritus of lost worlds. Onto the stones in *Cruthni 1*, the pattern of a fingerprint is embedded. This mark, a signature of 'scientific' identity, offers some sense of a 'true' identity, but this image simultaneously speaks to the fluidity of personal and cultural character. *Cruthni 1*, for all its scientific validations, speculates upon the 'stories' created in historical chronicles, and their claims to authenticity. In which case, the fragile border between history and myth is explored and challenged.

This thread is extended in *Cruthni 11* where an arm and hand, holding a primitive abacus, descends into the constructed scenario. Here, the sense of a formal calculation of character and identity is delivered, with all its assumptions of veracity. The final reflection, in *Cruthni 111*, presents the DNA molecular structure within the fractured landscape. With this scenario, the paradigm of hard science is offered as empirical exactitude in determining identity.

However, the entirety of this particular triptych remains located within an ambiguous and ruptured landscape. The background in the photographs are by turn stormy, ominous and opaque. Science, then, may offer these principles of identity, but they are situated within a space that creates uncertainty and dispute. Colvin evidently recognises the relativism in accounts of identity, so that there are 'truths' and there are beliefs; and these poles create doubt and, sometimes, discord.

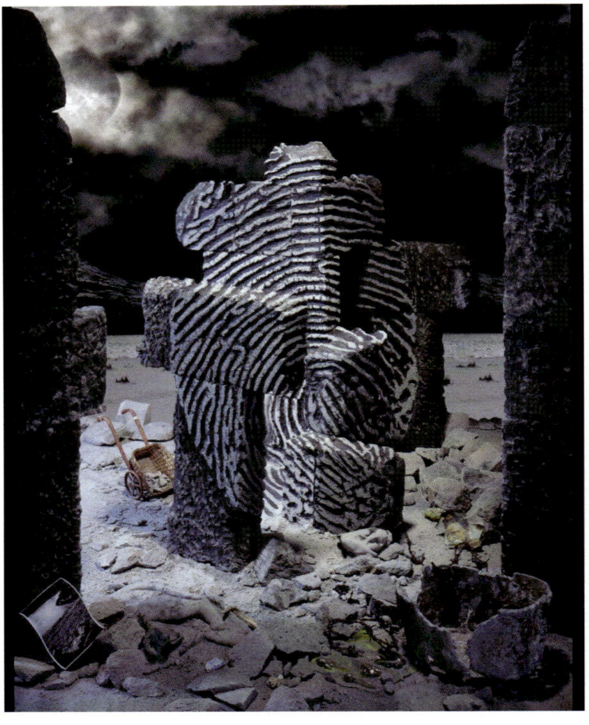

Colvin would further explore these ambiguities with his series of images titled *Fragments*. This group of eight photographs was a core component of his *Ossian* project. Yet, if the *Blind Ossian* and *Cruthni* elements of this project focussed on the sober aspects of this intellectual construction, *Fragments* returned to the dynamic of the comic.

The set for this series of photographs was, again, a dark and broken prospect with what appears to be the corner of an abandoned sitting-room. This derelict, ashen space contains a scree of rubble amongst which can be found a host of symbolic items: an inflatable globe to signal the interaction of world cultures; a torn confection packet that reveals the word 'Celt'; a packet of picture hooks with the lettering attenuated to reveal the word 'Pict', while related detritus includes a commonplace lamp, an ornamental lion and an old record player.

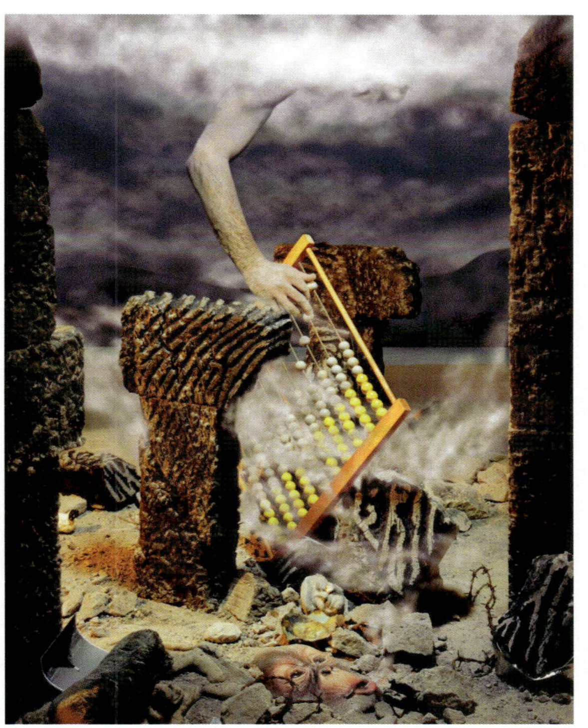

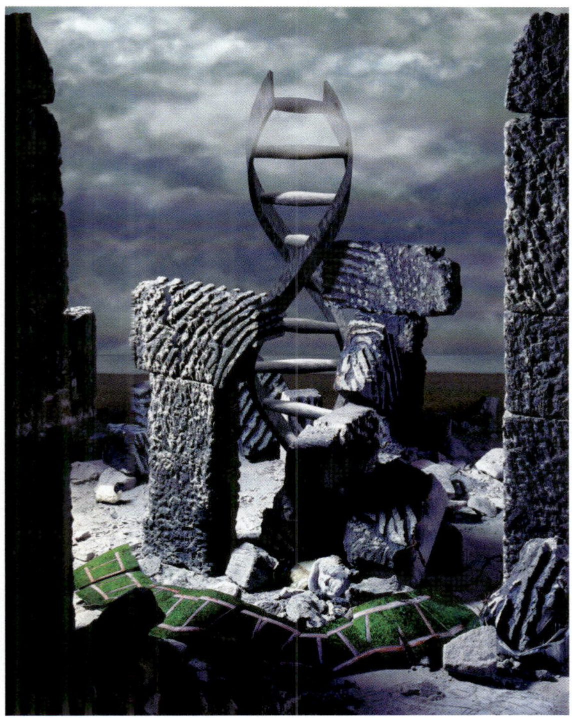

Cruthni I; Cruthni II; Cruthni III,
2002

The centrepiece of this tableau is a slide projector, with attendant screen. This looks towards a mirror, partially covered by a ragged cloth. Onto this, in the first three images from *Fragments*, the Maori face that was half-hidden in the *Blind Ossian* series is writ large. However, as the series progresses, this image gradually transforms into a caricature 'Highland Laddie'; a plaster ornamental head that was a popular decoration in the 1950s and 1960s. In *Fragment vii,* this 'Highland Laddie' image gradually fades, so that in *Fragment viii,* only the broken wasteland of the background set remains.

This tragi-comic scenario is replete with subtle references and meanings. The use of the romanticised Maori head, complete with tattoos, refers, in part, to the notion that Macpherson had discovered in Ossian a 'noble savage'. The currency of this idea was familiar in Enlightenment philosophy, and indeed James Boswell, Samuel Johnston's interlocutor, would call Macpherson 'The Sublime Savage'. Equally, the ornate tattoos on this figure would reference a correspondence with the patterns of Celtic design. The 'Highland Laddie' head represented the degraded sense of Celtic and Highland culture as represented within kitsch culture. The conjoining of these references signifies a nuanced reflection upon the broader theme within the *Ossian* series; that the search for essential identities is misconceived, for the global interaction of peoples and cultures is substantive. Given these conditions, these seemingly concrete identities mingle and dissolve.

'Identity', however, remains a powerful agency in the contemporary psyche. And, driven by culture, history and myth it can fall into animus. In the *Ossian* series, Colvin would explore this dynamic in his work titled *Twa Dogs*.

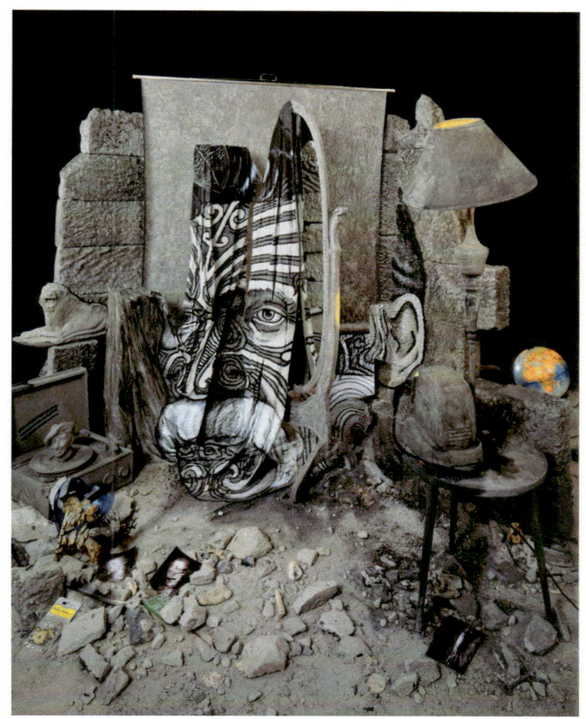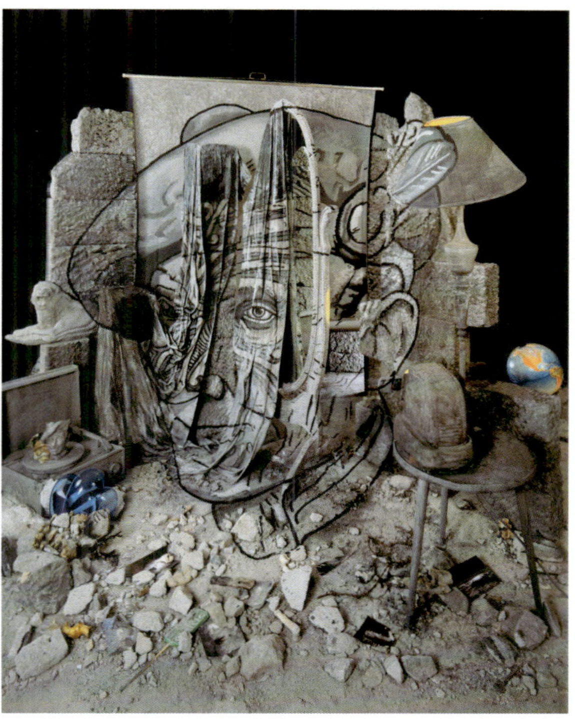
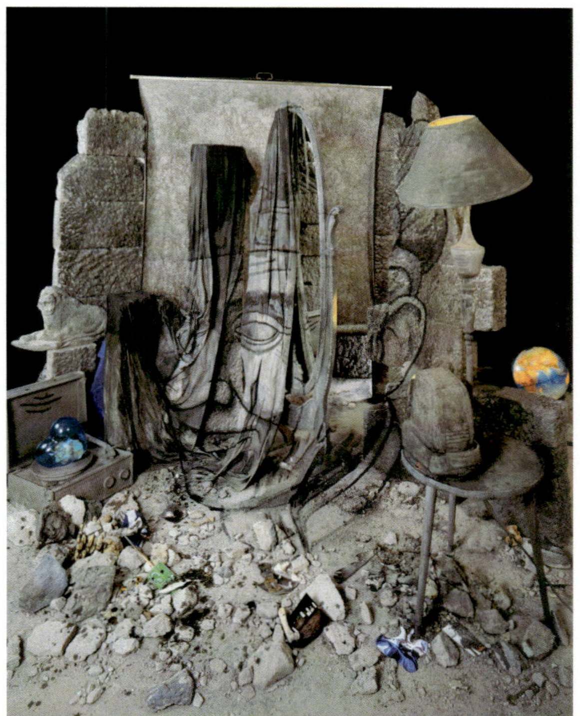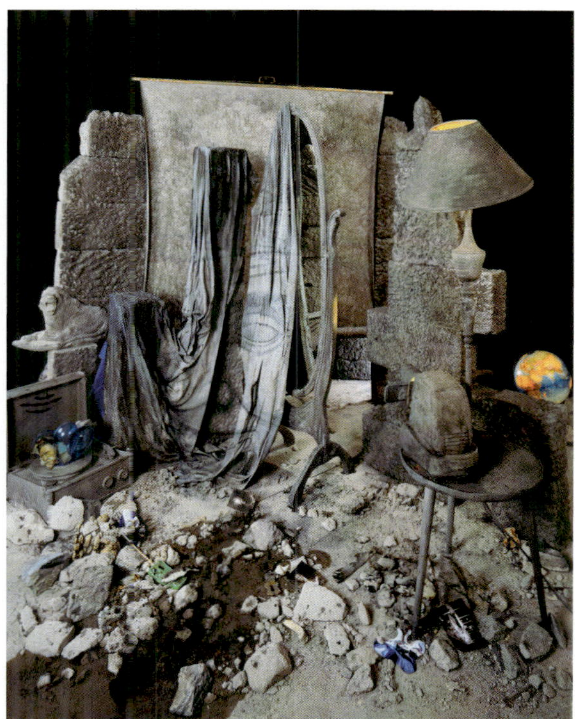

Fragment I; Fragment IV; Fragment VI; Fragment VII,
2002

Twa Dogs is a rumination on the poem by Robert Burns titled 'The Twa Dogs'. Here, Burns had created a comic work that was written as a dialogue between two dogs; one 'o' high degree' and the other 'a ploughman's collie'. Hence, the discourse concerned social class and, underlying this, a discussion on the nature of human society. In Burns' work, the dogs are named Caesar and Luath. Caesar, of course, represented the classical world and, as Burns notes, 'nane o' Scotland's dogs', whereas Luath was named 'After some dog in Highland sang/Was made lang syne, lord knows how lang'. In fact, Luath was the name of Cuhullin's dog in Macpherson's *Fingal*. It was, moreover, the name of Burns' own favourite collie, and so the return to Macpherson's *Ossian* is realised in this subtle association.

Colvin, however, has reprised this theme in terms of a more contemporary conflict concerning 'identity'. In the first instance, he explores the disconnect between Celtic and British identity and extends this into a reflection on the duality of Highland and Lowland culture. This becomes keyed in to a meditation on the two historic languages of Scotland, Gaelic and Scots-English, then surfaces as a fundamental, atavistic dualism; the contest between Glasgow Celtic and Glasgow Rangers football clubs.

In *Twa Dogs,* Caesar, renamed in Colvin's work 'Kaiser' and Luath become the signifiers of tribal identities and implacable factions. In Colvin's tableau, the scene is enacted around a modern domestic hearth; though, evidently, this is the set of Ossian's fractured megalith now reconstructed as a homely fireplace. The dogs guard the dismal symbols of their conflict and identities. Kaiser stands atop a Glasgow Rangers towel, Luath on a Celtic floor covering; an empty 'Gaels' honey jar is juxtaposed to some orange sweets, while each dog's feeding bowl is filled, ironically, with the branded novelties of the opposing tribe. Everywhere the grim sectarianism is reprised and proclaimed. And, whereas in Burns' poem the two dogs, after a long deliberation on the nature of human life, are reported to '...up they gat, an' shook their lugs/Rejoiced, they were na men, but dogs', the absurd segregation in Colvin's narrative remains immutable.

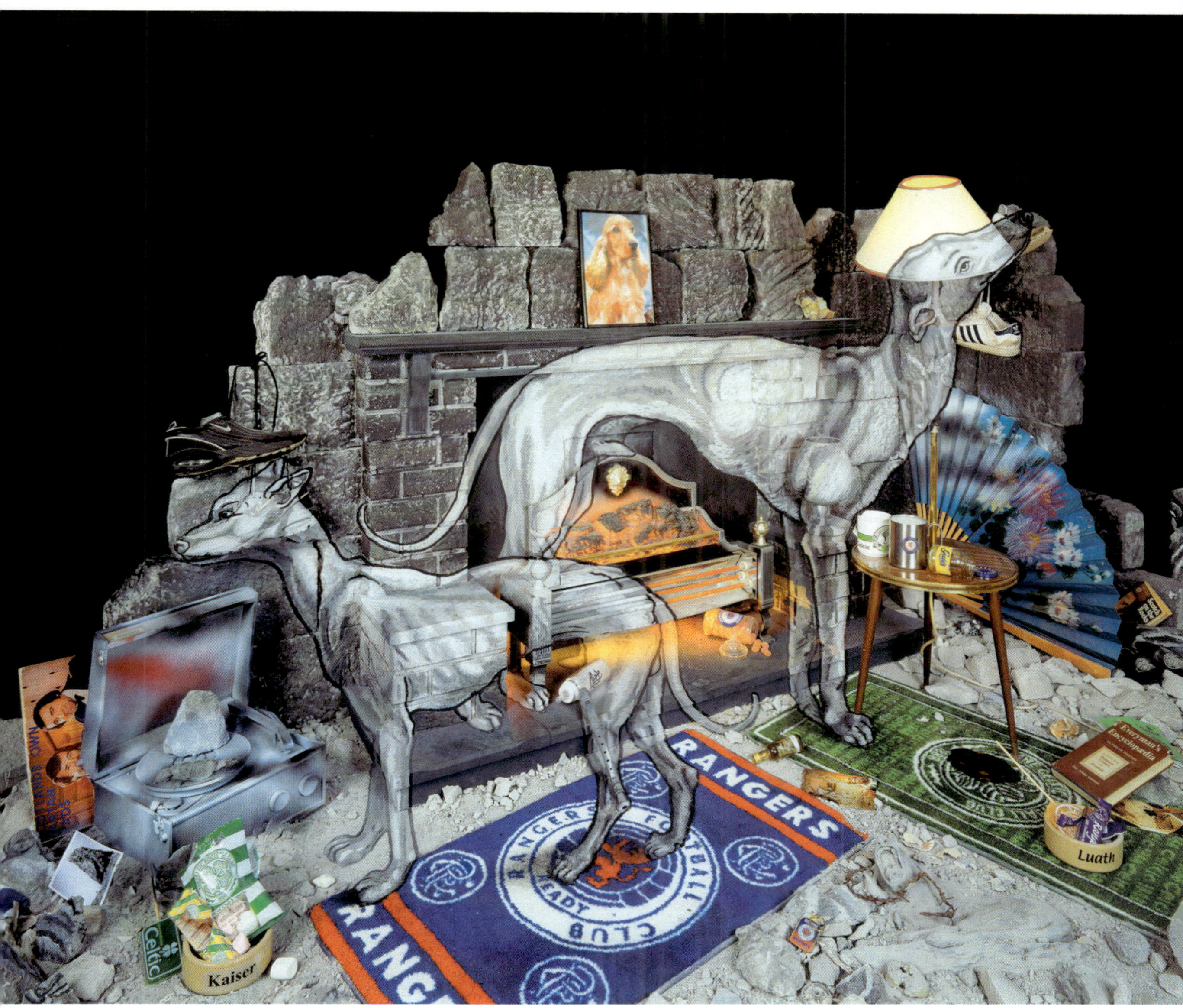

Twa Dogs,
2002

Throughout the *Ossian* project, Colvin was exploring the nature of identity in the modern period. He recognised both the importance of this construct in the contemporary world and its layered complexity. In reflecting upon this, he explored the concept as varied cultural phenomena, rooted in historical accounts but manifest as stories that had the omniscient power of myth. Macpherson was, evidently, a cultural phenomenon, but he presented his Ossian as historical fact and this became a mythic fable. Colvin's *Ossian: Fragments of Ancient Poetry* was created to celebrate this extraordinary illusion and to search through its manifestations and mysteries. It was this sense of the near occult nature of these mythologies that he would explore in subsequent studies of Robert Burns and Charles Edward Stuart.

Robert Burns was both a contemporary of James Macpherson and an admirer. Indeed, he had declared Ossian to be 'the prince of Poets'. It was logical then that, in conjunction with *Twa Dogs*, Colvin created a portrait of Burns to complement his *Ossian* series. This *Portrait of Robert Burns (after Archibald Skirving)*, from 2001, takes the little-known chalk drawing by Archibald Skirving as its model. This latter work was itself based on the renowned painting of the poet by Alexander Nasmyth, and it might be suggested that this trail of adaptations from Nasmyth's painting to Skirving's drawing and on to Colvin's photograph is an echo of the 'translations' evident in Macpherson's poems of Ossian.

Colvin's *Portrait of Robert Burns (after Archibald Skirving)* is, however, an ingenious construction that pays homage to the bard and is replete with allusions to his canonical works. The set itself resurrects the monoliths of the *Blind Ossian* works and builds these into a tableau to which a bookcase and a classical column are added. The bookcase, most evidently, references Burns' role as writer, while the classical column creates a shorthand note relating to his place in the world of the Enlightenment. The head of Burns is portrayed across the bookcase and his shoulders flow

Portrait of
Robert Burns
(after Archibald Skirving),
2001

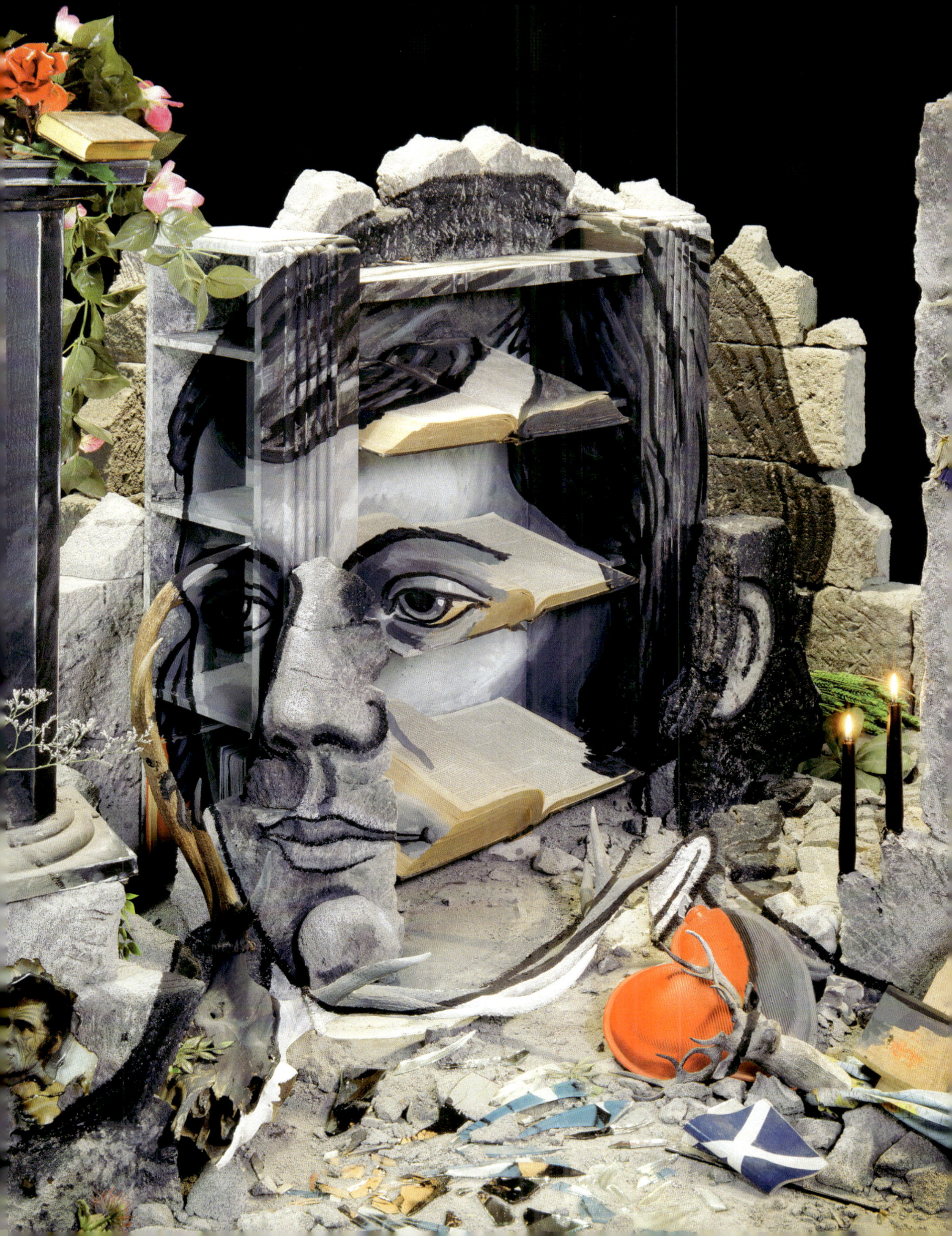

down into the symbolic debris of the foreground. Here, a red hot-water bottle in the shape of a heart provides a cushion for a model stag's head: it surely references the verse 'My heart's in the Highlands, my heart is not here/My heart's in the Highland's a-chasing the deer'. Discreetly positioned behind the poet, a bundle of green bulrushes can be glimpsed: a note that alludes to the beautiful song *Green grow the rashes, O*. Atop the column, a book and a posy of flowers is placed, with the 'red, red rose' prominent: a quotation that requires no annotation. The image is a joyous, tragi-comic celebration of the poet that recognises his place within the broader narrative of the Ossian myth and, in some degree, views the bard as the heir to Ossian.

Overall, Colvin's *Ossian: Fragments of Ancient Poetry* was a complex, subtle, challenging and invigorating project that proved to be something of a landmark in his development as an artist. It was an ambitious creation that combined the inventiveness of his working method with an intellectual panorama that was inspirational. It also deepened his fascination with the interrelationship of art and poetry and this, coupled with his attraction to the nature of myth in the contemporary narrative of Scotland, compelled him towards a more expansive reflection on the cult of Robert Burns.

The *Portrait of Robert Burns (after Archibald Skirving)* was the first in a sequence of photographs and objects that Colvin would create as he explored the world of Burns and his labyrinthine cultural associations. Burns was a natural fit for Colvin and Colvin's art. Burns' stature was epic, his reputation was global and his character was legendary. Moreover, as a poet, he straddled boundaries. He utilised both the English and the Scots language. He moved in the world of classical forms while being a champion of the vernacular. He explored the serious, and even the tragic, while being acclaimed for his wit and comic verse. He spoke to the local while acknowledging the global. He aspired, in all these things, to recognise the glorious ambiguity of being human.

Colvin revealed this universalism in his works on Burns, and notably in his photograph *Burns Country* from 2012. This was completed for his exhibition titled *Burnsiana* held, appropriately, in the Robert Burns Birthplace Museum in Alloway during 2013. The setting for *Burns Country* is a simple corner in a room decorated with floral wallpaper; a bright sunshine yellow in tone. In this set an open and carved display stand for trinkets and ornaments is juxtaposed with a standard lamp, and with a three-legged table. All are redolent of 'homely' furnishings from the post-war period. An ornamental stag's antlers and a guitar are set against these props, while the foreground is replete with books, a Mauchline Ware box, flagons, a lit candle and some gathered grass folded into a nest complete with a half-hidden model of a harvest mouse. These symbolic objects are accompanied by ornamental bird figurines, placed on the table and in the display stand. Across this tableau, a portrait of Burns, visionary and handsome, is created. Surrounding the head a painted laurel-leaf garland encompasses the poet.

Here is Robert Burns in his 'country'. Colvin has noted how the image

> evokes the rural idylls and scenes you often see engraved in Burns editions…with…a bard figure, within a landscape.[10]

The references to Burns as a countryman and ploughman are abounding in this image. Foliage and shrub in the background, model birds flitting through the scene with notations of their song written into the set and the guitar remembering the poet as an exquisite songsmith.

Burns Country is a joyous and evocative image, part homily and part kitsch. Interestingly, the tonal range in the painting of the poet's face moves towards the blue end of the spectrum. This thought was reprised in Colvin's photograph *Blue Burns* (2013). Here, Burns' portrait is painted across an impressive floor-standing globe, his face blue and his lips a vivid

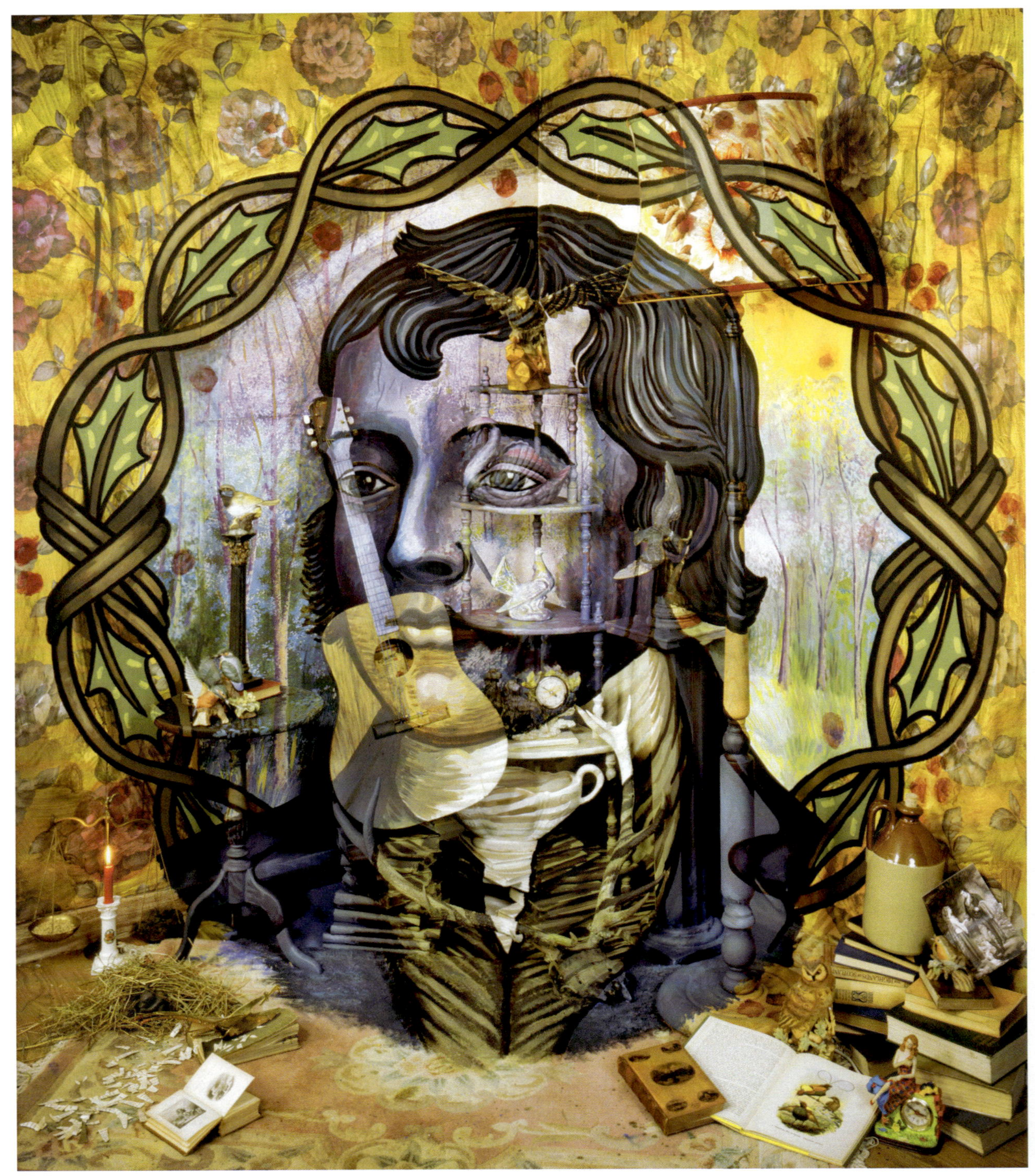

Burns Country,
2012

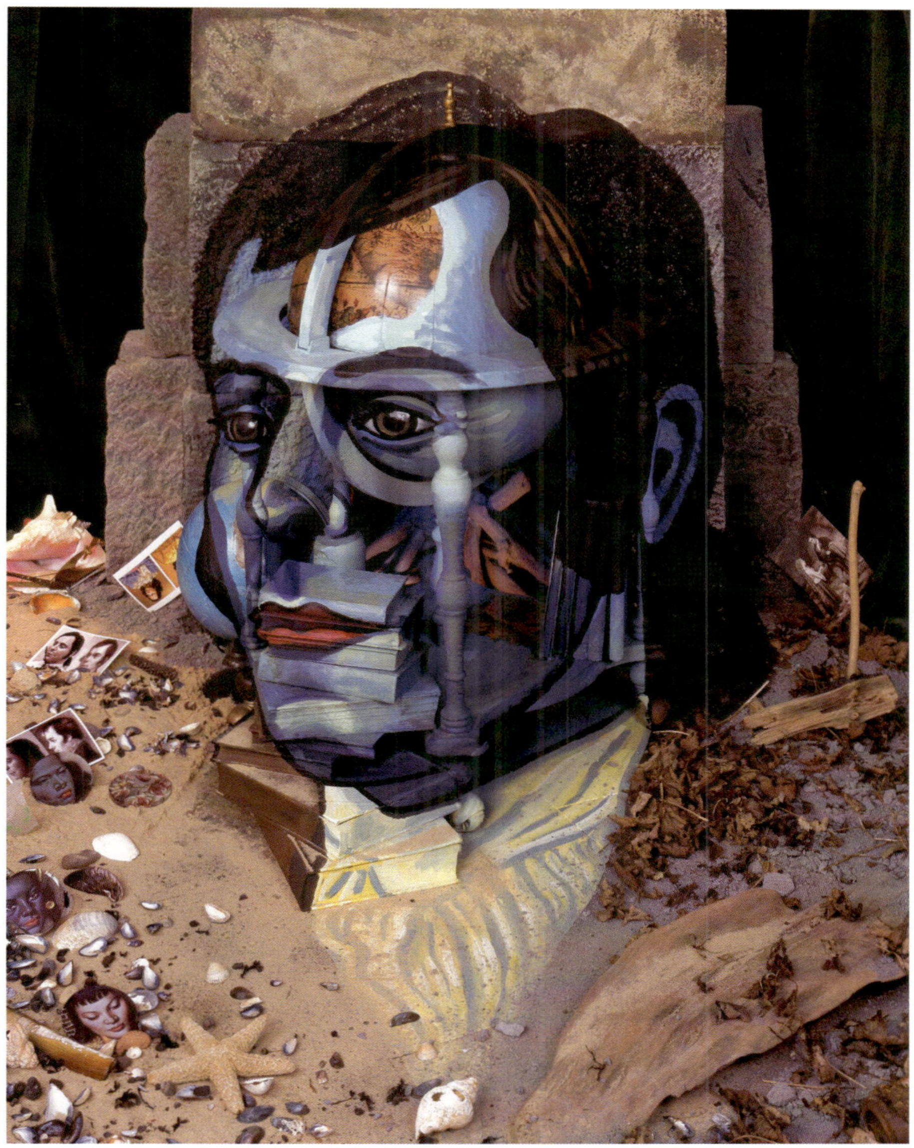

Blue Burns,
2013

red. Of course, Colvin is again referencing the international success of Vladimir Tretchikoff's mass-produced print, *Chinese Girl*, from 1953. Provocatively, the poet is presented as a martyr to his international celebrity, a global figure, but stranded in a seashore landscape of flotsam and jetsam, his life's work being levelled into a wrack of kitsch ornament.

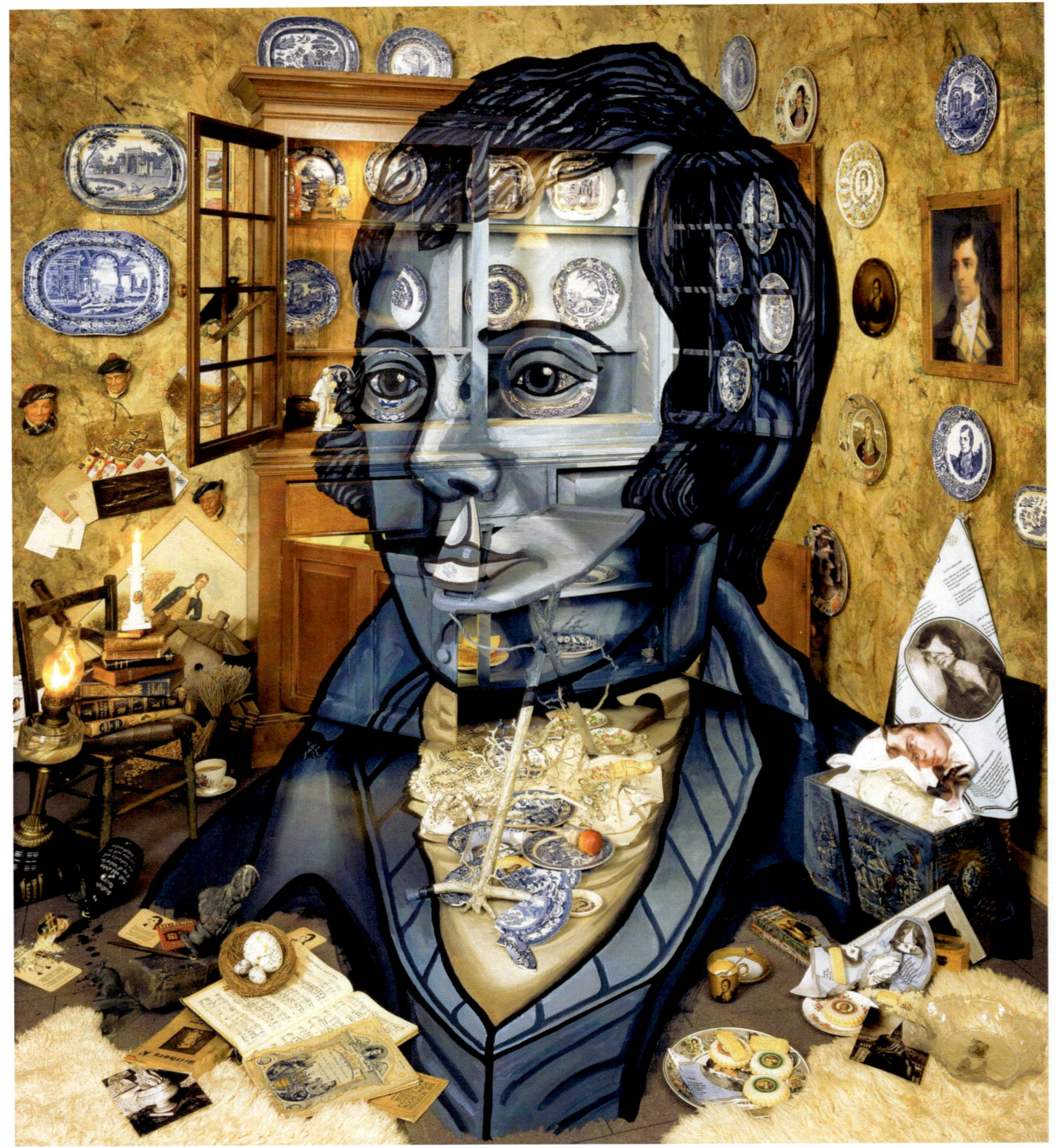

Burnsomania,
2017

Colvin was sensitive to this 'kitschification' of Burns, both in respect of the poet's reputation and of his works. Indeed, he found the representation of Burns within popular culture something of a positive dynamic. This he celebrated in his Burns works, and no more so than in *Burnsomania* (2017). *Burnsomania* gives a kaleidoscopic review of the ways in which the Scottish nation, and the world beyond, has celebrated Robert Burns. In the corner of his studio, Colvin has created a set that is decorated with a display cabinet, with chairs, with various rugs and lamps and even an ironing-board complete with the iron. Around this furniture, he has arrayed every kind of Burns-inspired knick-knack, bauble and curio: commemorative plates, prints, books, table cloths, cups and goblets, statuettes and Burns-club certificates. On the wall to the right, there is a print modelled on Alexander Nasmyth's portrait of the poet from 1787. It is this portrait that Colvin has used for his overpainting of the set with his expressive image of the bard.

Burnsomania is an extraordinary celebration of Burns and what he has come to represent in Scottish, and world, culture. Colvin's work certainly highlights the 'mania' for Burns but recognises this as a colourful and positive energy, even in its most kitsch manifestations. Indeed, when he exhibited this work in the exhibition titled *Museography*, held in Dundee's McManus Gallery in 2017, he presented it as an installation. The image was reproduced in a round format and surrounding the work was an array of 12 ceramic plates. Seven of these plates were mass-produced objects memorialising the bard, but five of the plates were reproductions of Colvin's own photographs, now printed onto porcelain.

This device of printing his photographs onto commemorative ceramic plates was a deepening of Colvin's fascination with the interaction of fine art with popular culture. In 2012, he reproduced two of his most intriguing images, *Negative Sublime 1* and *Negative Sublime 11*, both first created as photographs in 2001, but now produced as decorated dinner plates.

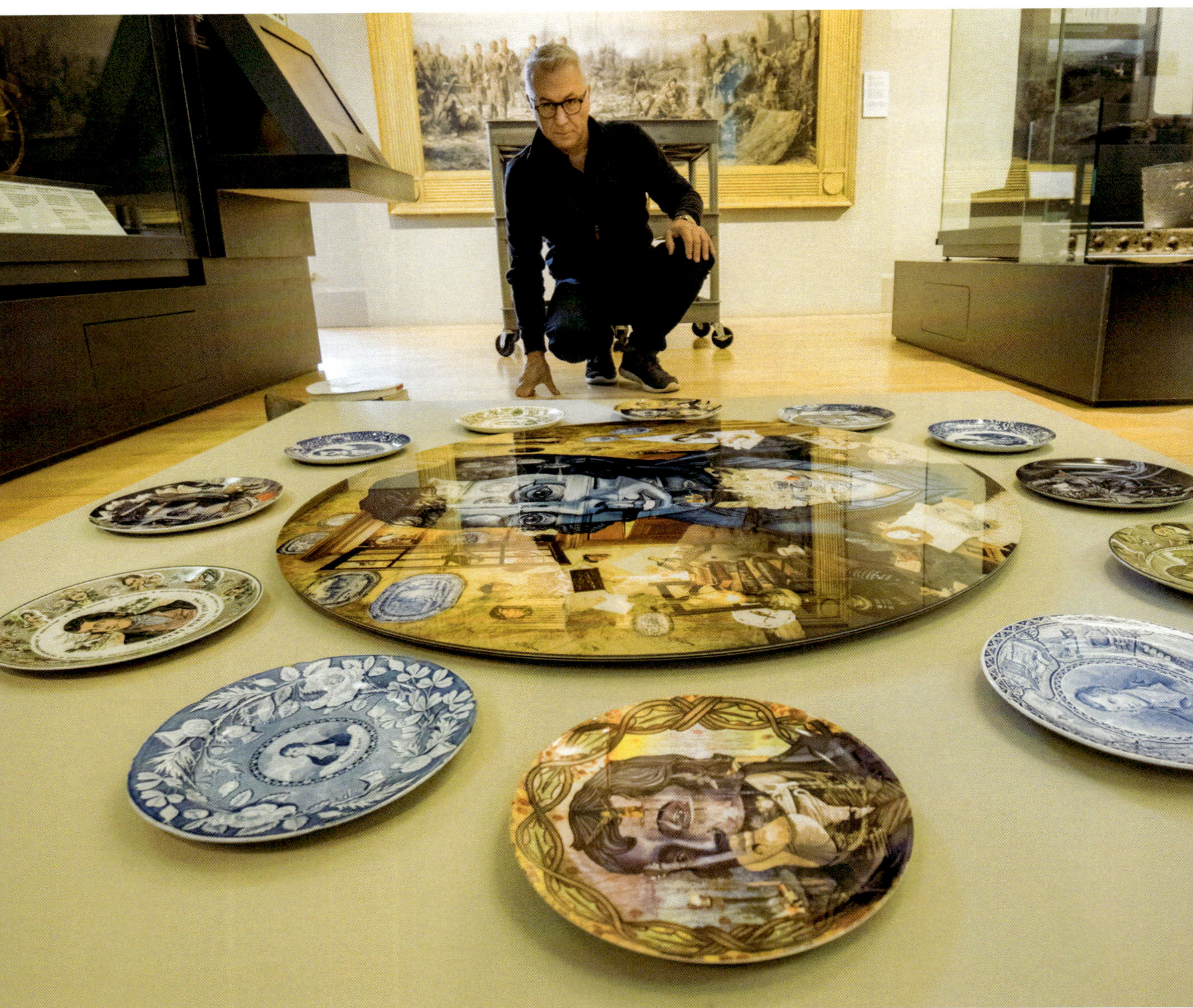

Calum Colvin installing the expanded Burnsiana at the McManus Galleries, Dundee,
2017

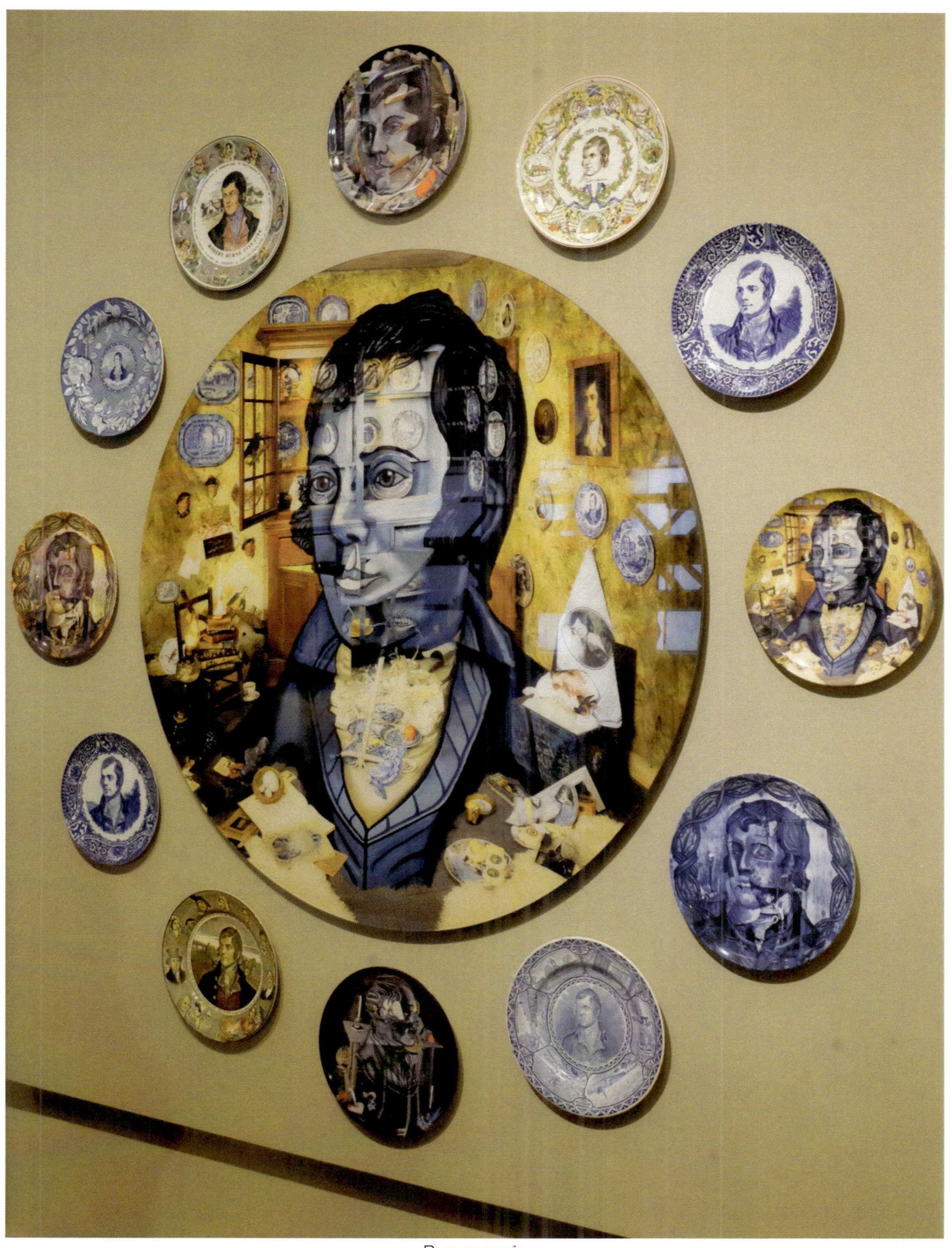

Burnsomania
(installation, McManus Gallery, Dundee},
2017

These works offer portraits of Robert Burns and of Lord George Gordon Byron, the Romantic poet with estates in Aberdeenshire. Placed side by side, the protagonists in the two works seem to be in conversation, though they never met for Byron was a mere eight years old when Burns died in 1796. In Colvin's fantastical world, they echo one another in style and form and share their common ideals and values.

Colvin's *Negative Sublime 1* is one of his fine portraits of Robert Burns. The setting is the poet's writing desk, piled with books and with an open volume of poetry on his book stand. In the set, a spade, hammer and 'graip' record Burns' role as a farmer and 'ploughman poet'. The tone of the room is dark and grey though it is lit with an anachronistic paraffin lamp and a candle. On the floor, an hour-glass, a cubic saltire and a skeletal mask speak to subjects of mortality and history. The bard himself is painted across the set as a profile figure in tones of grey, almost a photographic negative. In the bottom right-hand corner, the pewter tankard that supports the candle reflects an anamorphic image, a grinning head, or skull.

The 'negative sublime' in the title refers to the darker threads in creative practice. That sense of struggle in 'making' and the need to embrace every human emotion in the creation of art. Simultaneously, it recognises that this engagement with the negative is resolved in the positive achievement of a visionary work, much as the analogue photographic negative produces the positive image.

Negative Sublime 11 offers a portrait of Byron. It is a parallel to the related image of Burns and occupies the same set, with desk, chair, book stand, candles and lantern. Equally, this work shares the idea of dark struggle as the root of creative practice. The sense that an engagement with the negative can be resolved in sublime art. The symbolic insignia surrounding the infamous Romantic poet 'mad, bad and dangerous to know' turns on his dual identity as a Scot, through his mother's connection with the Gordon estates in Aberdeenshire, and also a British poet. And so, the saltire is juxtaposed to the Union flag in the bottom left of the image. Although toned as a photographic negative, the intense highlights of red in the portrait reference Byron's political radicalism and romantic engagement with independence movements, most especially in Greece. Like the portrait of Burns in *Negative Sublime 1*, the image is replete with intimations of mortality. Indeed, both poets died in their 30s.

The connections Colvin has made between poets has been a compelling aspect of his practice, though it is a truth that these poets often only interacted in his imagination. In fact he has consistently juxtaposed Burns with James Macpherson, Walter Scott, and even Hugh MacDiarmid. Equally, he saw this mooted connection between Burns and Byron as meaningful. The image *Dirt and Deity*, produced for the *Burnsiana* exhibition, reveals the significance of these associations.

Dirt and Deity was modelled on a silhouette portrait of Burns created by the artist Samuel Houghton during the poet's lifetime, in 1790. The work is a prized exhibit in the Robert Burns Birthplace Museum. The silhouette is not quite the romantic young man painted by Nasmyth, and the museum acknowledges that it

shows that he (Burns) had a distinctive nose.[11]

However, Colvin has long been interested in the more dissident visions of the poet. In this instance, he reproduces a silhouette image, set atop a projector stand piled with books, antlers and a sickle. The background wallpaper is the same that has appeared in *Burns Country* and buried in the image there are singing birds, a harvest mouse and a lit candle at the centre of the poet's brain. Evidently, this is a homage to Burn's creative imagination.

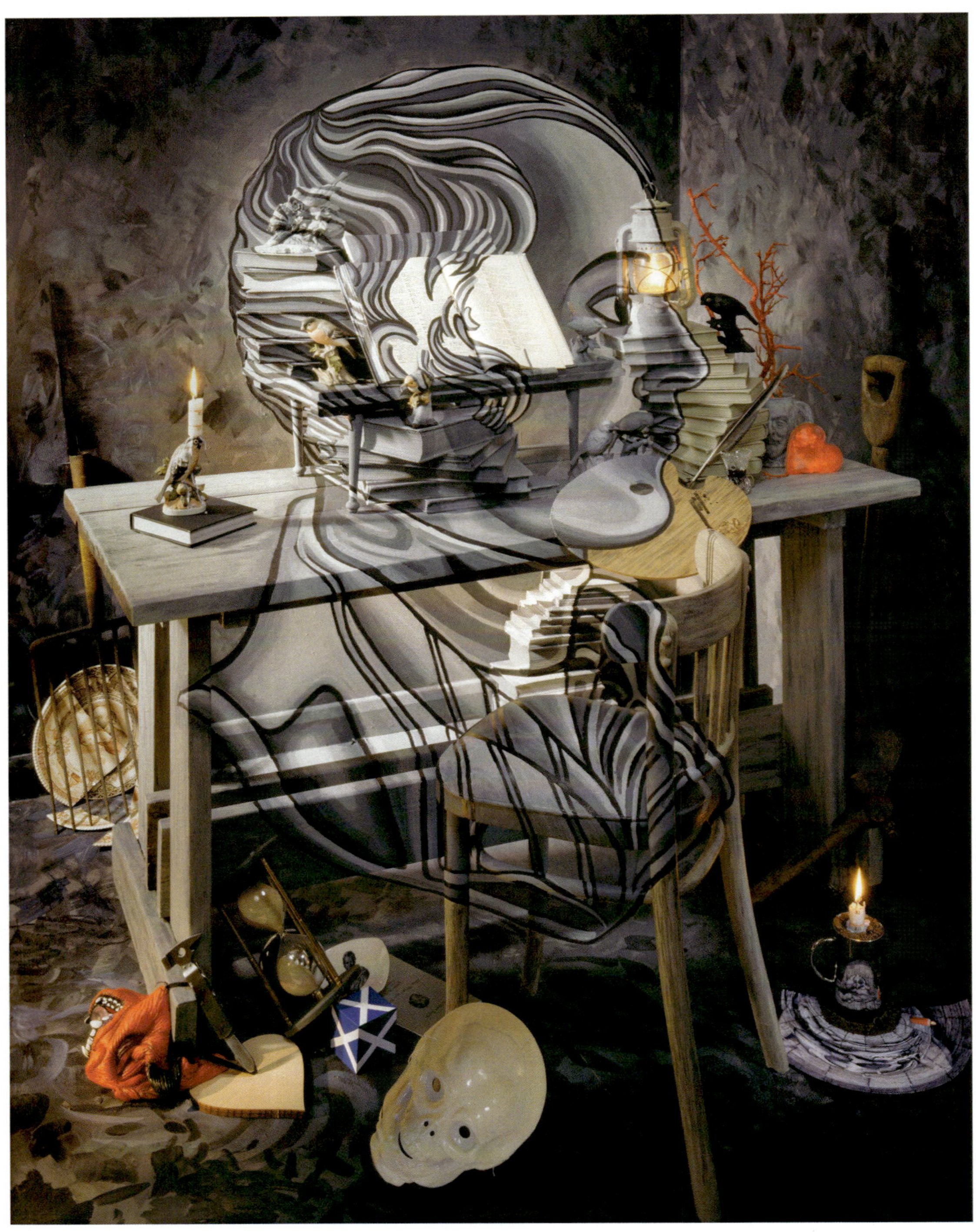

Negative Sublime I,
2001

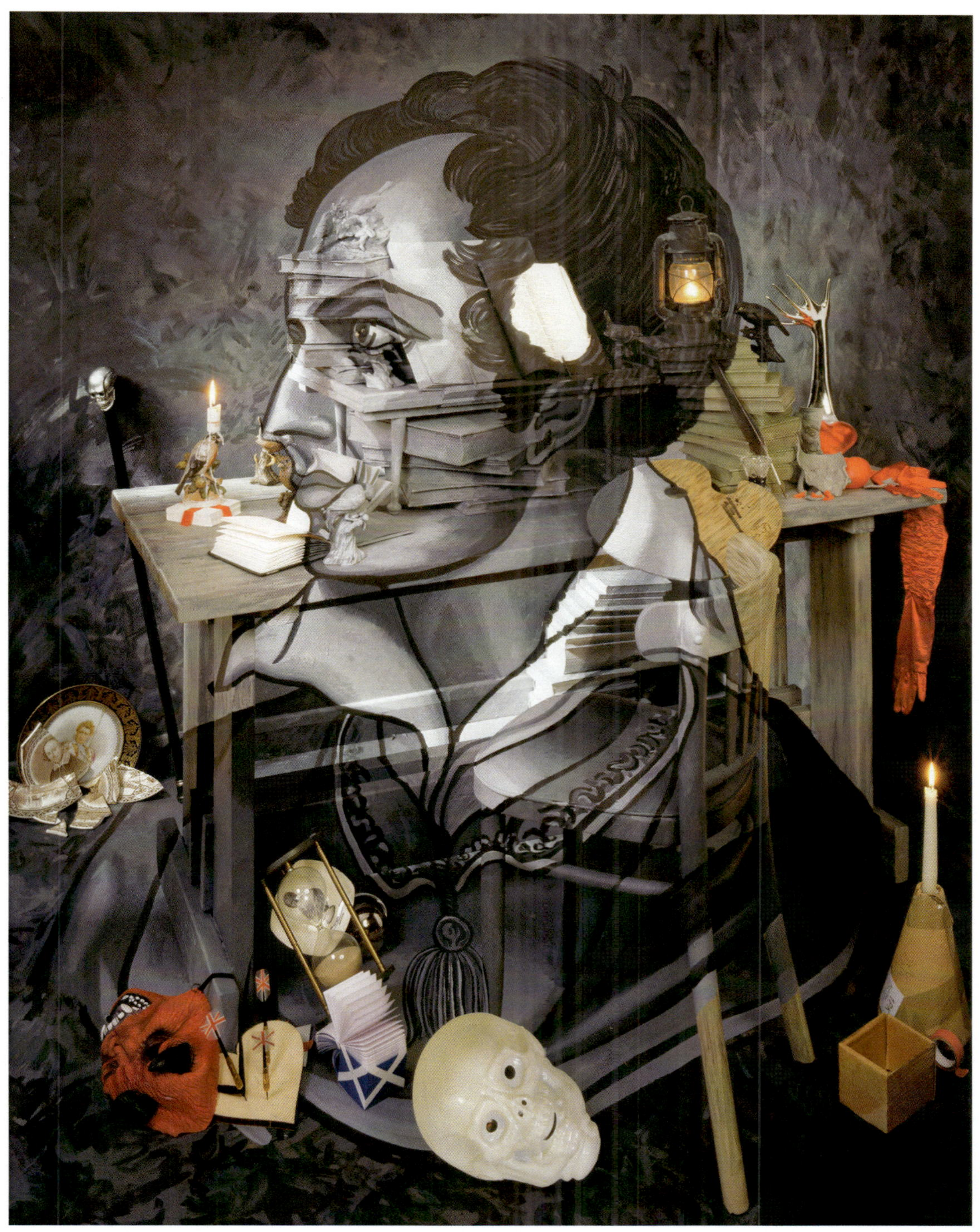

Negative Sublime II,
2001

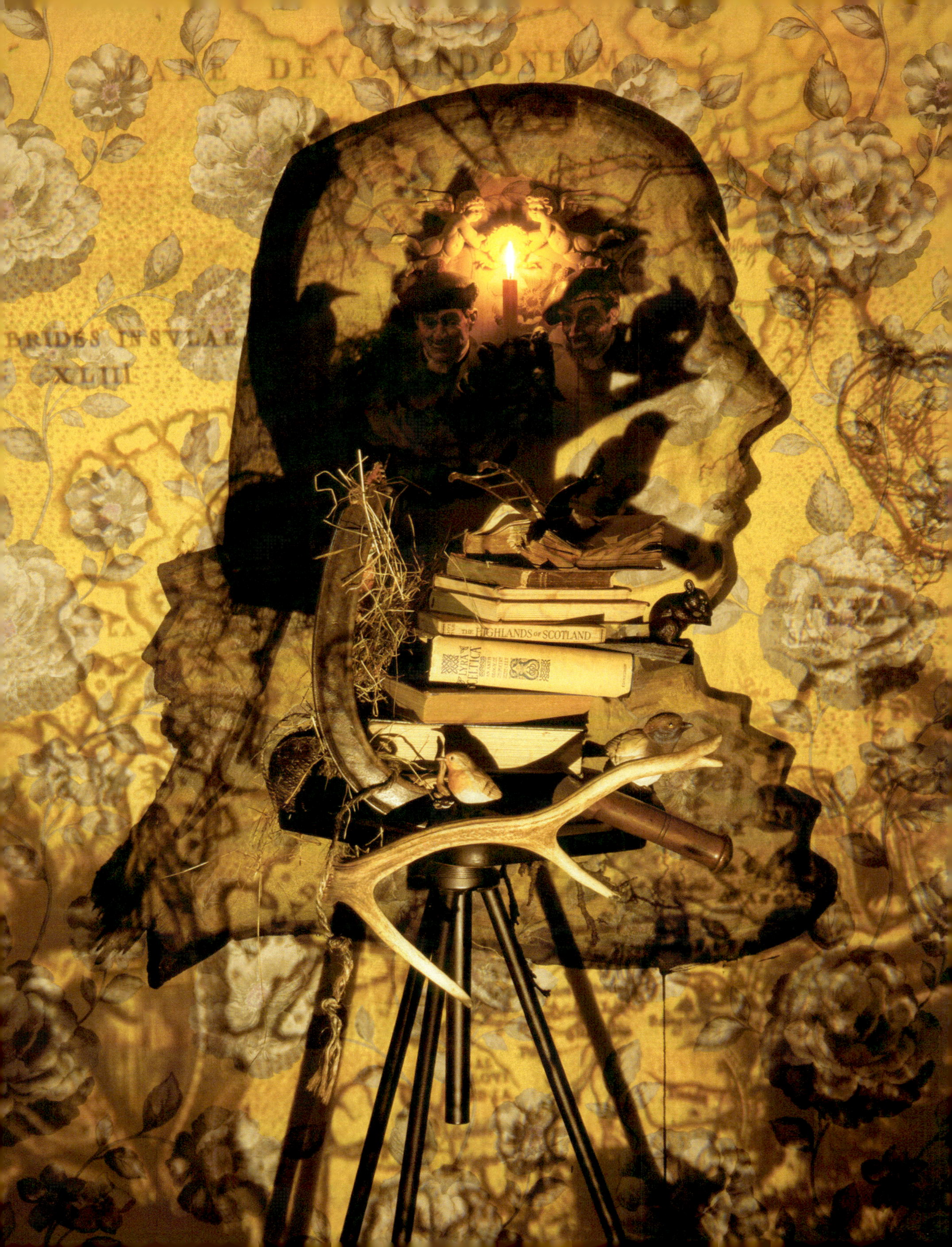

MARE DEVO...DONIUM
BRIDES INSVLAE
XLIII
THE HIGHLANDS of SCOTLAND
LYRA CELTICA

However, it is the title of the piece that is most revealing. In the December of 1813, Byron made an entry in his journal. This was written following his reading of some of Burns' letters. Byron wrote

> They are full of oaths and obscene songs. What an antithetical mind! - tenderness, roughness - delicacy, coarseness - sentiment, sensuality - soaring and grovelling, dirt and deity - all mixed up in that one compound of inspired clay![12]

Manifestly, Byron saw something of a kindred spirit in Burns, and it is these two 'antithetical minds' that Colvin has connected within his *Negative Sublime* photographs.

There is also something of a dissenting voice that is shared by these poets, and certainly a rebellious spirit. Manifestly, Burns came to represent not only an esteemed national bard and a personality ripe for exploitation in every kind of whatnot, but the symbolic representation of a dissenting cultural identity and political rebellion. Colvin probed this aspect of the Burns cult in many of his works but none more so than in the piece titled *Twa Plack* (2009).

Careful study of this photograph reveals that the set is painted as a misty and clouded background, but the portrait of Burns is drawn across as a spectral model horse. This is a discarded fairground ride, once ready to jostle and bounce its passenger for the price of a small coin. The model horse is named Rebel, and this title had been painted at its base. The paraphernalia surrounding the poet include some piled books, some corn stooks and a digital clock with the time set at 20:09. A closer study shows a small stamp in the lower left corner with a portrait of Burns written across a saltire. This stamp is the key to the work. It represents the 'Twa Plack' postage stamp of the title.

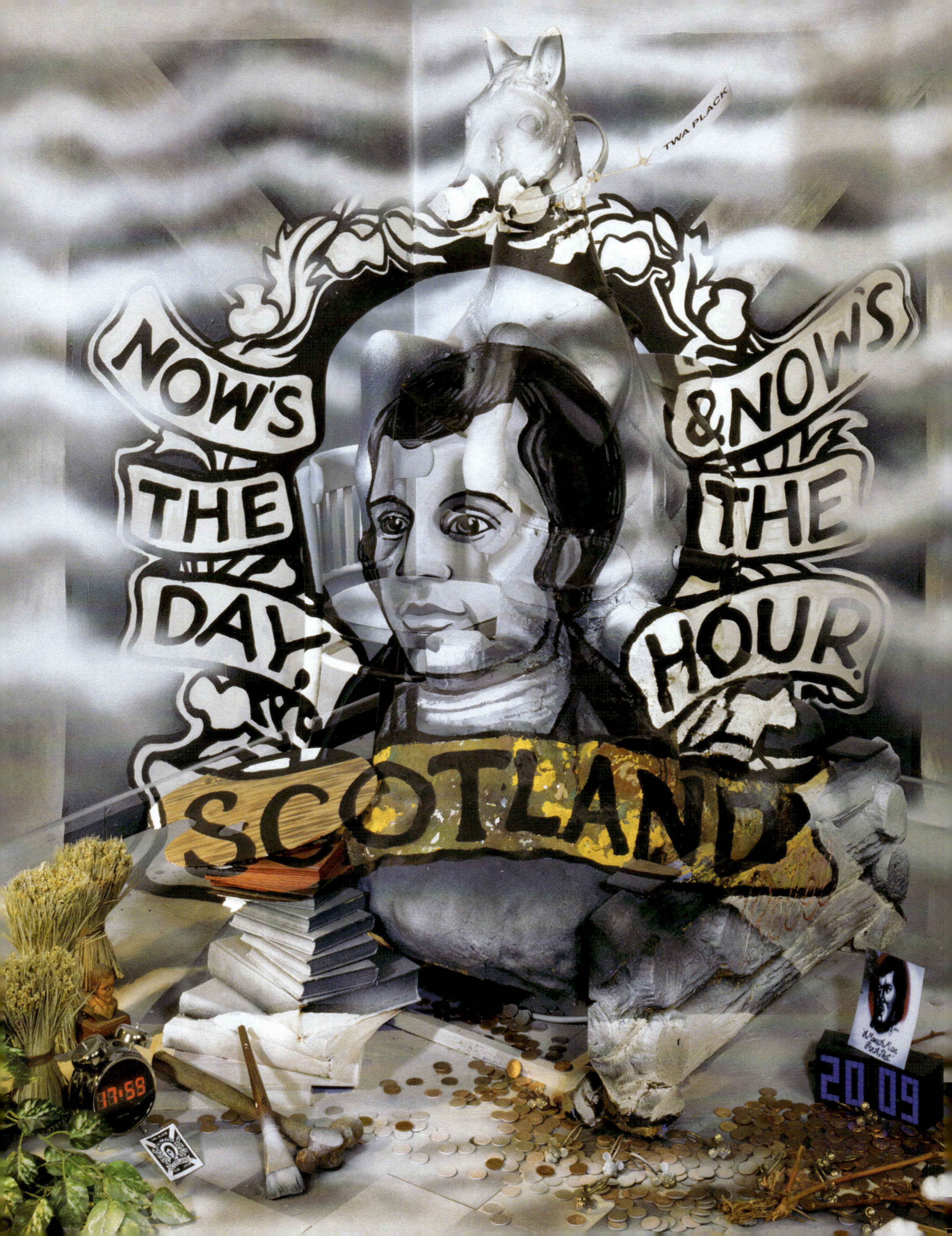

TWA PLACK
NOW'S
THE
DAY
&NOW'S
THE
HOUR.
SCOTLAND
17:58
20 09

In 1959, a Scottish nationalist group known as the Scottish Secretariat had proposed that the bicentenary of Burns' birth might be commemorated in an official stamp. This proposal was rejected. Nevertheless, an unofficial stamp was created by this group, the 'Twa Plack', a 'plack' being an old Scottish coin of little value. The stamp was 'minted' in small numbers and distributed in the streets and stuck on public buildings, a kind of samizdat intervention.

Colvin was keen to celebrate this act of rebellion and created his own work. He stretched the commemoration from 1759, the year of Burns' birth, to 2009, the year of the photograph's creation and he emblazoned his image with words from Burns' rousing song *Scots Wha Hae*. Here was Burns presented as the signifier of dissent and rebellion, in some degree, a model for change in the contemporary period.

As Colvin moved on from his fascination with Robert Burns, this notion of rebellion found a new focus in the form of Charles Edward Stuart 'Bonnie Prince Charlie', the heir to 'The King Across the Water' and 'The Young Pretender'. The realisation of this fascination would be made manifest in his exhibition, *Jacobites by Name*, presented in the Scottish National Portrait Gallery through the winter of 2015 and the spring of 2016. Of course, 2015 was the 300th anniversary of the Jacobite Rising of 1715. This rising, led by John Erskine, the Earl of Mar, was in support of James Francis Edward Stuart, the deposed James VII and II, and his claim to the throne of Great Britain and Ireland, against the ascendancy of the Hanover dynasty. The insurgency collapsed by 1716, but the long tail of this discontent led to the more profound rising of 1745 initiated by James' son Charles Edward Stuart.

The portrait gallery has long held a distinguished collection of images that document and celebrate the Jacobites and their supporters, and these are ceremoniously displayed in the rarefied atmosphere of the Jacobite

Twa Plack,
2009

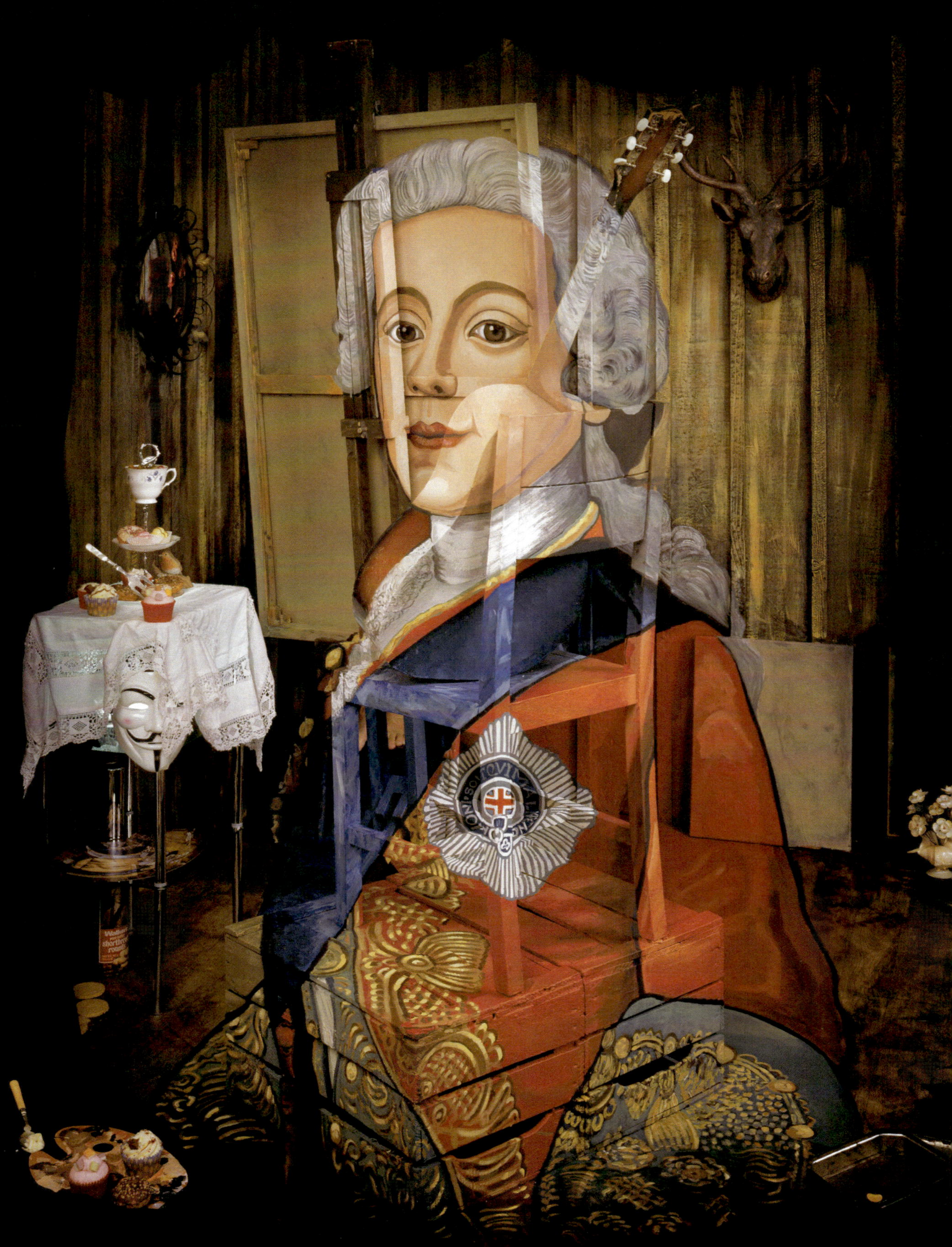

Gallery. Colvin was invited to create a series of interventions within this gallery that would reflect upon the portraits and their import. Naturally, he did this in a manner that created subtle allusions, engaged with ingenious metaphors, and dissected sometimes tangled, sometimes secret histories. His method was to review and then rework the grand portraits displayed in the collection, and to juxtapose his imaginative photographic inventions to the original paintings. The exhibition, in its insurrectionary reordering of the austere and tasteful Jacobite Gallery, presented a magnificently rebellious review of the stately insurgents.

The portraits Colvin chose to examine and reevaluate were principally those of the romantic, romanticised and dashing Charles Edward Stuart. He had been a favoured subject of many Continental painters and his face had become an alluring signifier of thwarted adventurous idealism. In respect of this, Colvin's *Portrait of Charles Edward Stuart (after Liotard)*, as previously noted in respect of its iteration as an anamorphic image, is a fine invention. The original work was created by the Swiss artist Jean-Étienne Liotard and is a formal study of the 'Young Pretender' completed in 1737. Colvin has taken this image and adapted it, giving it a context that sings of wild thoughts and associations.

The image is painted over a set that speaks of the artist's studio and is decorated with a stag's head, a guitar and, incongruously, a number of cake-stands. The stag's head references the Highland landscape of the young Prince's supporters, and the locus of his escape after the calamitous Battle of Culloden in 1746. The guitar represents the music that has mythologised 'Bonnie Prince Charlie'. But the cakes are a subtle reference to the 'Land o' Cakes'. This phrase was used by Robert Burns to intimate Scotland the nation and, before Burns, by the poet Robert Fergusson. It most probably relates to the habit of Scottish soldiers to carry an iron plate, or griddle, while on campaign. This was accompanied by oatmeal, and so became the

Portrait of
Charles Edward Stuart
(after Jean-Étienne Liotard),
2015

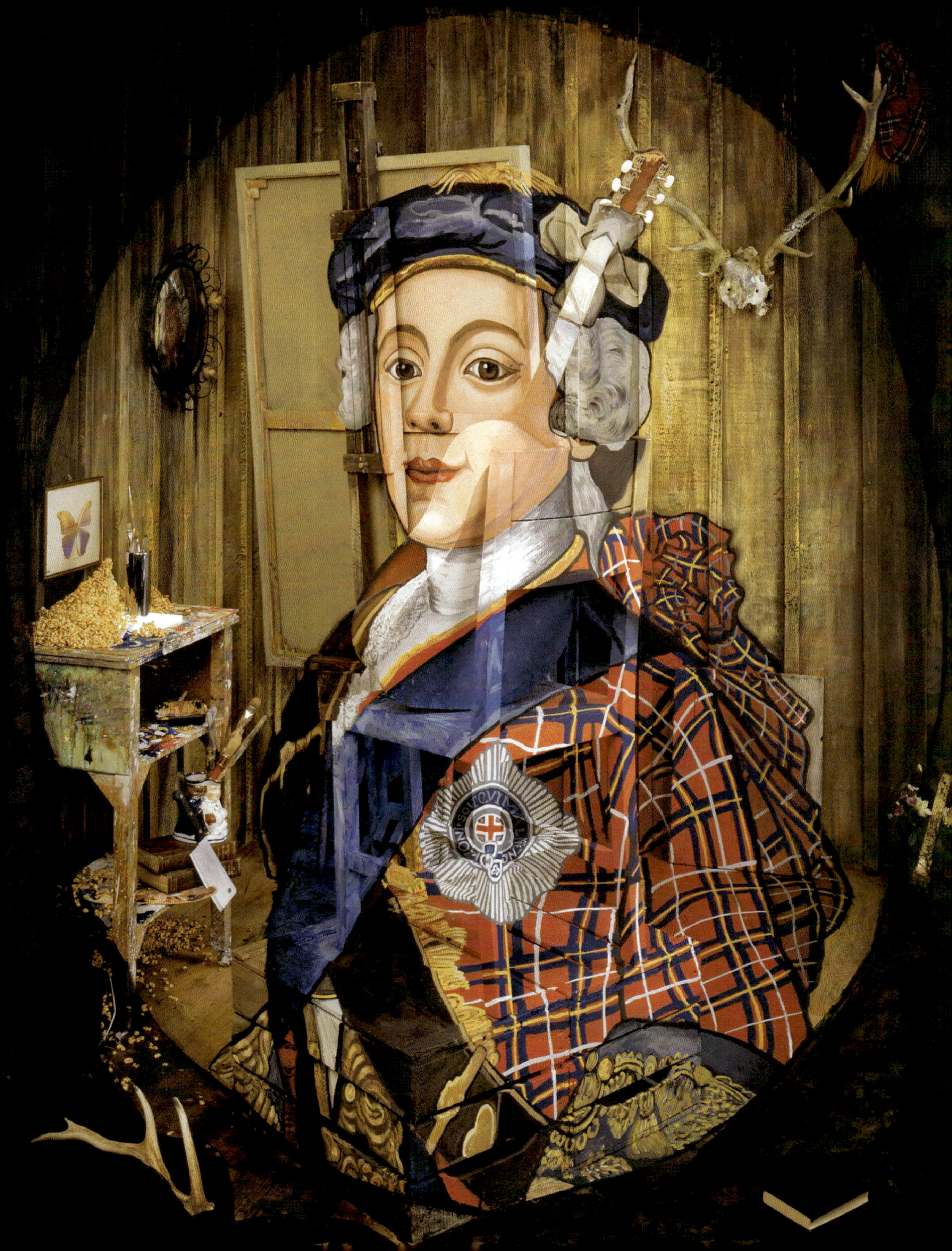

'cake' that sustained their expeditions. In Colv.n's work, the bizarre decorated cake-stands become symbolic of the rebellious Highlanders and the broader failure of the campaign. Associations that further recall the merciless persecution of the Highland armies by 'Butcher' Cumberland, the British general in the campaign and the youngest son of the incumbent George II.

In extending this thread of thought, Colvin's portrait of *Charles Edward Stuart (after Mosman)* adapts the set of the Liotard portrait. William Mosman was a portrait painter born in Aberdeen. He travelled to Rome in 1732 to study painting and returned to ply his trade in Edinburgh in 1738. His portrait of Charles Edward Stuart was most probably painted around 1750 and so after the Prince was again exiled to Rome. It is a mythic image with the Prince, young and handsome, in martial garb. His leather cross-belts are set to carry his weapons, he wears a tartan jacket and the 'white cockade', that emblem of Jacobite affiliation, sits on his bonnet. Colvin has recognised all of these insignia and highlights their splendour. Amongst the 'props' in this image, the guitar is reiterated but the larger context is the easel with reversed canvas and the palette, paints and brushes, as well as the mirror. Here, the work of the artist becomes a subject for the portrait and, especially, the ways in which the artist constructs an identity for the subject. Within this creation, then, the notion of the 'Bonnie Prince' as a romantic and heroic figure is reconstructed, celebrated and subtly abstracted.

Naturally, in this project, Colvin was often drawn to the more eccentric images within the Jacobite Gallery. Colvin's photographic pastiche of the curious *Harlequin* portrait of Charles Edward Stuart is gathered from a coloured print engraved by the little-known etcher G. Will. The unique feature of this portrait is that the tartan uniform of the Prince has been translated into a harlequin outfit. It is thought that this absurd pattern was created because of a simple misunderstanding in the discussion of what exactly constituted a 'tartan'. In which case, the heroic Prince

Portrait of
Charles Edward Stuart
(after William Mosman),
2015

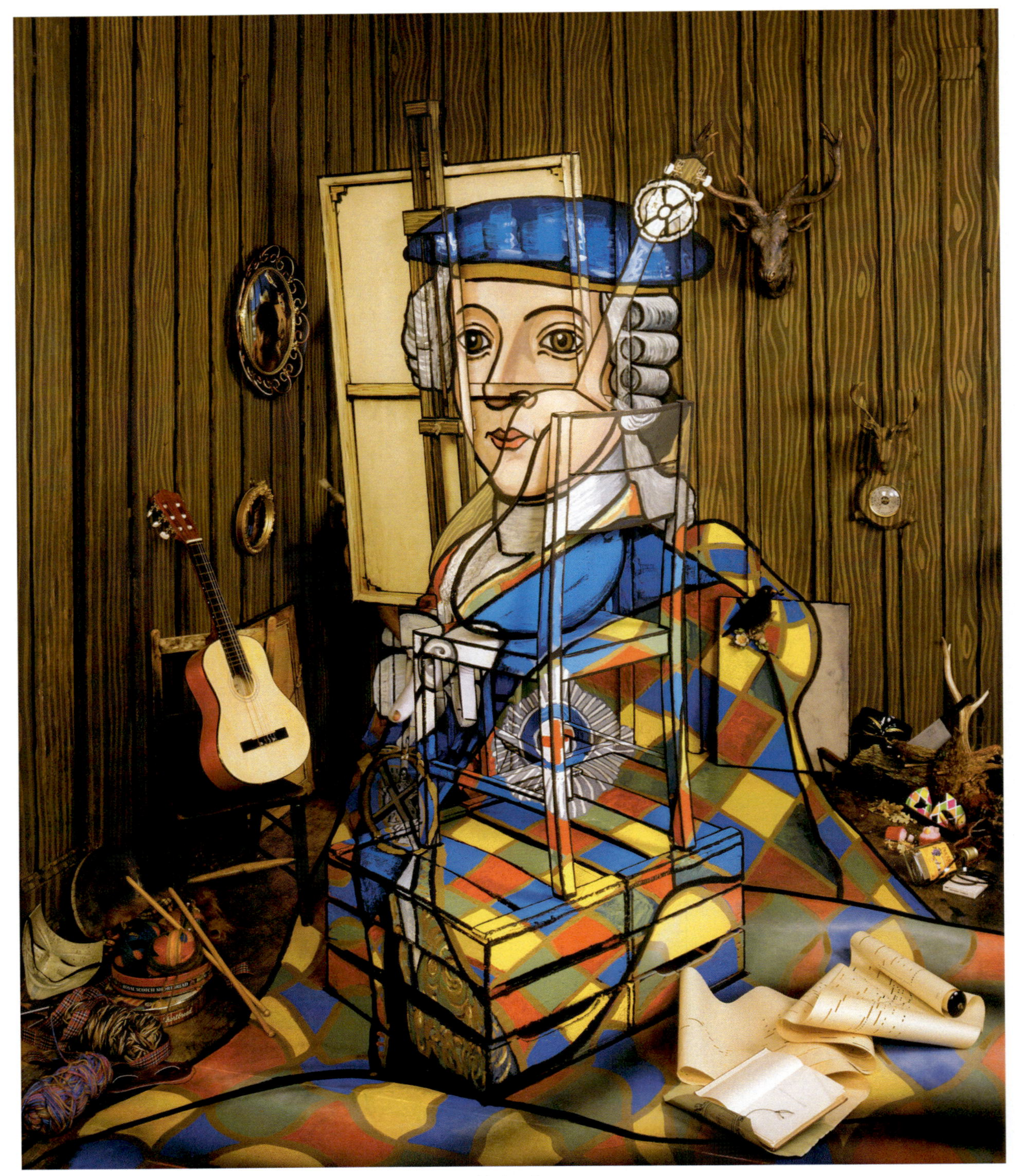

Harlequin,
2015

becomes a comedic figure through a simple mistranslation. Equally, it chimes with Colvin's thoughts on the ways in which aspects of history are overlain with layers of misdirected speculations and cockeyed thinking. Moreover, in this work, Colvin again includes the memento objects of the folk tradition. These accent the manner in which the tropes of academic history are contorted in souvenir keepsakes, so that the 'story' of Scotland's chronicle is written as a gimcrack reliquary in plates, tea-towels, glass trinkets, cups and mugs, novelty ornaments and every kind of gallimaufry.

Two of the more intriguing images from this project are the beguiling photographs *Betty Burke* and *Jenny Cameron*. Famously 'Betty Burke' was the Prince himself, in flight after the defeat at Culloden and protected by the heroic Flora Macdonald. Macdonald had persuaded the Prince to dress as her Irish maid, Betty Burke, and planned his retreat 'over the sea to Skye'. Colvin's ethereal portrait of the cross-dressing Prince is taken from an engraving by J. Williams; completed in 1746, the year of his exile firstly to France, and latterly to Rome. The spectral image of the Prince is written across a set that is familiar from the regal portraits but here the guitar takes centre stage, an allusion to the many songs that lamented the Prince's loss. Markedly, the image is faithful to Williams' representation; the calico dress, the delicately laced cuffs, the cowled bonnet covering all but the graceful face. *Betty Burke* is, indeed, an extraordinarily subtle and elegant portrait.

In contrast, the portrait study of the mysterious *Jenny Cameron* is altogether more fantastical. Appropriately, the story of Jenny Cameron is rife with misdirections, dead-ends and distracting diversions. She may, or may not, have been a singular hero of the Jacobite Rising, raising and leading a small cohort in the cause of the Stuarts. She was probably, though possibly not, a consort of the Prince. She may have been an Edinburgh milliner, mistakenly imprisoned as a Jacobite supporter, and eventually dying a lost and destitute

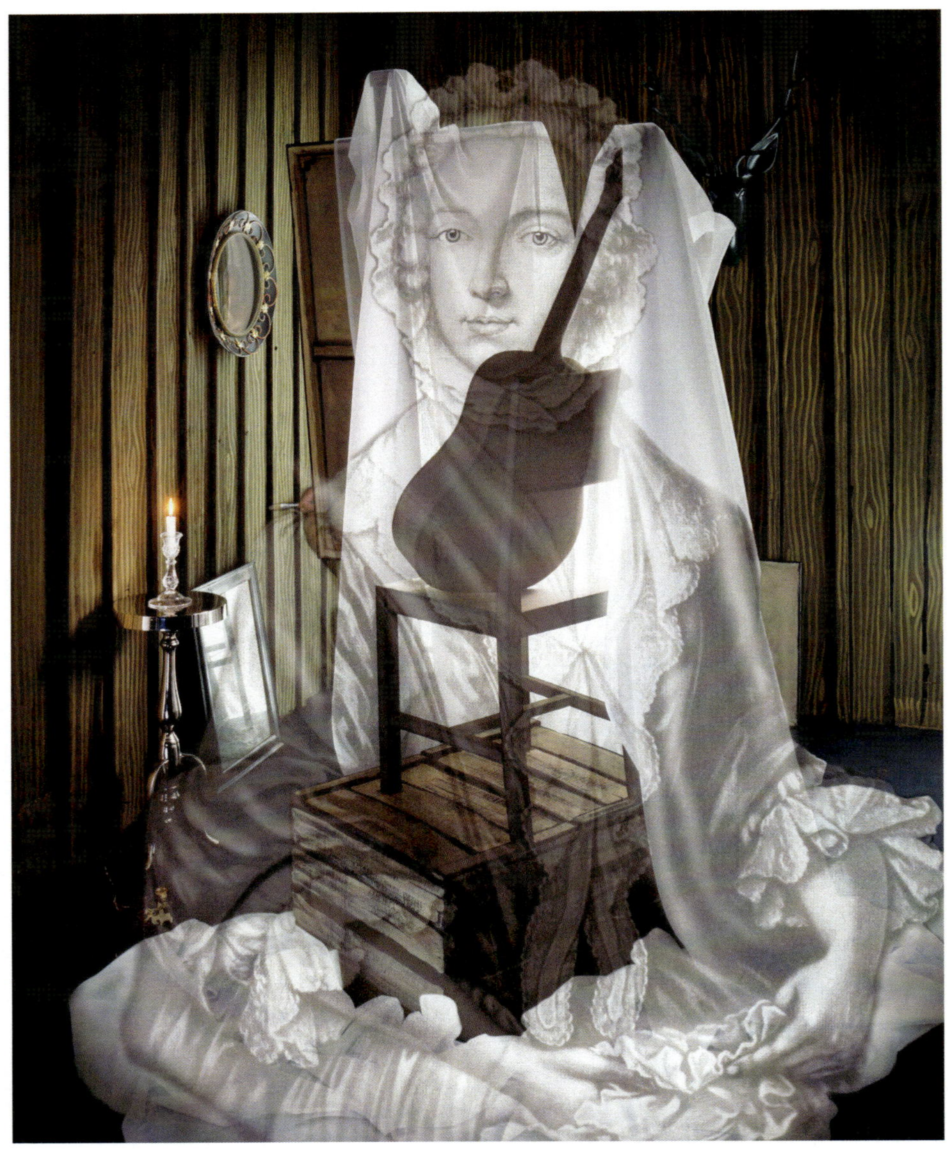

Betty Burke,
2015

soul on the streets of Edinburgh. Certainly, the figure of 'Jenny Cameron' was a celebrated personage in the iconography of Jacobite art. Perhaps aptly, Colvin has selected an engraving by an unknown artist as the model for his remarkable photographic invention. The central motif is a wooden mannequin holding a sword, 'Jenny Cameron' as the Amazonian warrior. The mannequin has no head, but this is replaced by a computer screen.

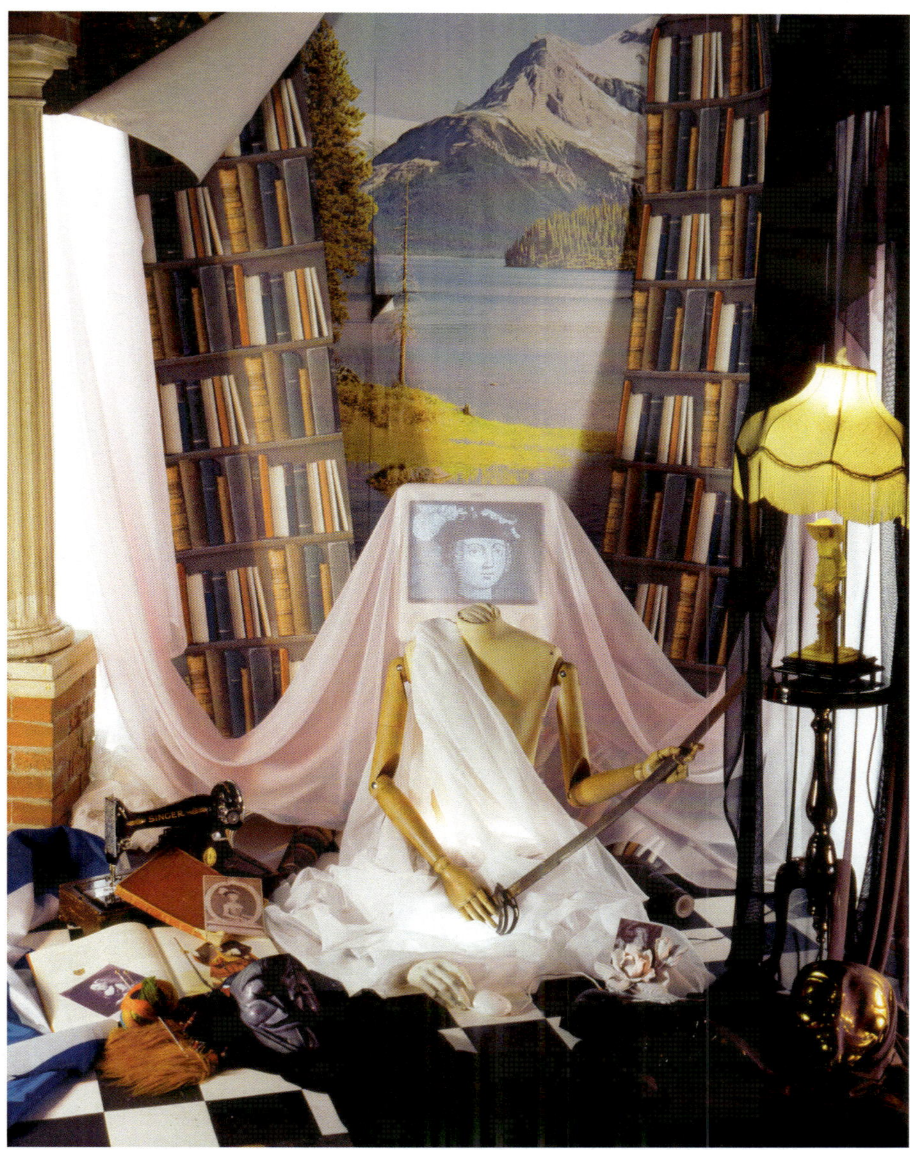

Jenny Cameron,
2015

The screen holds the image of Cameron's face taken from the anonymous engraving. Surrounding this construction, the paraphernalia of associated regalia speaks to the mystery that is 'Jenny Cameron', while bracketing the doll-like figure are two sheets of wallpaper in the style of library shelving with books, evidently a reference to many exotic accounts of this mythic individual.

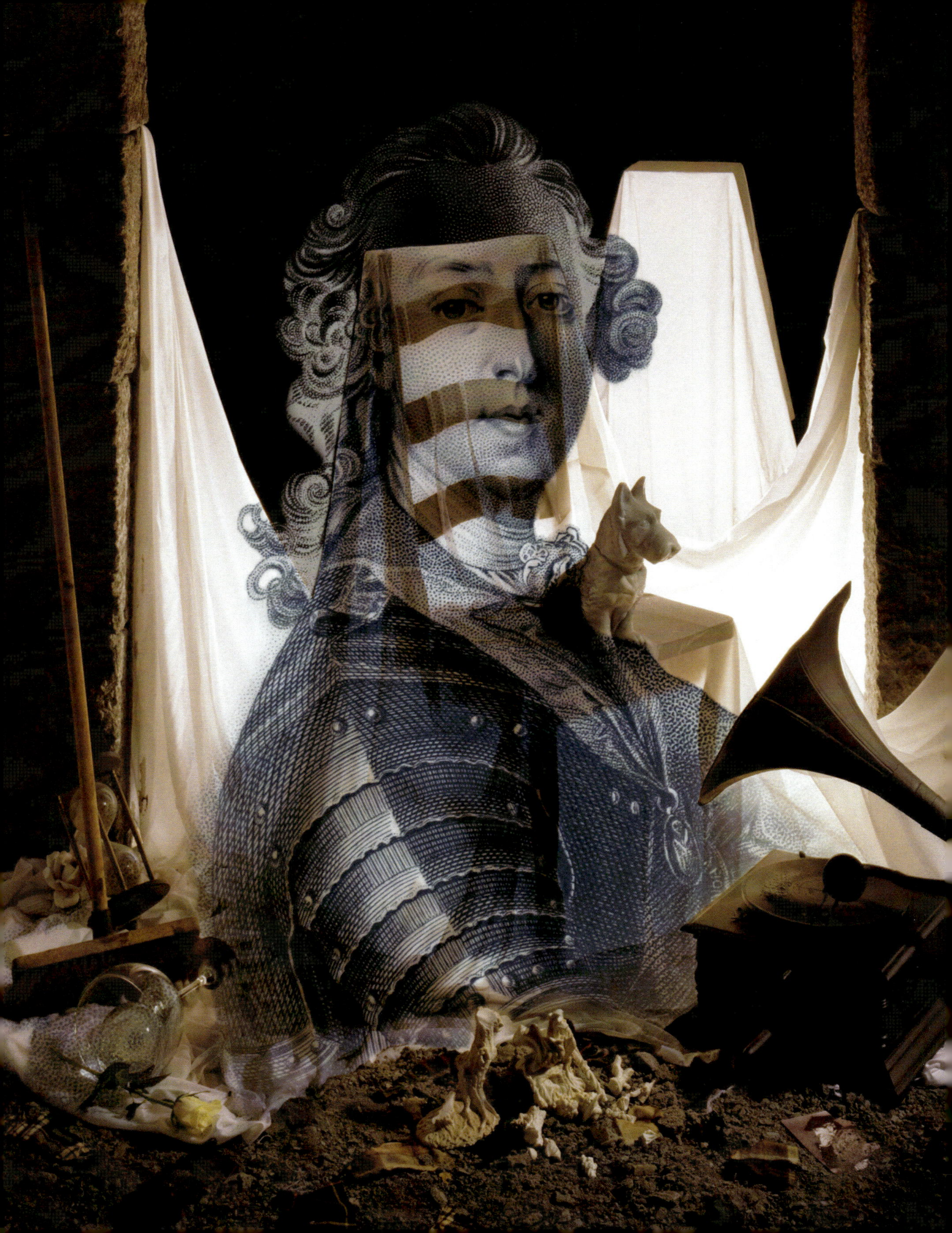

Of course, the Jacobite cause would end in calamity and misfortune, both for the Prince and for the Highlands of Scotland. Charles Edward Stuart would end his days an exile in Rome under the protection of the Pope. The details of his later life have been reported as the subject of tragedy, and certainly of decline. Colvin reflects upon this in two works from *Jacobites by Name*: *Lochaber No More I* and *Lochaber No More II*, both completed in 2014.

The title is a famous refrain from Jacobite history. It refers to the exile of Charles Edward Stuart in 1746. Following the legendary flight of the Prince through the Highlands and Islands he would eventually leave Scotland on a French frigate. He departed from Loch nan Uamh in the area of the Western Highlands known as Lochaber. He would not return.

Colvin selects an etching and a late portrait of the Prince as his prototypes for the images in the Lochaber works, the first of the young Prince in armour, by the German engraver Johann Georg Wille, and the second of the aged exile, by the Irish portrait painter Hugh Douglas Hamilton.

Both works are held in the Scottish National Portrait Gallery, and Colvin creates the same set to embrace these two images of the youthful Prince and the ageing refugee: an ethereal background with a diaphanous hanging cloth, a vintage gramophone complete with horn, a Scotty dog ornament intent upon the song, a brush that sweeps away the fractured incidents in the foreground. The subject is time, and its passing. Indeed, Colvin creates a third work in this series, the previously cited *Lochaber No More, Anamorphosis*. An intriguing work that unites the two images, youth and age, in a transitional passage that records the cruelties of history and time.

Lochaber No More I,
2014

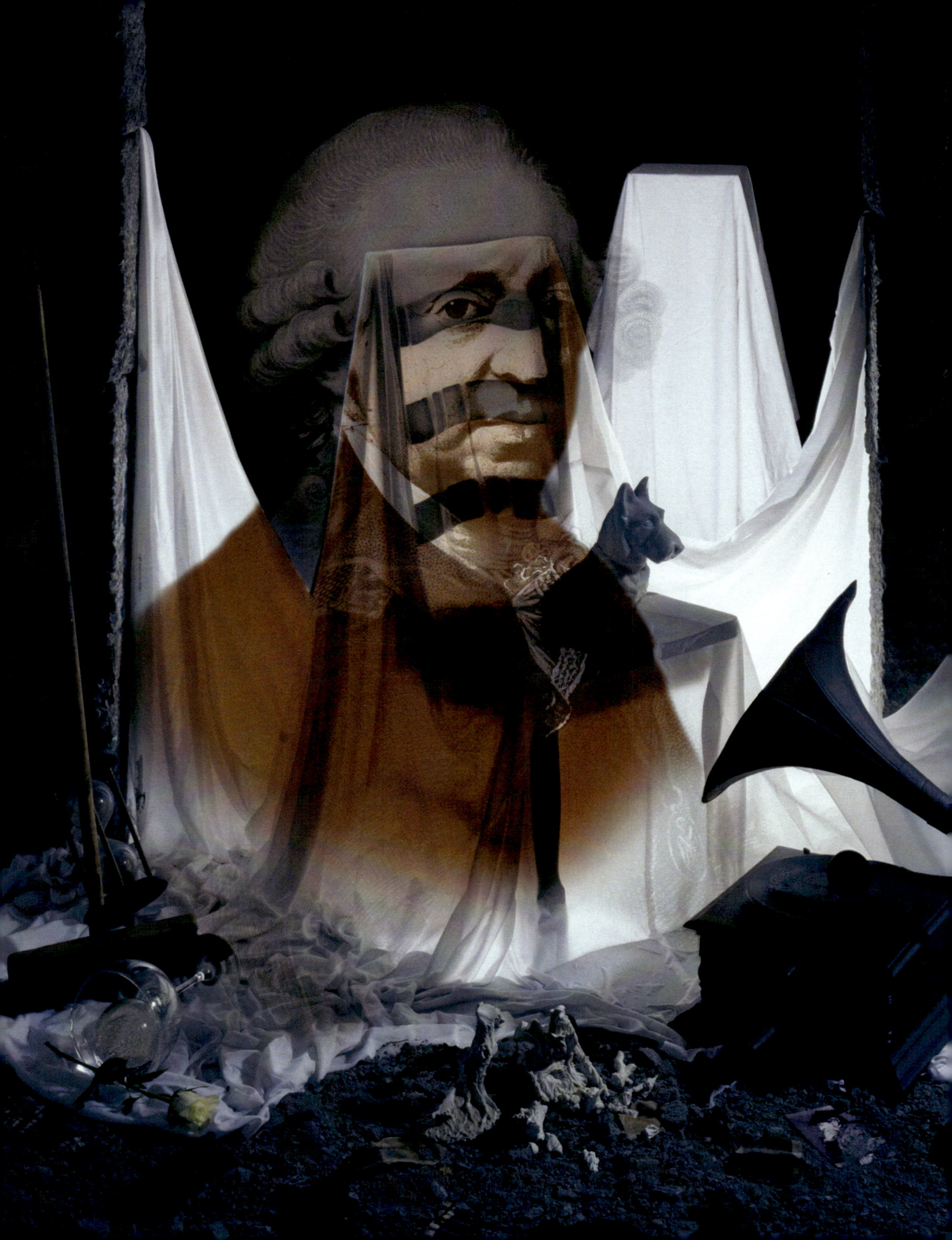

Colvin, in reflecting upon this project, evidently became more concerned with the ways in which a mythology might be established and then fade. James Lawson has commented that

> Because of the palimpsestical nature of Colvin's final pictures, there is a quality of transparency to their content. Presences are ghostly. The portraits, transformed by Colvin's process, take on an air which we realise they always possess and which by a switch of the mind becomes manifest – their spectral air.[13]

This is an acute observation, and it might be extended to recognise that Colvin is speaking of the ways in which accretions to the historical chronicle shift into a mythic story telling that dissolves the empirical moment into a misted, only half-glimpsed landscape.

This recognition was realised in the group of works, *Pretender i–iv* (2014) from the *Jacobites by Name* series. Here, the heroic Prince is first seen in armour and tartan plaid. His portrait is written across a landscape of rock and his sword is placed against a copper plate depicting a galleon in full sail, a portent of his fate. As the image progresses, the accent falls on the rocky landscape and the Prince's face is decorated with turf and heather, motifs that relate to the landscape of his escape after Culloden. Gradually, the Prince fades and the fairground horse Rebel appears. Indeed, he was always there, the bedrock of the Prince's portrait. But, in *Pretender iv*, Rebel is all that remains, rearing majestically in the broken landscape. And so, what had been an historical episode evaporates, leaving only a symbolic marker of the byzantine narrative.

Lochaber No More II,
2014

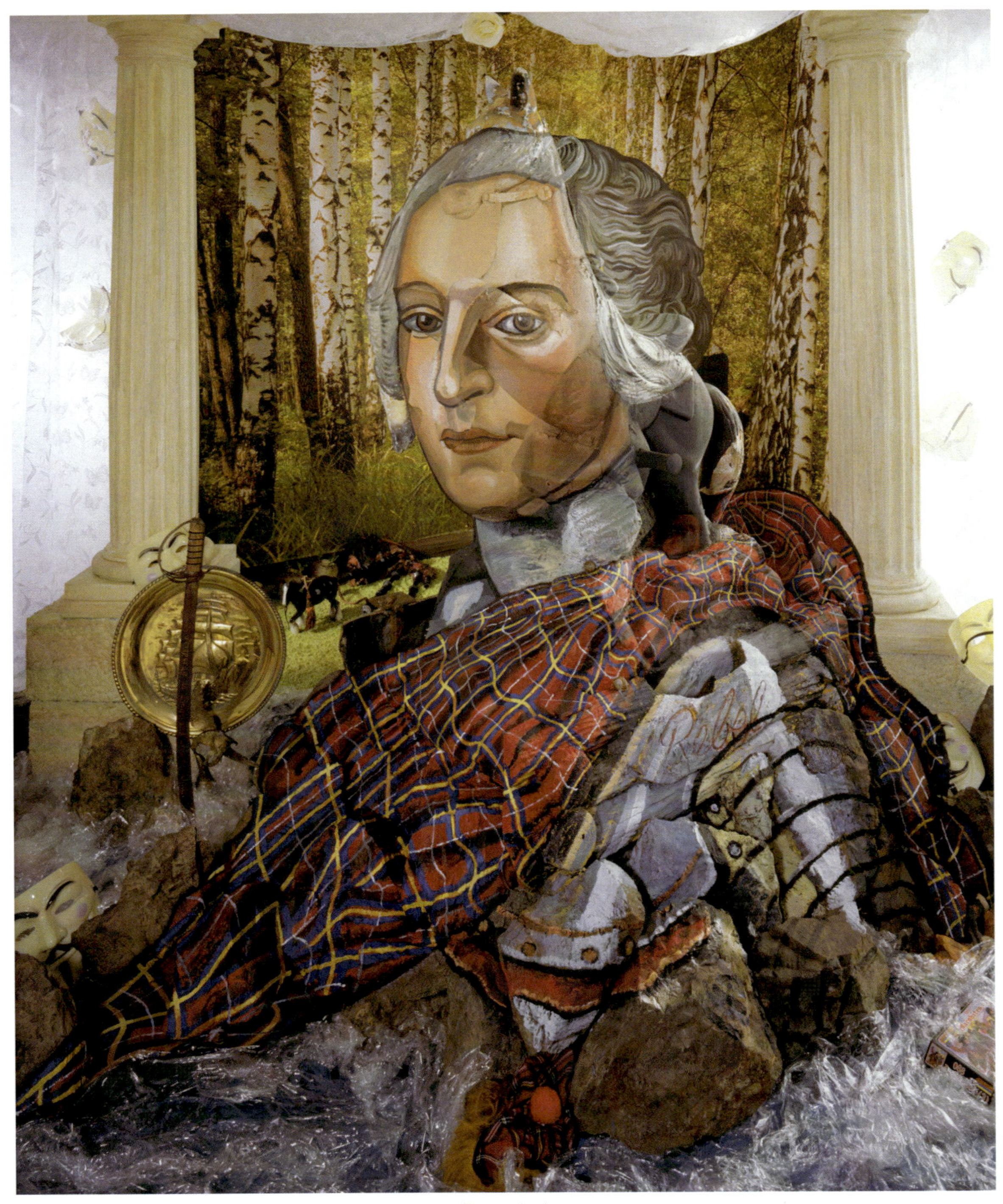

Pretender I,
2014

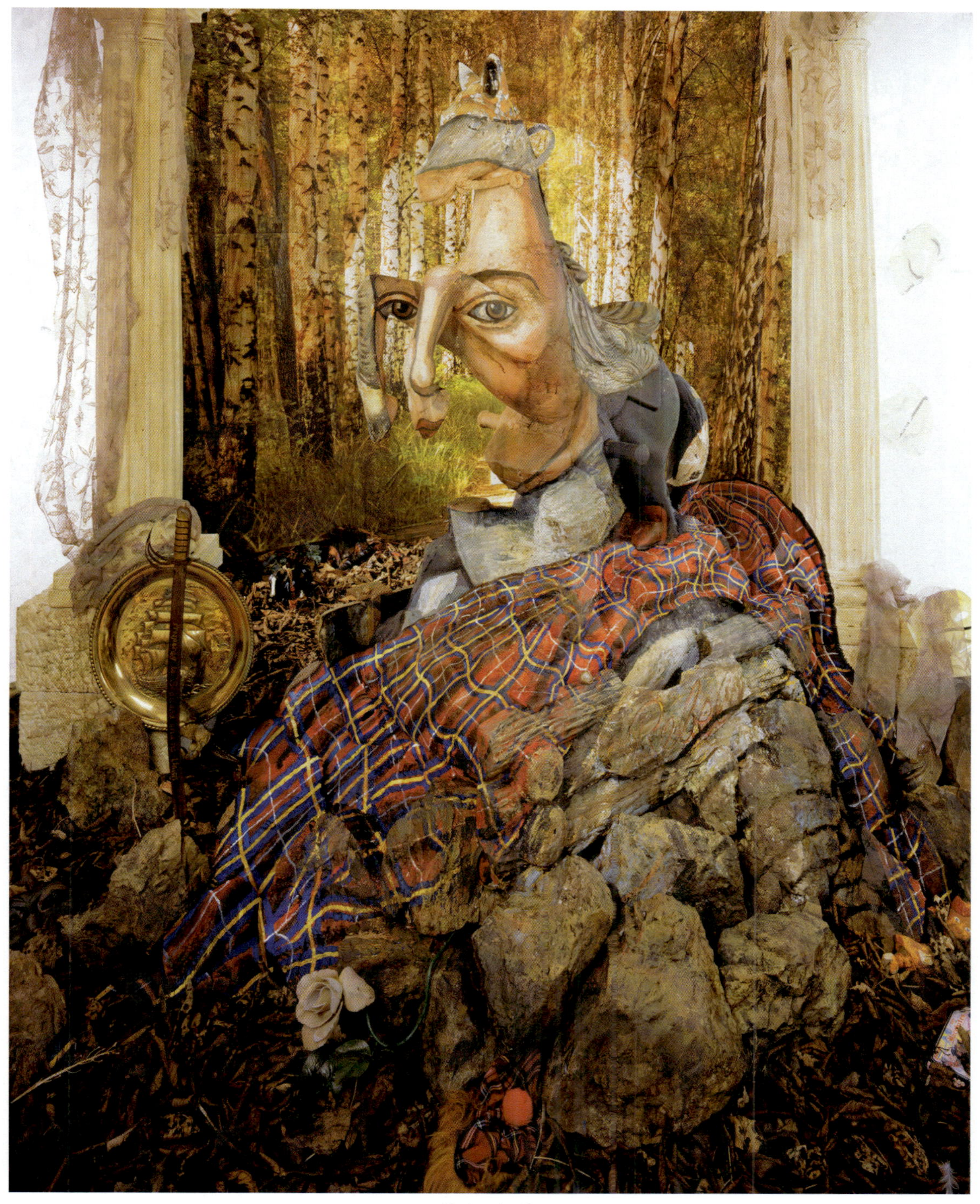

Pretender II,
2014

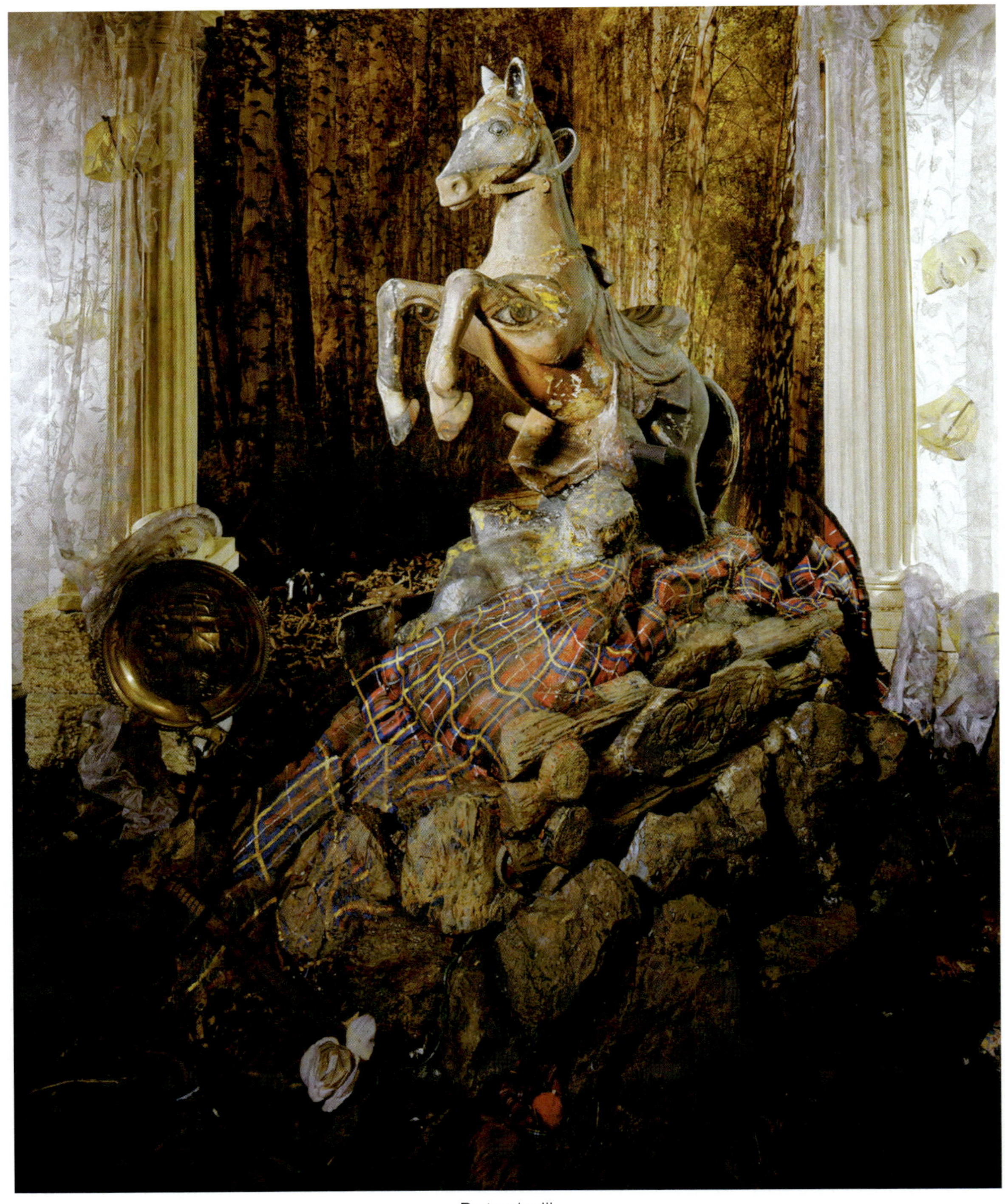

Pretender III,
2014

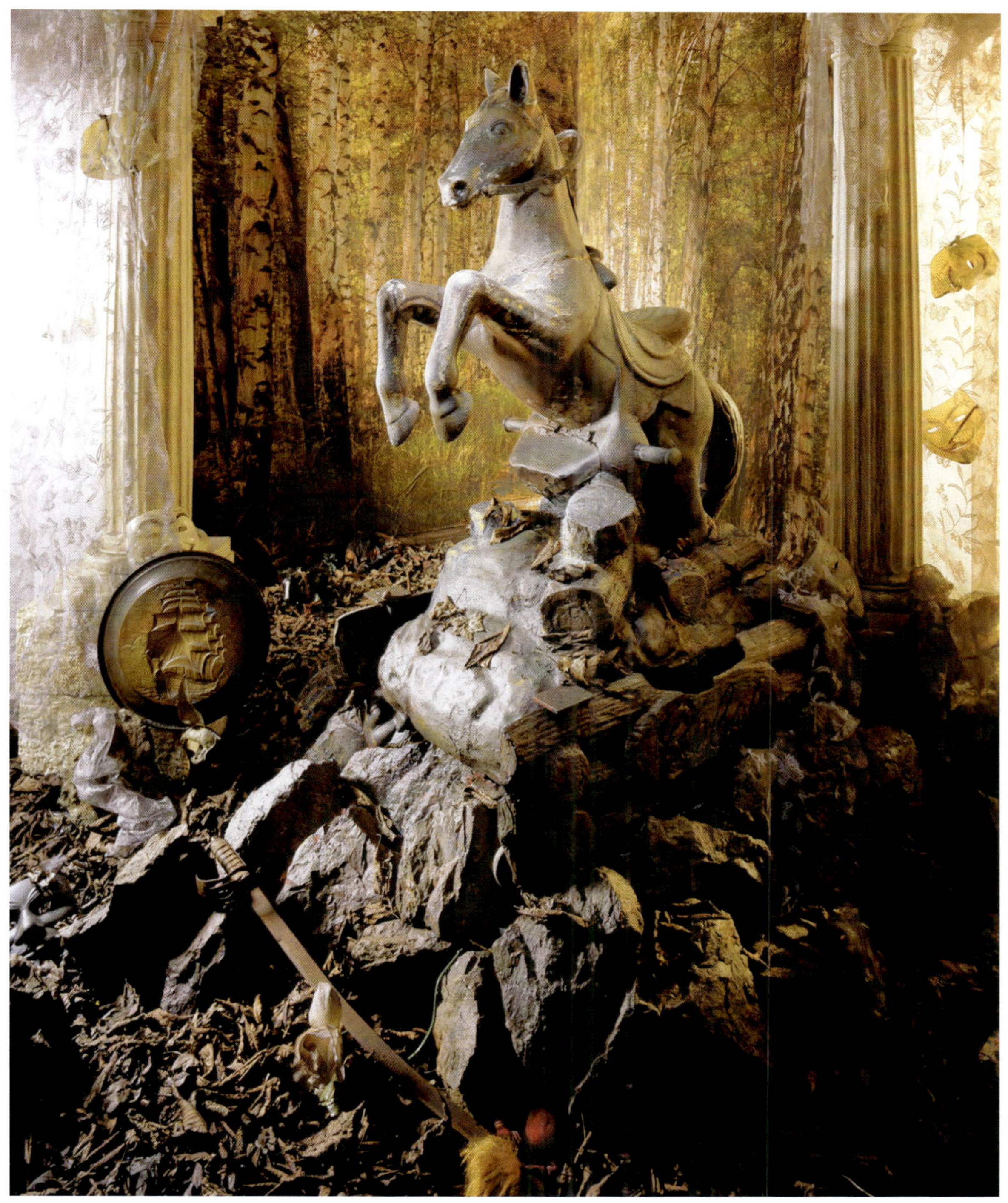

Pretender IV,
2014

These were three impressive exhibitions, visionary in their conception, daring in their execution, and stimulating in their presentation. As projects of work, they shared the sense of reflecting upon the past as a means of understanding, and even challenging, the present. For, in each case, the individual photographs raised issues and questions that remain relevant in the modern period. It might be said that the mood of *Ossian: Fragments of Ancient Poetry* was melancholic; the character of *Burnsiana* was comic, though tempered with a spirit of deep passion; while the atmosphere in *Jacobites by Name* was poignant and tragic. Collectively, each project moved between substance and shadow, the sense of a thing known and recognised, but fleeting and ethereal; a kind of dream vision. In this way, they each spoke to contemporary experience, exploring, creatively, the broken landscape between knowing and not knowing. This is surely their intrigue and their triumph, and the signal component of Colvin's talent.

Calum Colvin, artist

The fascinating, often baroque, pathway of Calum Colvin's development as an artist has been remarkable. He has moved with an extraordinary dexterity between subjects and themes, thoughts and actions, concepts and intuitions. At each junction in this journey, he has searched for the passage that has afforded most challenge and he has embraced that danger. This sense of adventure has been the root of his creativity, the notion that each twist and turn is an opportunity, and that every uncertainty and hazard is the place where the imagination can engage with the world.

The trajectory of this convoluted route has taken him from a wide-eyed incredulity at the absurdity of the social world to a rarefied sense of enlightened reflection. In this progression, the exploits of his Action Man avatar presented a kind of mock-heroic odyssey, a comically surreal expedition into the manifest folly of the modern world. These were works that explored the wild horizons of humanity's foolish dissipation, while simultaneously affirming the finest moments of human kind's imaginative vision; the very apotheosis of the artistic canon.

Latterly, his meditations on time and history, on culture and myth, signified a recognition of the constants in human experience. In these artworks, the sense of a critical intelligence comes to dominate, so that while there remained that desire to essay the febrile conditions of contemporary culture, this has been tempered by a subtle metaphysics that acknowledged the nature of time's passage, and of mortality. In which case, this creative odyssey shifts from a concern with journey to a fascination with advent; the mysterious moment of arrival.

Evidence of this ambitious mission is amply demonstrated in the comparison between his early and later photography. This is especially evident in the contrast between *Minotaur*, from 1989, and the project titled *Camera Lucida*, undertaken during 2012.

Minotaur is a diptych that includes a self-portrait. Of course, it references the awe-inspiring Greek myth wherein Minos, the King of Crete, is compelled to trap the terrifying Minotaur in a mystifying labyrinth constructed, with infinite skill, by Daedalus. The Minotaur, who is the progeny of the Cretan Bull and Minos' wife Pasiphae, is half man and half bull, the very epitome of priapic fury. Trapped in the labyrinth, the Minotaur is fed, by sacrifice, from the youth of Crete until Theseus, with the mindful guide of Ariadne's thread, navigates the labyrinth and slays the Minotaur.

Colvin's diptych is an epic of reference, symbol and allusion. The right-hand panel offers a view of the chaotic labyrinth: broken stone and debris, classical statuary, rocking horses, horns, effigies and even bagpipes. In this crazed pandemonium, an Action Man doll wears a bull's head, and this is complemented by the kilted avatar complete with rope; the symbolic token of Ariadne's thread. Here is the labyrinth in all its tumult and terror, with a distinctively Scottish Theseus venturing in its heartland.

The left-hand panel of this image, however, offers the self-portrait. Here, Colvin appears as Theseus; perhaps also as the Minotaur. Painted across the original construction, there are additions of a brick passageway – complete with a photograph of Elvis Presley, an Alpine landscape and a Tower of Babel. The man-bull figurine observes the scene while the avatar continues to search through the wrecked landscape. References to identity are strewn around: Highland pipers, multiple bagpipes, Oor Wullie illustrations. A glass eye and a plastic pork chop allude to the sacrifices that have been made to the Minotaur, while a stone decorated with a maze, an emblem for the labyrinth, prefigures the Celtic design that will appear in the *Ossian* series. The self-portrait is painted across this scene, occupying the centre of this comically savage stage.

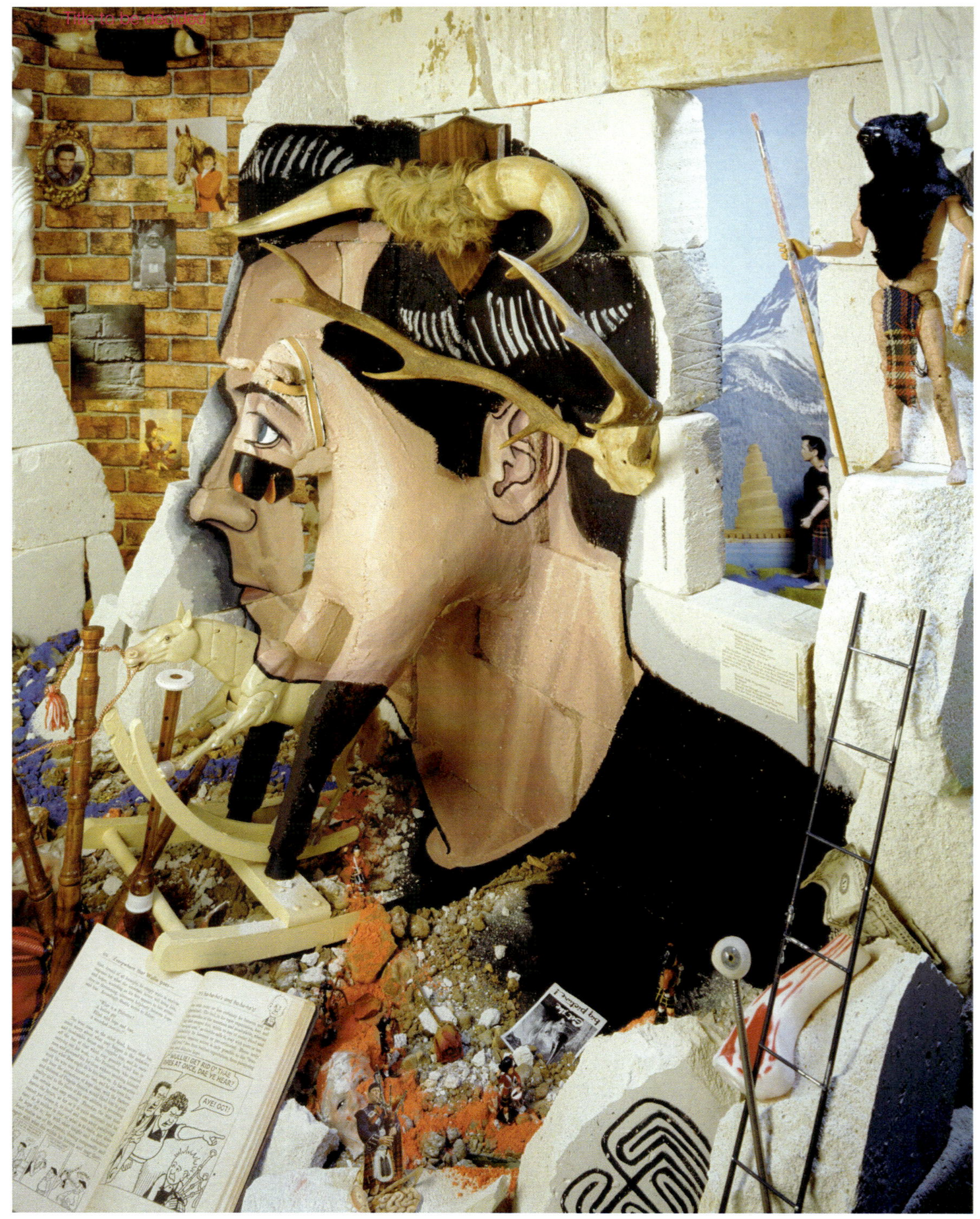

Minotaur,
1989

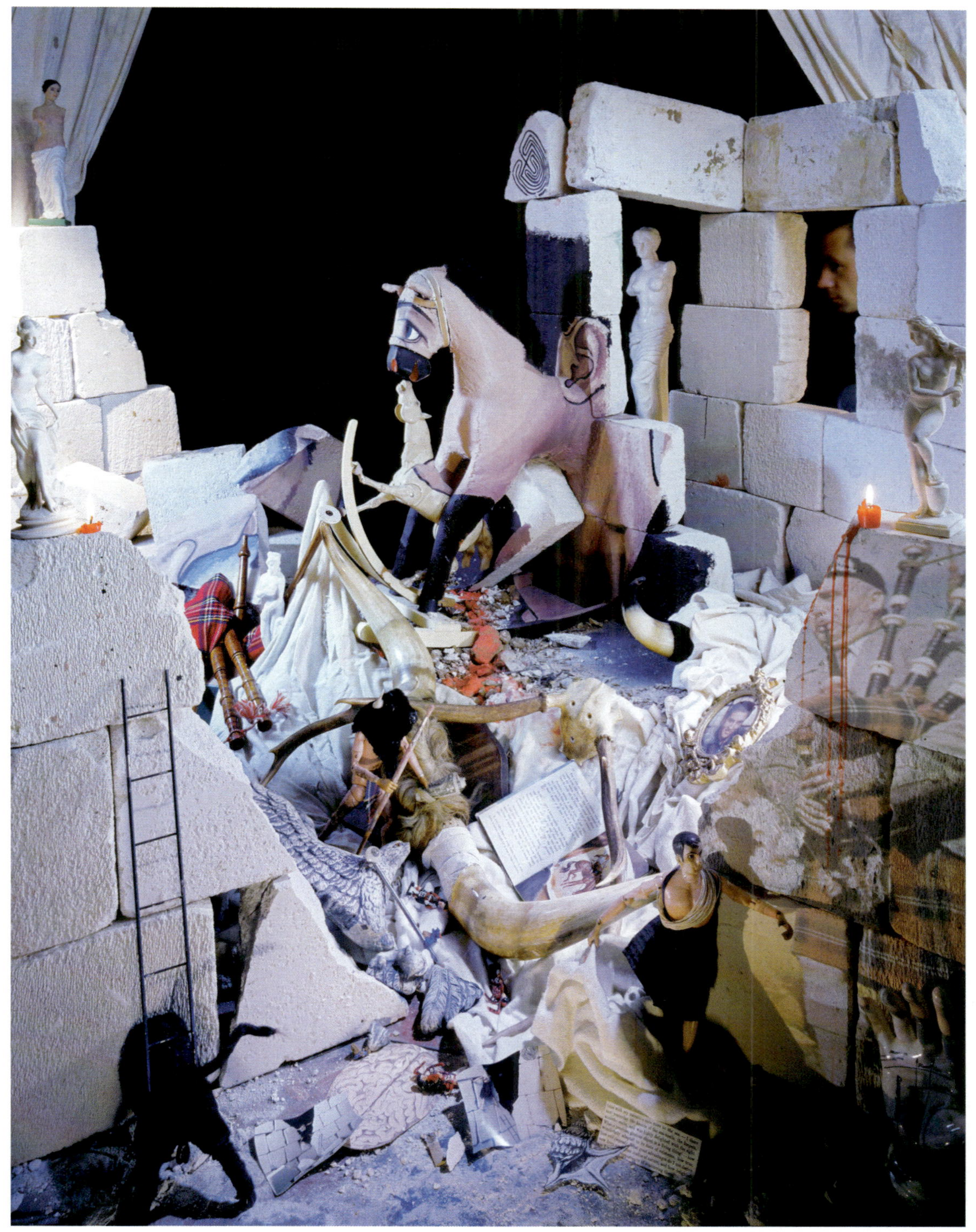

Minotaur,
1989

In *Minotaur,* Colvin gave the fullest expression to his sense of dislocation and estrangement. Certainly the diptych referenced his consciousness of difference and the fact of his alienation within a hyperkinetic social world. It also reflected the idea of a febrile and frantic culture wherein coherence and reason were lost to the noise of a frenzied babel. Within that context Colvin explored the fragmented imaginary of contemporary reality, and locked this into a contrasting antecedent that was shaped by a classical and canonical ethic. Intriguingly, he attained this, creatively, in a raw and visceral manner but also with that sense of wit and whimsy that embellished his vision. Nevertheless, at the deepest level, a work like *Minotaur* both embraced the mythic sense of human aspiration and declared the shattered fantasy that was the perceived world.

Minotaur was a turbulent and radical work. It both recognised and critiqued the hallucinatory nature of modern life, and it did so with an energy and imagination that gave voice to that condition of being. This can be juxtaposed to the *Camera Lucida* project, wherein a more introspective and even metaphysical quality becomes evident.

Camera Lucida consists of a suite of ten images completed during 2012. They illustrated a publication from the University of Dundee, titled *In Memoriam.* This anthology of writings and images was created to celebrate those individuals who had donated their bodies to scientific study. The relationship between art and science was, once again, significant here and Colvin developed this correspondence in his contribution to the publication.

With the generic title *Camera Lucida,* Colvin returned to the pre-history of photography as a medium, the *camera lucida* being a device historically used by artists to promote accuracy in drawing, and in perspective. While the *camera lucida* used light to generate the refracted and transcribed image its companion, the *camera obscura,* performed its magic through a tiny prick of light projected into a dark room. In which case, the dialectic between the 'light-room' and the 'dark-room' was established; and Colvin was surely sensitive to this resonant synthesis.

However, the title *Camera Lucida* also held a further signification. In 1980, the French semiotician and philosopher Roland Barthes had published *Camera Lucida: Reflections on Photography*. This beautiful, poignant book written by Barthes after his mother's death, and shortly before his own, is a search for the 'vision' of his mother as presented in his collection of photographs. He finds the connection between likeness and memory fraught, until discovering a photograph of his mother aged five. This he recognised as the mother he knew. But the emotional anguish of this experience aroused from Barthes a meditation on the contingent nature of photography, and the photograph *per se*, as a disabling encounter; a melancholy reflection on memory and mortality.

In 2012, Colvin was sensitive to all these connections, and the ways in which they chimed both with his creative concerns and the particular nature of the mission that was *In Memoriam*. In response to these feelings, he produced the suite *Camera Lucida*.

Camera Lucida 1 is created on an intimate set. It is a corner scene, with a wallpaper background in shades of umber and ochre. The set is populated by a standard lamp complete with an ornate shade decorated with faded flowers and foliage. Besides this sits a three-legged side table. The principal props are a small writing desk, an *escritoire*, accompanied by a wooden chair. On the desk there are some dried flowers, an hourglass, a picture frame and a cup and saucer. There are letters and notelets in the desk and scattered on the floor. A wooden walking-stick is propped against the writing-desk. On the floor, besides the strewn letters, there is a coloured image of a woman. Across this lower horizon, there are the assorted materials of knitting: pins and threads, balls of wool, lines of yarn.

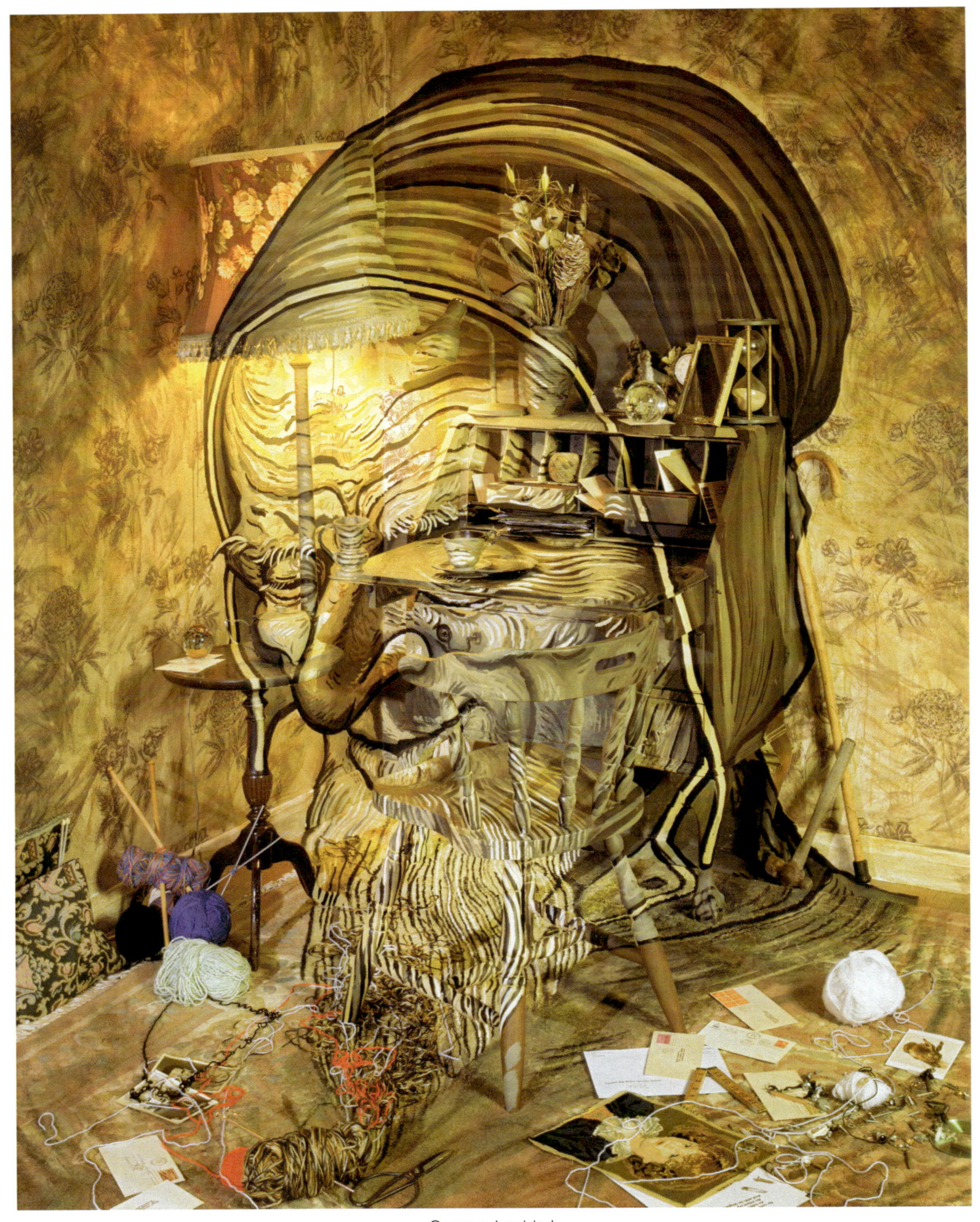

Camera Lucida I,
2012

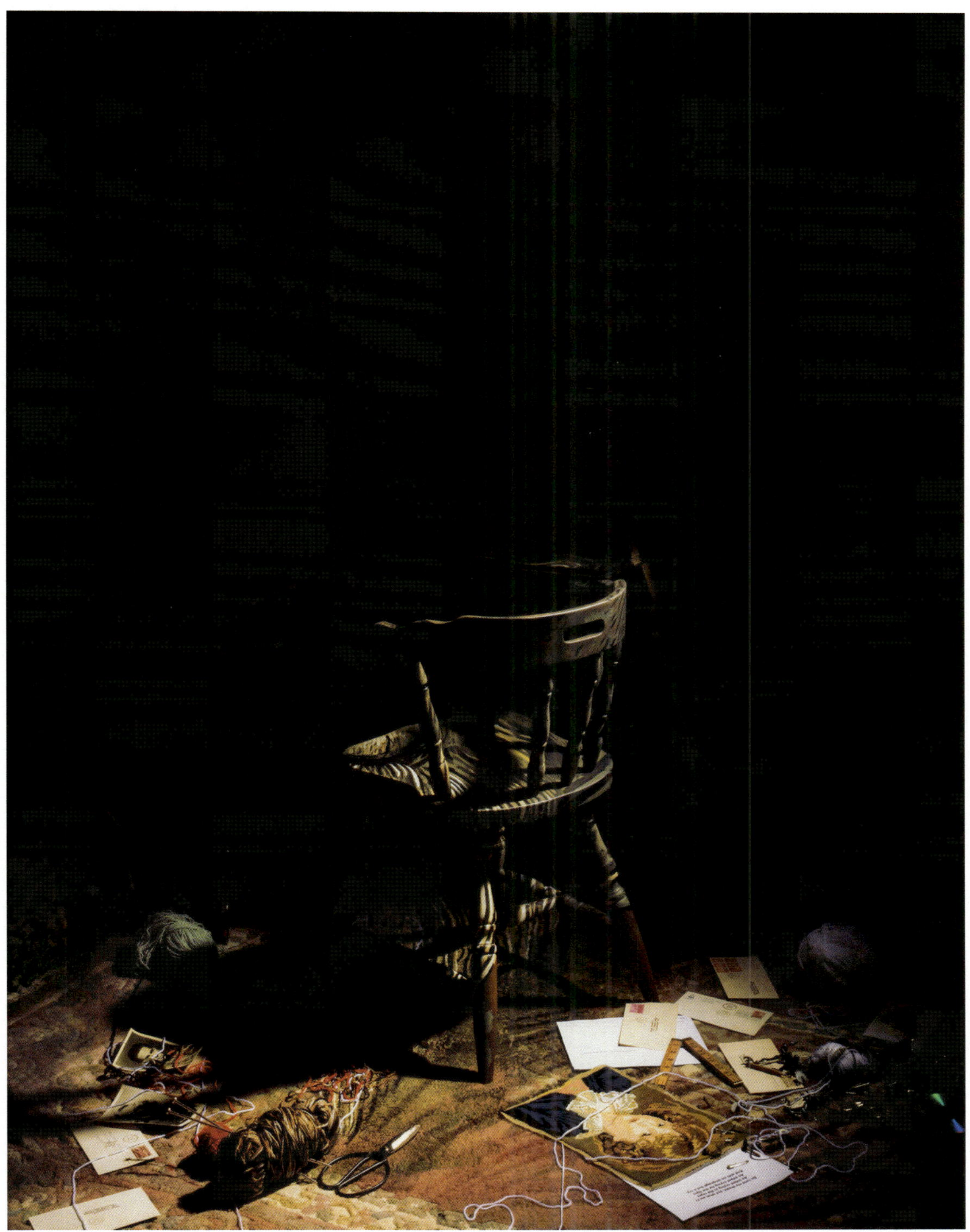

Camera Lucida VII,
2012

Onto this set Colvin has painted an old man's head, in fact, an appropriation of Albrecht Durer's *Head of an Apostle*. Durer's drawing, from 1508, was a sketch for a subject that would adorn the *Heller Altarpiece*: a work completed in combination with Matthias Grunewald, and now located in the Staatlich Kunsthalle in Karlsruhe, in Germany. Durer's image shows the aged apostle looking downwards with eyes half-closed, his long beard trailing to the lower edge of the drawing.

Colvin reverses Durer's image and paints it across the set of *Camera Lucida I*. The whole work has a mood of melancholy and decay. The apostle's beard is thin and his eyebrows bristling. The palette is autumnal, as is the sentiment in this photograph. Indeed, the work speaks of time and its passing. The scattered letters allude to former accords. The lines of wool record the patterns of associations and memories, the warp and weft of being and recollection.

In subsequent images within this suite, Colvin allows these objects and images to come to prominence and to fade. He plays with light and shade so that each element within the composition is given its due place, then dissolves from the scene. Consequently, in *Camera Lucida VII*, only the chair is visible, with a single ball of wool and few letters, the rest of the image cast into darkness.

Evidently Colvin is reflecting upon the nature of the camera and the photograph in *Camera Lucida*. This is an exposition of light and shade, the very substance of photographic practice. Equally, he is exploring the photograph's link to memory and memorialisation, the sense, intimated in Barthes' testament, that the photograph is a connection with the immutable conditions of presence and absence, that photography's essence is ineffable, its fundamental character mysterious, like 'being' itself.

This dialectic between the fervour of a photographic diptych like *Minotaur* and a subtle suite of images like *Camera Lucida* certainly describes an arc that moves from passionate engagement to reflective contemplation. Yet this contrast only touches upon the variety and range of Colvin's art. The themes, moods and emotions of his oeuvre are manifestly multiple and various. This is a restless creativity, a searching vision, and an intuition for active contest with the conditions of modernity. Always, this is tempered by a discerning consciousness, a critical intelligence that is attuned to the dreams and follies of human kind. Colvin pours these perceptions into his wondrous art, creating those magical images that remain replete with a beguiling meld of insight and joyous humour and enticing enigma.

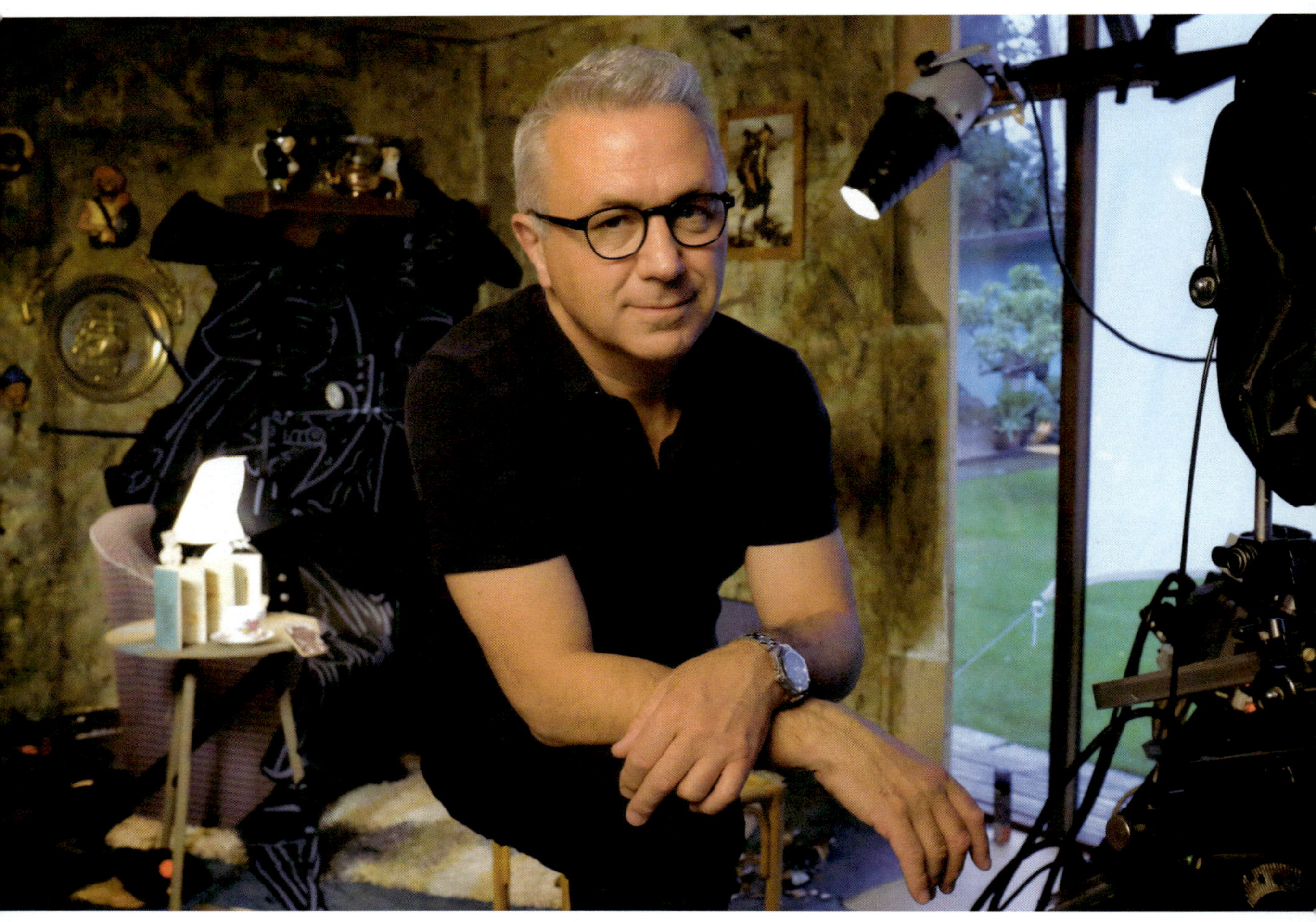

Calum Colvin in his studio

Acknowledgements

I would like to acknowledge the generosity of the Royal Scottish Academy
and the Sir William Gillies Bequest Fund in its support for this publication.

A number of photographers have kindly provided documentary images,
illustrative material and portrait studies for this book. In respect of this,
I am pleased to acknowledge the sterling work of Robin Gillanders,
Chris McLennan, Chris Park, Alan Richardson and Sandy Wood.

Finally, the designer of this book, Ian McIlroy, has worked tirelessly to
produce an eloquent and expressive publication, one that is worthy of its
subject. He is to be commended for his patience and selfless dedication.

[1] Hughes, Henry Meyric in Henry, et. al. 1987. *The Vigorous Imagination – New Scottish Art*, exhibition publication, Edinburgh: Scottish National Gallery of Modern Art, p.19.

[2] Normand, Tom. 1994. *An interview with Calum Colvin*, in 'Transcript – a journal of visual culture', vol. 1, issue 1, Dundee: University of Dundee, p.40.

[3] Mellor, David Alan. 1990. *Calum Colvin*, exhibition catalogue, Edinburgh: Fruitmarket Gallery, unpaginated.

[4] Normand, Tom. 1994. *An interview with Calum Colvin*, in 'Transcript – a journal of visual culture', vol. 1, issue 1, Dundee: University of Dundee, p.40.

[5] Lawson, James. 1998. *Sacred and Profane*, exhibition publication, Edinburgh: Scottish National Galleries, p.19.

[6] Mellor, David Alan. 1996. *A Package Flight to the Land of the Dead*, in Portfolio Magazine, no. 24, Edinburgh: Portfolio Gallery, p.49.

[7] Warner, Marina. 2006. *Phantasmagoria*, Oxford: Oxford University Press, p.153.

[8] Colvin, Calum. 2007. *Hybridization*, in History of Photography, vol. 31, no. 1, Jan Baetens and Hilde van Gelder eds., London: Taylor and Francis.

[9] Normand, Tom. 1994. *An interview with Calum Colvin*, in 'Transcript – a journal of visual culture', vol. 1, issue 1, Dundee: University of Dundee, pp.42–3.

[10] Colvin, Calum. Wilson, Rab. 2014. *Burnsiana*, exhibition publication, Edinburgh: Luath Press, p.18.

[11] Robert Burns Birthplace Museum, webpage, www.burnsmuseum.org.uk/collections/object_detail/3.8016

[12] Calder, Angus. 1989. *Byron and Scotland: Radical or Dandy*, Edinburgh: Edinburgh University Press, p.116.

[13] Lawson, James in Stafford, Jamie, Lawson, Wilson, 2016. *Jacobites by Name*, exhibition publication, Edinburgh: National Galleries of Scotland, unpaginated.

Baker, Christopher et. al. 1999. *A Companion Guide to the Scottish National Portrait Gallery*, Edinburgh: National Galleries of Scotland.

Boom, Mattie. 2001. *Still Lifes and Portraits*, Amsterdam: Rijksmuseum.

Brittain, David. 1986. Constructed Narratives, *Photographs by Calum Colvin and Ron O'Donnell*, exhibition catalogue, London: Photographers Gallery.

Brittain, David. Stevenson, Sara. 1990. *New Scottish Photography*, exhibition publication, Edinburgh: National Galleries of Scotland.

Clark, Alistair et. al. 2007. *Edinburgh Printmakers, 40 Years of Original Prints*, Edinburgh: Edinburgh Printmakers Workshop.

Colvin, Calum. Wilson, Rab. 2014. *Burnsiana*, Edinburgh: Luath Press.

Colvin, Calum. 2007. *Hybridization*, in History of Photography, vol. 31, no. 1, Jan Baetens and Hilde van Gelder eds., London: Taylor and Francis.

Colvin, Calum. 1998. *The Alchemical Canvas*, in Studies in Photography, Edinburgh: Scottish Society for the History of Photography.

Ferrero, Marianna. 2003. *2nd Triennale Internazionale D'Incisione*, exhibition catalogue, Turin: Citta di Chieri.

Gaskill, Howard et. al. 2007. *The Reception of Ossian in Europe*, London: Thoemmes.

Gattinoni, Christian. Vigouroux, Yannick. 2002. *Tableaux Choisis – La Photographie Contemporaine*, Paris: Editions Scala.

Gunn, Kirsty et. al. 2012. *In Memoriam*, Dundee: Dundee University Press.

Hare, Bill. 1993. *Scottish Painting*, Edinburgh: Talbot Rice Gallery.

Hartley, Keith. 1989. *Scottish Art since 1900*, exhibition publication, Edinburgh: Scottish National Gallery of Modern Art.

Haworth-Booth, Mark. 2004. *Things, A Spectrum of Photography 1850-2001*, London: Jonathan Cape.

Hennebohl, Rudolf. 2004. *Antike und Gegenwart, Daphne. Narcissus. Pygmalion*, Bamberg: C.C. Buchners Verlag.

Henry, Clare et. al. 1987. *The Vigorous Imagination – New Scottish Art*, exhibition publication, Edinburgh: Scottish National Gallery of Modern Art.

Kent, Sarah. 1989. *Through the Looking Glass*, exhibition catalogue, London: Barbican Gallery.

Langford, Michael. 1997. *Story of Photography: from its beginnings to the present day*, London: Focal Press.

Lawson, James. 1993. *Calum Colvin and Deadly Sins*, in Portfolio Magazine, no. 17, Edinburgh: Portfolio Gallery.

Lawson, James. 1998. *Sacred and Profane*, exhibition publication, Edinburgh: Scottish National Galleries.

Lemaistre, Isabelle Leroy-Jay. 2003. *Canova Psyche ranimee par le baiser de l'Amour*, Paris: Louvre Productions.

Macdonald, Murdo. 2000. *History of Scottish Art*, London: Thames and Hudson.

Maclean, Malcolm. Dorgan, Theo. 2002. *An Leabhar Mòr Gaidhlig/ The Great Book of Gaelic*, Edinburgh: Canongate Books.

Macmillan, Duncan. 2000. *Scottish Art 1440–2000*, Edinburgh: Mainstream Publishing.

McGeoch, Brian. Porch, Steven. 1996. *Looking at Scottish Art*, Wayland: BBC Education Scotland.

Mellor, David Alan. 1996. *A Package Flight to the Land of the Dead*, in Portfolio Magazine, no. 24, Edinburgh: Portfolio Gallery.

Mellor, David Alan. 1990. *Calum Colvin*, exhibition catalogue, Edinburgh: Fruitmarket Gallery.

Mellor, David Alan et. al. 1997. *On the Bright Side of Life: Zeitgenössische Britische Fotografie (British Contemporary Photography)*, exhibition publication, Berlin: NGBK.

Mellor, David Alan. 1988. *Romances of Decay, Elegies for the Future*, in 'British Photography, Towards a Bigger Picture', Aperture 113, New York: Aperture Foundation.

Normand, Tom. 1994. *An interview with Calum Colvin*, in 'Transcript – a journal of visual culture', vol. 1, issue 1, Dundee: University of Dundee.

Normand, Tom. 2002. *Calum Colvin's Ossian: Fragments of Ancient Poetry*, exhibition publication, Edinburgh: National Galleries of Scotland.

Normand, Tom. 2007. *Calum Colvin's Ossian*, in Next Level: Art/Photography/Ideas, edition 12, Edinburgh: Creative Scape Ltd.

Normand, Tom. Galloway, Janice et. al. 2014. *Calum Colvin: The Magic Box*, artists book, Edinburgh: Edinburgh Printmakers Workshop.

Normand, Tom. Wade, Nicholas. 2009. *Natural Magic*, exhibition publication, Edinburgh: Royal Scottish Academy.

Normand, Tom. 2007. *Scottish Photography: a history*, Edinburgh: Luath Press.

Normand, Tom. 1993. *The Seven Deadly Sins and the Four Last Things*, exhibition catalogue, Edinburgh: Portfolio Gallery.

Ogee, Frederic et. al. 2008 *Ossian, Then and Now*, Interfaces: Image, Texte, Language, no. 27, Worcester, Massachusetts: Holy Cross.

Pohlmann, Ulrich. Stevenson, Sara. Lawson, James. 1994. *Revisions*, exhibition publication, Munich: Nazraeli Press.

Prieto Gonzalo, Pilar. 2003. *Zombis, Castrados, Mantis Y Deformes, Notas Para una Exploracion de la Postfotografia*, Murcia: Association Murciana de Criticos de Arte.

Rötzer, Florian. Burgin, Victor. Rosler, Martha et. al. 1996. *Photography after Photography*, exhibition catalogue, Michigan: University of Michigan.

Salmon, Dimitri. n.d. *Ingres et les Modernes*, Montauban: Musée Ingres.

Stafford, Fiona. Jamie, Kathleen. Lawson, James. Wilson, Rab. 2016. *Jacobites by Name*, exhibition publication, Edinburgh: National Galleries of Scotland.

Stevenson, Sara. Forbes, Duncan. 2001. *A Companion Guide to Photography in the National Galleries of Scotland*, Edinburgh: National Galleries of Scotland.

Stevenson, Sara et. al. 1995. *Light from the Dark Room*, exhibition publication, Edinburgh: National Galleries of Scotland.

Vowinckel, Andreas. 1993. *The Two Ways of Life and Other Photographic Works*, exhibition catalogue, Karlsruhe: Badischer Kunstverein.

Westerbeck, Colin. Mellor, David Alan. 1991. *The Two Ways of Life*, exhibition catalogue, Chicago: Art Institute of Chicago.

Luath Press Limited

committed to publishing well written books worth reading

LUATH PRESS takes its name from Robert Burns, whose little collie Luath (*Gael.,* swift or nimble) tripped up Jean Armour at a wedding and gave him the chance to speak to the woman who was to be his wife and the abiding love of his life. Burns called one of 'The Twa Dogs' Luath after Cuchullin's hunting dog in Ossian's *Fingal*. Luath Press was established in 1981 in the heart of Burns country, and now resides a few steps up the road from Burns' first lodgings on Edinburgh's Royal Mile.
Luath offers you distinctive writing with a hint of unexpected pleasures.

Most bookshops in the UK, the US, Canada, Australia, New Zealand and parts of Europe either carry our books in stock or can order them for you. To order direct from us, please send a £sterling cheque, postal order, international money order or your credit card details (number, address of cardholder and expiry date) to us at the address below. Please add post and packing as follows: UK – £1.00 per delivery address; overseas surface mail – £2.50 per delivery address; overseas airmail – £3.50 for the first book to each delivery address, plus £1.00 for each additional book by airmail to the same address. If your order is a gift, we will happily enclose your card or message at no extra charge.

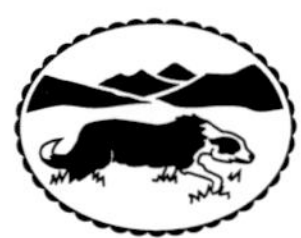

Luath Press Limited
543/2 Castlehill
The Royal Mile
Edinburgh EH1 2ND
Scotland
Telephone: 0131 225 4326 (24 hours)
Fax: 0131 225 4324
email: sales@luath.co.uk
Website: www.luath.co.uk